"OUR HOU:
1400 Josephine
Denver, Colorado

Formerly known as "the Bosworth House," this home is the chapter house of Assistance League of Denver® and Denver Historical Landmark #73. This proud old turn-of-the century home, with its Colorado redstone foundation and chimneys, its multi-gabled roof with decorative valances, the arched upper balcony and the galleried front porch, exemplifies the taste and life style of Denver's early aristocrats.

In 1966, Assistance League of Denver® purchased the property as a meeting place and to house part of its philanthropic projects and activities, and as a preservation project to help secure Denver's architectural heritage.

Extensive restoration occured in 1974 and 1975. These efforts were recognized by the Denver Historical Landmark Commission in January 1975. In April 1976 The Mayor's Committee of 19 FOR 76 endorsed the Bosworth House as a Heritage Project of the Centennial-Bicentennial Celebration.

In 1991 the auditorium was redecorated and the kitchen completely modernized. A new facility for H.E.L.P. was added on.

Assistance League of Denver® is very proud of this vintage residence and dedicated to its maintenance and preservation.

About the cover:

The original painting, "Our House," was commissioned by Assistance League of Denver® and painted by Colorado artist, Margaret E. Jensen. The watercolor painting captures the charm of the house during the annual fundraiser, "Christmas at Our House." Color prints are available for purchase. You may purchase a print by contacting Assistance League of Denver® by telephone at (303) 322-5205 or by Fax: (303) 322-5205, or write: "Our House" Prints, Assistance League of Denver®, 1400 Josephine Street, Denver, CO 80206.

ASSISTANCE LEAGUE OF DENVER®

Assistance League of Denver® is one of 90 chapters of National Assistance League and was organized in 1953. Each chapter is identified with its own philanthropic projects which address the needs within its community and that community benefits from all funds raised by the chapter. Mile High Professional Auxiliary was founded by 12 professional women in 1989. In order to finance its projects, Assistance League of Denver® operates a thriftmart at 1331 East Colfax and holds two major fundraisers yearly.

Assistance League of Denver® Philanthropic Projects Include:

FINE ARTS — Six outstanding students enrolled in the Denver School of the Arts are awarded a cash grant to help with their education.

OPERATION SCHOOL BELL — Needy children are provided with a basic wardrobe of new clothing and shoes. Recipients are referred by school social workers. 1500 to 1700 are clothed each year. New clothing and the program is at 1331 E. Colfax.

HELP — (Hospital Equipment Lending Program). At the request of a physician, social worker or visiting nurse, equipment is loaned to needy persons free of charge. Hundreds of pieces of equipment are loaned as long as needed by each individual.

HOSPITALITY HOUSE — On Wednesdays senior citizens are invited for refreshments at the chapter house and to participate in various activities.

MEMORIAL SCHOLARSHIPS — Educational grants are awarded to women students attending Community College of Denver.

MYCVA (Minorou Yasui Community Volunteer Awards) — A.L.D. was selected to be administrative sponsor of this committee created in 1976 by the Denver Mayor's office. Outstanding volunteers are recognized with a ceremony, media publicity and cash grant for the charitable organizations they serve.

ASK — Clothing and grooming kits distributed to assault victims at Denver General Hospital. Complete clothing and kits for as many as 400 to 500 victims per year.

Mile High Professional Auxiliary Philanthropic Projects Include:

ALD-O-BEAR — The Auxiliary furnishes teddy bears to be given to children experiencing a traumatic incident to which emergency personnel respond.

OPERATION SCHOOL BELL BOOKS — The Auxiliary project furnishes recreational reading material for children, in an effort to increase their desire to read as well as their reading comprehension. Books are included with clothing for needy children.

An Expression Of Our Thanks

Assistance League of Denver® has long enjoyed the reputation of a membership who are not only excellent cooks, but enjoy the spirit of creating enjoyment for the many guests who have been entertained at "our house." Our events are often centered around food, and we have often been asked for our recipes. For this reason, a committee was created to collect, test, and enjoy the many recipes found in this book. The book was compiled over a two year period to allow for the best recipes and the best test results.

The committee of "Recipes from our House" wishes to thank all who have helped in the preparation of this cookbook by way of sharing and testing recipes. We hope everyone has as much fun using the book as we had putting it together for you. We have endeavored to combine the practical with the unusual in order to provide an outstanding book of favorite foods that will be treasured and enjoyed by all.

We hope you will share copies of our book with your friends, family and loved ones for those special "one of a kind" gift solutions. We have provided ordering information in this book for your convenience. Thank you for supporting Assistance League of Denver®.

Sincerely,

Charlotte Weinberger, President, 1996-97
Jeannine Lincoln, Chairman

Commmittee Members of "Recipes From Our House"

Chairman .... Jeannine Lincoln
Vice Chairman .... Mary Hanneman
Marketing .... Kathy Finger
Inventory .... Phyliss Campbell

Lorraine Allred	Patti Askew	Jan Bradberry
Lois Burnett	Anne Bush	Meredith Chapman
Martha Crawford	Joan Deem	Donna Faraci
Virginia Flye	Sondra Harden	Debra Fagan-Heikens
Patricia Hodder	Norma Johnson	Renee Linton
Martha Mull	Joyce Patterson	Joey Pereira
Lynne Pettyjohn	Helen Rose	Connie Smith
Joyce Spaulding	May Torizawa	

ASSISTANCE LEAGUE OF DENVER®
Membership, Contributors and Testers

— A —

Elaine Aarons
Margaret Ailshie
Elinor Albrecht
Angela Alexis
Polly Allen
Winnie Allen
Lorraine Allred
Kay Amberg
Elly Andersen
Beverly Andrews
Babe Arnold
Betty Arp
Patti Askew

— B —

Gladys Bader
Joan Bailey
Ruth Bailis
Betty Baker
Elaine Baker
Nancy Bakker
Olive Bangle
Rose M. Barrett
Mary Barry
Annette Beaird
Norma E. Besant
Barbara Beymer
Vera Bierbach
Joan Birkenmayer
Elaine Bishop
Anne L. Blackburn
Merida Blackwell
Viola E. Boothby
Marjorie Bowen
Jan Brackney
Jan Bradbury

Barbara Bramley
Peg Brandle
Jay Breen
Billie Marie Brennan
Pattie Brick
Flo Brooks
Lu Brown
Marion Brown
Midge Brown
Doris G. Buchanan
Daisy L. Buhrmaster
Lois Burnett
Dee Burroughs
Anne Bush

— C —

Joyce Cairns
Bettye Callahan
Lee Camerson
Phyllis Campbell
Shirley Canada
Jean Carl
Barbara Carlson
Marie Carlson
Kaye Carney
Virginia Carpenter
Peg Carey
Elizabeth Carrick
Meridith Chapman
Elaine Chew
Arlene Christensen
Marian Christman
Sue Margaret Chrysler
Twila Coe
Anna Marie Cook
Hilda Cook
Carol Coughran

Patricia Cowan
Bettie L. Craddock
Martha Crawford
Bernadine Creer
Louise Crosby
Angie Crowder
Fran Cuneo

— D —

Mary Dahlager
Marjorie Davis
Peg Davis
Joan Deem
Maxine Devore
Della Dickman
Ellen Dimberg
Cindy Donnelly
Fran Dorward
Mary Dougherty
Ann H. Dowler
Audrey Dugdale
Carolyn Dunn
Lynn Dyrenforth

— E —

Marilyn Ehrhardt
Marie Erickson
Lucille Erlewine
Lody M. Eshe
Gladys Evers

— F —

Jane G. Fagan
Donna Faraci
Freda K. Feeney
Kathie Finger
Judy R. Fish
Audrey A. Fisher

Virginia Flye
Margaret Frank
Jolie Fraterelli
Maxine Fulton

— G —

Ann H. Gabree
Grace Gehret
Patti Giese
Kay Gilbert
Ernestine Gipson
Helen Godfrey
Jane C. Goodwin
Virginia Gorham
Elizabeth Grady
Diane Gras
Rachel Graves
Margaret Green
Margaret Gumz

— H —

Fran Hadley
Darlene Hall
Nancy J. Hall
Jane Halstead
Doris L. Hanan
Mary Hanneman
Billie Hansen
Katherine Haraway
Sondra Harden
Joan Harris
Margot Hartmann
Tommie Hatcher
Midge Hauser
Suzanne Hess
Sheila Hiner
Betty Hines
Elaine Hix

Jan Hobbs
Patricia Hodder
Lucile M. Hoglund
Patricia Holloway
Ann M. Howard
Jean Hughes
Carol Hull
Martha G. Hull
Lucy Hulwick
Kathleen Humphrey
Evelyn Huseby
Sue H. Hval
Helen Hyman

— J —

Billie Jackson
Gladys E. James
Irma James
Lucille M. James
Perry E. James
Bonnie Johnson
Carole Johnson
Norma R. Johnson
Pat Johnson
Ruth Johnson
Ara Johnston
Verna Johnstone
Pat Jones
Pat Jones
Eva Lee Jordan

— K —

Kathryn M. Kaiser
Jean Karr
Nicola Jean Kearns-Beattie
Carla Kem
Nancy Kerr
Grace Killin

Winifred Kitts
Shirley Kleiber
Shirley Klotz
Barbara Kotlarek
Frankie Krstich
Kathy K. Krusnik
Gerry Kulp
Vonnie Kurz

— L —

Rose Marie Labriola
Mary Langehough
Eleanor Lear
Brenda Leisey
Betty Lewis
Irene Lewis
Mary Meisner Lewis
Jeannine M. Lincoln
Renee Linton
Lavona Long
Mickie Lym
Florence Lyons

— M —

Dorothy Macintosh
Alice Maercklein
Constance Malone
Ellen Marchand
Alexandria Mauvais
Virginia McCoy
Anne McElroy
Evelyn McElroy
Margaret Ann McFall
Jean McLaughlin
Ilamae Smoot McNair
Norma Meade
Barbara Meyer
Maudie Millet

Pat Mills
Mary Moore
Theresa Moore
Ann Morehead
Sherill Morgan
Beverly Morris-White
Marjorie Morroni
Martha Mull
Betty Ann Mumey
Peg Munroe
Mona Murray
Mabel Musgrave

— N —

Frances Naylor
Leola M. Naylor
Dorothy Nelson
Esther Nelson
Patricia Nelson
Hilda Newton
Lillian Nicoletti

— O —

Ruth O'Connell
Joanne O'Day
Marguerite O'Day
Lindsey O'Shaughnessy
Barbara G. Oliver
Virginia Olson
Arlene Olvey

— P —

Joyce Parker
Mary Lou Parks
Joyce Patterson
Joey Pereira
Jane Perkinson
Virginia Perrott
Lynne Pettyjohn

Armeda M. Plank
Margie Platz
Jean S. Plumb
Dorothy Plunkett
Jeanette Preston
Martha Pribyl
Katie Pridonoff
Emma Lou Purvis

— Q —

Judy Quinn

— R —

Mary Rasmuson
Pat Reed
Joy Reese
Carol Slifer Reetz
Renny F. Regan
Maja Reid
Roberta Reineman
Bette Reno
Helen Rizer
Dorothy Roberts
Esther Robertson
Susan Ronald
Frances Root
Helen R. Rose
Jeanie Roth
Doni Rouse
Patricia Lee Rudd
Donna Rugg
Mary Ellen Ryan

— S —

Dorothy Schorr
Beth Schultz
Kathleen Scullion
Dorothy N. Scyrkels
Elsie Seay

Gerry Seep
E. J. Self
Eloise Semmelmeyer
Denise K. Sever
Jill Shaver
Linda E. Simmons
Sue Simos
Barbara Woody Smith
Connie J. Smith
Swan Snow
Betty Snyder
Lee Soggin
Joyce Spaulding
Dori Stack
Helen Standlee
Joanne Starbuck
Wilhelmina M. Stemmer
Mable Stevens
Tina Steward
Pam Stith
Lollie Stoecker
Joan Stringfield
Judith K. Stromberg
Jane Ellen Strottman
Carolyn Strutton
Mary Jean Sullivan
Patricia Ann Sumter
Alice Swanson

— T —

Wanda D. Taylor
Dodi Thomas
Betty Thompson
May Torizawa
Reba Treat
Jo O. Treece

— V —

Vernice Van Duzer
Clara Van Genderen
Joan Van Wyk
Cissy Vanek
Virginia Vincent
Beverly Vogler

— W —

Kay Walker
Barbara Wehrle
Charlotte Weinberger
Betty Welch
Ruth Westbrook
Wilma Wheeler
Elizabeth White
Pam Wiegand
Louise Williams
Wanda Williams
Catherine Wilson
Jerre Wilson
Kay Wilson
Sue Wood

— Y —

Pat Yelland

— Z —

Hertha Zagari

PALS OF ASSISTANCE LEAGUE
1996-1997

Jack Allen
Mel Allen
Glen Allred
Ken Andrews

Jerry Barrett
Alan Brown

Gray Davis
Virgil Dickman

John Ehrhardt
Bill Evers

Don Fisher
Gordon Flye
Allan Fulton

Jerry Garbarino
Aaron Green

Ronald L. Harris

Harold Johnson
Carl Jones

Dean Karr

Bud Mauvais
Tom Mull

Nick Nicoletti

Bill O'Day

Pete Peterson
Gene Pridonoff

Jim Reese
Lloyd Rizer

Jay Snow
Ed Spaulding

Don Weinberger
Bobby Williams

MILE HIGH PROFESSIONAL AUXILIARY OF ASSISTANCE LEAGUE OF DENVER®
Membership, Contributors and Testers

Barbara N. Allen
Jean Brickell
Pat Brickell
Nelva Caton
Mary Ann Connors
Barbara Ellis
Maxine Facca
Debra J. Fagan-Heikens
Jacqueline Goreham
Christine Graf
Suzanne Hamilton
Barbara Higgins
Bobbet Hines
Connie Hirz-Hernick
Sarah Hotchkiss-Porter
Marlene Lind
Nadine Mantooth
Kristi Martinez
Gail Mitchel
Nancy Moore
Dana Mumey
Janet Nagl
LeAnn Nelson
Susanna Orzech
Susan Rager
Margaret Rizer
Ann Sanchez
Della Swanson
Susan Tilton
Linda Weber
Marlys White

TABLE OF CONTENTS

FAVORITE RECIPES
FROM MY COOKBOOK

Recipe Name	Page Number

Appetizers, Beverages

FOOD QUANTITIES FOR 25, 50, AND 100 SERVINGS

FOOD	25 SERVINGS	50 SERVINGS	100 SERVINGS
Rolls	4 doz.	8 doz.	16 doz.
Bread	50 slices or 3 1-lb. loaves	100 slices or 6 1-lb. loaves	200 slices or 12 1-lb. loaves
Butter	½ lb.	¾ to 1 lb.	1½ lb.
Mayonnaise	1 c.	2 to 3 c.	4 to 6 c.
Mixed filling for sandwiches (meat, eggs, fish)	1½ qt.	2½ to 3 qt.	5 to 6 qt.
Mixed filling (sweet-fruit)	1 qt.	1¾ to 2 qt.	2½ to 4 qt.
Jams & preserves	1½ lb.	3 lb.	6 lb.
Crackers	1½ lb.	3 lb.	6 lb.
Cheese (2 oz. per serving)	3 lb.	6 lb.	12 lb.
Soup	1½ gal.	3 gal.	6 gal.
Salad dressings	1 pt.	2½ pt.	½ gal.
Meat, Poultry, or Fish:			
Wieners (beef)	6½ lb.	13 lb.	25 lb.
Hamburger	9 lb.	18 lb.	35 lb.
Turkey or chicken	13 lb.	25 to 35 lb.	50 to 75 lb.
Fish, large whole (round)	13 lb.	25 lb.	50 lb.
Fish, fillets or steaks	7½ lb.	15 lb.	30 lb.
Salads, Casseroles, Vegetables:			
Potato salad	4¼ qt.	2¼ gal.	4½ gal.
Scalloped potatoes	4½ qt. or 1 12x20" pan	8½ qt.	17 qt.
Mashed potatoes	9 lb.	18-20 lb.	25-35 lb.
Spaghetti	1¼ gal.	2½ gal.	5 gal.
Baked beans	¾ gal.	1¼ gal.	2½ gal.
Jello salad	¾ gal.	1¼ gal.	2½ gal.
Canned vegetables	1 #10 can	2½ #10 cans	4 #10 cans
Fresh Vegetables:			
Lettuce (for salads)	4 heads	8 heads	15 heads
Carrots (3 oz. or ½ c.)	6¼ lb.	12½ lb.	25 lb.
Tomatoes	3-5 lb.	7-10 lb.	14-20 lb.
Desserts:			
Watermelon	37½ lb.	75 lb.	150 lb.
Fruit cup (½ c. per serving)	3 qt.	6 qt.	12 qt.
Cake	1 10x12" sheet cake	1 12x20" sheet cake	2 12x20" sheet cakes
	1½ 10" layer cakes	3 10" layer cakes	6 10" layer cakes
Whipping cream	¾ pt.	1½ to 2 pt.	3 pt.
Ice Cream:			
Brick	3¼ qt.	6½ qt.	12½ qt.
Bulk	2¼ qt.	4½ qt. or 1¼ gal.	9 qt. or 2½ gal.
Beverages:			
Coffee	½ lb. and 1½ gal. water	1 lb. and 3 gal. water	2 lb. and 6 gal. water
Tea	1/12 lb. and 1½ gal. water	1/6 lb. and 3 gal. water	1/3 lb. and 6 gal. water
Lemonade	10 to 15 lemons, 1½ gal. water	20 to 30 lemons, 3 gal. water	40 to 60 lemons, 6 gal. water

APPETIZERS, BEVERAGES

OFFICIAL ALD "OUR HOUSE" WASSAIL

1 gal. tea (seep 10 bags 10 minutes)
1 gal. apple cider
1 gal. Ocean Spray holiday punch
1 (6 oz.) can frozen orange juice
   concentrate
1 (6 oz.) can frozen lemonade
   concentrate

1 c. brown sugar
Spice ball (wrap 1 Tbsp. whole
   cloves + 1 Tbsp. whole
   allspice in cheesecloth; tie with
   string. Steep with tea and add
   to other liquids).
1 tsp. nutmeg

Simmer together for 20 minutes. Float apple, orange, or lemon slices on top. Freezes well. Keep some to simmer to make your home smell like Christmas.

For an alcoholic touch, wine enhances the flavor.

20 MILE PINK PUNCH

1 large (46 oz.) can pineapple juice
2 c. boiling water
2 (3 oz.) pkg. strawberry jello
6 c. cold water

½ c. sugar
1 (12 oz.) can frozen orange juice
1 (12 oz.) can frozen lemonade
1 qt. ginger ale

Add boiling water to jello. Stir until dissolved. Add cold water and juices. Add ginger ale just before serving. Garnish punch bowl with slices of lemon or orange. Add ice ring if desired. Serves 35 to 40.

RECEPTION PUNCH OF THE ROCKIES

1 large bottle champagne
½ c. sugar
1 c. fresh lemon juice

2 c. apple juice
2 c. orange juice

Chill champagne at least 4 hours. Combine other ingredients and stir until sugar is dissolved. Chill well. Just before serving, add champagne. *Quick, easy, and good.*

AN OLD-FASHIONED PUNCH BOWL

1 c. sugar
⅓ c. water
1 fifth bourbon

Equal amount carbonated water
1 Tbsp. bitters
Orange and lemon slices

Boil sugar and ⅓ cup water for 2 minutes. Cool. Pour all ingredients over ice in bowl. Garnish with orange and lemon slices.

HURRICANE PUNCH

32 oz. reconstituted hurricane
   cocktail mix or Hawaiian
   Punch
2 oz. dark rum

1 oz. Welch's orchard passion fruit
   juice mix (undiluted)
Lemon juice to taste
Ice

Garnish with oranges and maraschino cherries.

ISLAND FRUIT PUNCH

Preparation time: 5 minutes.

2¼ c. orange juice
1 c. pineapple juice
½ c. light rum

¼ c. fresh lime juice
2 Tbsp. grenadine syrup

Combine first 4 ingredients in a pitcher; stir well and chill. Fill 4 glasses with orange juice mixture. Slowly pour 1½ teaspoons grenadine syrup down inside of each glass (do not stir before serving). Yield: 4 cups (serving size 1 cup).

Note: For a nonalcoholic punch, omit rum and use 2½ cups orange juice and 1¼ cups pineapple juice.

SPARKLING CRANBERRY BLUSH

3 c. cold water
2 (48 oz.) bottles cranberry juice
  cocktail, chilled
2 (6 oz.) cans thawed lemonade
  concentrate (undiluted)

2 (750 ml) bottles Brut champagne,
  chilled

Combine the first 3 ingredients in a punch bowl and stir well. Add chilled champagne and stir gently. Serve immediately. Yield: 6 quarts (serving size ¾ cup).

SANGRIA BLANCA

7 c. dry white wine, chilled
1 c. Cointreau
½ c. sugar
Ice cubes

2 bottles club soda (10 oz.)
2 oranges, sliced
2 lemons, sliced
4 limes, cut in wedges

Combine wine, Cointreau, and sugar until well blended in glass pitcher. When ready to serve, stir in ice and soda. Add fruit and serve. Makes 12 servings.

TAHITIAN PUNCH

1¼ c. sliced banana
1¼ c. sliced strawberries, chilled
1¼ c. sliced peeled papaya, chilled
1 c. sliced peeled mango, chilled

1 c. orange juice, chilled
1 c. crushed ice
1 (8 oz.) ctn. plain nonfat yogurt

Place all ingredients in a blender and process until smooth. Serve immediately. Yield: 1½ quarts (serving size 1 cup).

SCARLET DUCK

1 qt. cranberry juice
1 (⅘) bottle Cold Duck

1 (28 oz.) bottle 7-Up

Have all ingredients cold. Add to punch bowl in order given. *Do not stir.* Beautiful and delicious! *Simple!* Makes 20 (4 ounce) servings.

MILE HIGH WHITE WINE PUNCH

2 large bottles dry white wine
1½ c. Curacao Liqueur
½ c. superfine sugar
2 oranges, thinly sliced

2 lemons, thinly sliced
2 limes, thinly sliced
24 strawberries
1 (28 oz.) bottle club soda

Halve 12 strawberries and place in an ice ring, freezing 2 to 3 hours or overnight. Combine the wine and Curacao in a punch bowl. Stir in sugar until dissolved. Add the sliced fruits and 12 of the strawberries; cover and chill for at least 1 hour. Just before serving, add club soda to punch bowl, mixing gently. Remove ice ring from mold and float in punch bowl. Yield: 1½ quarts. Sugar measurement may be varied.

WHITE WINE PUNCH

1 c. superfine sugar
1 c. orange juice
½ c. orange liqueur
2 lemons, thinly sliced
1 (1 liter) bottle club soda

1 c. fresh lemon juice
2 bottles dry white wine (cold)
1 navel orange, sliced thinly
Ice ring

Stir together sugar, lemon juice, and orange juice until sugar dissolves. Add wine and liqueur. Stir well. (At this point, mixture can be stored in refrigerator for future use.) Pour into punch bowl. Add lemons, oranges, club soda, and ice ring. Stir well. Serves 20 or more punch cups.

HOT APPLE PUNCH

2 (12 oz.) cans frozen unsweetened
  apple juice concentrate,
  thawed (undiluted)
1 qt. water

2 c. fresh cranberries
2 (3 inch) sticks cinnamon
6 whole cloves

Prepare apple juice according to package directions. Pour into Dutch oven and add rest of ingredients. Bring to a boil; cover. Reduce heat and simmer 30 minutes. Strain mixture, discarding cranberries and spices.

Beautiful color! Serve in clear glass cups. Also great before Thanksgiving dinner.

KAHLUA PARTY PUNCH

16 oz. (2 c.) Kahlua
1 (12 oz.) can frozen apple juice
  concentrate
4 oz. (½ c.) lemon juice
Small chunk ice
1 (25.4 oz.) bottle sparkling apple
  juice

1 qt. bottle club soda or lemon-lime
  beverage
1 (750 ml) bottle dry champagne
Thin lemon and small orange slices

Have all ingredients well chilled. Combine Kahlua with undiluted apple juice concentrate and lemon juice. Pour over small chunk ice in punch bowl. Add sparkling apple juice and club soda or lemon-lime beverage. Add champagne and stir gently. Add lemon and orange slices for garnish. Kahlua, apple juice concentrate, and lemon juice may be mixed and refrigerated the day before. Recipe may be increased without adjustment. Party on! Makes about 1 gallon (30 half-cup servings).

PEACH MIMOSAS

2 c. peach nectar, chilled
1⅓ c. orange juice, chilled
⅔ c. grenadine syrup

1 (750 ml) bottle Brut champagne, chilled

Combine peach nectar and orange juice in a pitcher and stir well. Spoon 1 tablespoon grenadine syrup into each of 10 champagne glasses.

Add ⅓ cup of the orange juice mixture to each glass and top with chilled champagne. Serve immediately. Yield: 10 servings.

ALWAYS THERE DAIQUIRIS

1 gal. rum
2 qt. (8 c.) water
⅓ c. Karo syrup

3 (6 oz.) lemonade, frozen
3 (6 oz.) limeade, frozen

Mix in large freezer plastic pail with lid. Place in freezer and dip out as needed.

BANANA-ORANGE DAIQUIRI

Preparation time: 5 minutes.

1½ c. sliced banana
½ c. light rum
½ c. bottled sweet-and-sour
   cocktail mix

¼ c. thawed orange juice
   concentrate
30 ice cubes
Orange slices (optional)

Place first 4 ingredients in blender, and process until smooth. With blender on, add ice cubes, 1 at a time and process until smooth. Serve immediately. Garnish with an orange slice if desired. Yield: 5 cups (serving size 1 cup).

GINGER BEER COCKTAIL

Ginger beer is a carbonated beverage that tastes like a stronger version of ginger ale. It is made both with and without alcohol.

¾ c. orange juice
4 (11.5 oz.) bottles ginger beer
1 medium cucumber, cut lengthwise
   into thin strips

1 medium Red Delicious apple, cut
   into thin wedges
1 medium orange, cut into thin
   wedges

Combine all ingredients in large pitcher; stir well. Serve over ice. Yield: 2 quarts (serving size 1 cup).

PINEAPPLE PLEASURE

1½ c. sliced strawberries, chilled
1¼ c. sliced banana
1¼ c. pineapple juice, chilled

1 c. orange juice, chilled
1 c. crushed ice
2 Tbsp. honey

Place all ingredients in a blender and process until smooth. Serve immediately. Yield: 5 cups (serving size 1 cup).

TIKI SHAKE

Preparation time: 5 minutes.

2¼ c. ginger ale, chilled
2 c. pineapple sherbet, softened

2 Tbsp. fresh lime juice
Lime slices (optional)

Combine the first 3 ingredients in blender, and process until smooth. Garnish with lime slices, if desired. Serve immediately. Yield: 4 cups (serving size 1 cup).

HAWAIIAN EYE OPENER

½ (12 oz.) can frozen pineapple juice
   concentrate, thawed

2 small bananas, cut up
2 c. ice cubes

Place the pineapple juice concentrate and bananas in a blender container. Cover and blend till smooth. With blender running, add ice cubes, a few at a time, through the opening in the lid. Blend till smooth and frothy. Makes 4 servings (3 cups).

TROPICAL CITRUS SANGRIA

Preparation time: 6 minutes. Microwave time: 1 minute.

2 Tbsp. sugar
2 Tbsp. cognac or brandy
1¾ c. dry white wine, chilled
4 lemon slices
4 lime slices

4 orange slices
1 (10 oz.) bottle club soda, chilled
Additional lemon, lime, and orange
   slices (optional)

Combine the sugar and cognac in a 1 quart glass measure. Microwave at HIGH 1 minute or until sugar dissolves, stirring after 30 seconds. Add wine and fruit slices; stir well. Cover and chill.

To serve, add club soda, and stir gently. Serve with additional fruit slices, if desired. Yield: 3 cups (serving size ¾ cup).

KIR ROYALE

1 c. creme de cassis, chilled
2 (750 ml) bottles Brut champagne,
   chilled

Combine creme de cassis and champagne in a large pitcher; stir gently. Serve immediately. Yield: 7½ cups (serving size ¾ cup).

LO-DO-BOURBON CAPPUCCINO

2 c. hot brewed coffee
2 Tbsp. brown sugar

2 c. 2% lowfat chocolate milk
2 Tbsp. bourbon

Combine coffee and brown sugar, stirring until brown sugar dissolves. Stir in lowfat chocolate milk and bourbon; cover and chill.

To serve, dip rims of 4 stemmed glasses in water and then in sugar to coat rims. Pour 1 cup cappuccino into each glass. Yield: 4 cups (serving size 1 cup).

GINGERED FRUIT DIP

1 (8 oz.) pkg. cream cheese, softened
1 (16 oz.) jar marshmallow creme
¼ tsp. powdered ginger
¼ tsp. grated orange rind

Whip first 4 ingredients together. Serve in a bowl on a tray surrounded with fresh fruit: Pineapple chunks or spears, strawberries, orange sections, apple wedges, and bananas.

This tray of hors d'oeuvres will disappear fast!

TEX-MEX DIP

3 medium size ripe avocados
2 Tbsp. lemon juice
½ tsp. salt
¼ tsp. pepper
1 c. sour cream or IMO
½ c. mayonnaise or salad dressing
1 pkg. taco seasoning mix
2 cans bean dip
1 (8 oz.) pkg. shredded Cheddar cheese
1 c. green onions, chopped
3 medium size tomatoes, coarsely chopped
1 (6 oz.) can pitted olives, chopped
Large round tortilla chips

Peel, pit, and mash avocados in blender with lemon juice, salt, and pepper. Combine sour cream, mayonnaise, and taco seasoning and mix in another bowl.

Spread bean dip on a large shallow platter or 9x13 inch glass pan. Top with avocado mixture. Sprinkle with chopped onions, tomatoes, and olives. Cover with shredded cheese. Serve chilled or at room temperature with round chips.

NUTTY BROCCOLI SPREAD

1 (10 oz.) box Birds Eye chopped broccoli
4 oz. cream cheese, softened
¼ c. grated Parmesan cheese
1 tsp. dried basil
¼ c. chopped walnuts
1 loaf frozen garlic bread

Preheat oven to 400°F. Place broccoli, cream cheese, Parmesan cheese, and basil in mixing bowl, food processor, or blender; process until ingredients are mixed (do not overmix). Add walnuts; process 3 to 5 seconds to blend. Split garlic bread lengthwise. Spread broccoli mixture evenly over cut bread. Bake 10 to 15 minutes or until bread is toasted and broccoli mixture in heated through. Cut into bite-size pieces; serve hot. Yield: 2 cups.

YUMMY YUMA ARTICHOKE DIP

2 (6½ oz.) jars or cans artichoke hearts, drained
2 c. lowfat mayonnaise
1 c. lowfat sour cream
¾ c. grated Parmesan cheese
1 tsp. Tabasco sauce
½ tsp. garlic powder
1 c. imitation crab (optional)
1 small can chopped chilies (optional)

Chop or mash artichoke hearts until slightly stringy. Add all other ingredients and mix thoroughly. Place in baking dish or casserole dish. Spread mixture evenly and sprinkle with additional Parmesan cheese. Bake at 350° for 30 minutes or until bubbly.

Great for large gatherings. Serve warm with baked tortilla chips, Melba rounds, and/or large carrot slices.

MEXICAN CHEESE DIP
(Quick and easy)

1 lb. Velveeta Mexican cheese   1 (15 oz.) can chili without beans

Cut cheese into small cubes and place in microwave container. Heat and stir until cheese is almost melted, then add the chili without beans. Heat in microwave until dip is completely melted. Serve with corn or tortilla chips. Dip is best if kept warm. May reheat. *Great for a sporting event!*

CHEESE HORSERADISH DIP
(Zippy dip!)

1 lb. Velveeta cheese   5 dashes of Tabasco
4 oz. (Blue label) Silver Spring   1 c. mayonnaise
    horseradish

Cube cheese and place in microwave-safe container. Melt and stir approximately 3 minutes. Add additional ingredients. Serve with crackers.

Option: May be divided and frozen. Great to take to a party. *Very addictive!*

GOOD LUCK "MEXICAN" SALSA

1 large ripe avocado, peeled,   1 can black-eyed peas, drained
    seeded, and cut into ½ inch   1 large tomato, seeded and diced
    cubes   1 oz. Italian salad dressing (lowfat)
2 bunches green onions, sliced

Prepare onions, peas, and tomato; combine with Italian dressing. Marinate at least 2 hours. Add prepared avocado to preceding. Serve with "Scoops" (Fritos type cracker). Makes approximately 3 cups of dip. *Refreshing. Excellent presentation!*

MIZ-ZIPPI PECANS

1 lb. pecan halves   ¼ c. butter or margarine
1 Tbsp. chili powder
1 large clove garlic, crushed (in one
    piece)

Put pecans in heavy pan with seasoning and butter. Cook over medium heat, stirring often until crisp and lightly browned. Remove garlic. Drain nuts; sprinkle with coarse salt. Cool. Store airtight.

BUTTER PECAN POPCORN

Because there's no boiling syrup, you won't need a candy thermometer to make this crunchy treat.

8 c. popped popcorn (about ⅓ to ½ c. unpopped)
Nonstick spray coating
½ c. broken pecans
2 Tbsp. margarine or butter

⅓ c. light corn syrup
¼ c. instant butter pecan pudding mix
¾ tsp. vanilla

Discard unpopped popcorn kernels. Spray a 17x12x2 inch roasting pan with nonstick coating. Place the popped corn and pecans in the pan. Keep warm in a 300° oven while making coating.

Melt margarine or butter in a small saucepan. Remove saucepan from heat. Stir in corn syrup, pudding mix, and vanilla. Pour syrup mixture over popcorn. With a large spoon, gently toss the popcorn with the syrup mixture to coat.

Bake popcorn, uncovered, in a 300° oven for 16 minutes, stirring halfway through baking. Remove the pan from the oven. Turn mixture onto a large piece of foil. Cool popcorn completely. When cool, break into large pieces. Store leftover popcorn, tightly covered, in a cool, dry place for up to 1 week. Makes about 9 (1 cup) servings.

GREEN VEGETABLES WITH TARRAGON CREAM DIP

Enough young tender asparagus or green beans for group to be served
Fresh tarragon leaves

Sour cream
Salt and pepper
Tarragon vinegar to taste

Make early in the day to allow time to mellow. Blanch the vegetables in boiling water. Cook until just tender (2 to 4 minutes). Plunge immediately into iced water; drain and chill. Strip the leaves of tarragon from the stems. Mince finely. Mix into the sour cream; add the salt, pepper, and vinegar to taste.

To serve, put the cream in a bowl and set in center of a large tray. Arrange the vegetables neatly around the bowl. Guests will pick up a stem and dip into the bowl.

CHEESE CRISPIES

1 c. soft butter
1 c. grated sharp Cheddar cheese

1 c. flour
1 c. crispy rice cereal

Mix ingredients together either by hand or use food processor with pulse action until dough forms a ball. Roll dough into small balls by hand. Place on baking sheet and press with fork. Bake in 375° oven for 10 to 15 minutes. Store in airtight container. Great gift for hostess!

Option: Can be made into long narrow roll, covered in plastic wrap and chilled until firm, 2 hours. When ready to bake, cut into ¼ inch slices. Place on ungreased baking sheet and bake as preceding.

POTTED SHRIMP

½ lb. (2 sticks) plus 4 Tbsp. butter,
  cut into ¼ inch bits
½ tsp. mace
½ tsp. ground nutmeg
⅛ tsp. cayenne pepper

1 tsp. salt
1 lb. shelled, cooked tiny fresh
  shrimp (60 or more) or
  substitute 2 c. drained, canned
  tiny shrimp

In a 1½ to 2 quart saucepan, clarify ¼ pound of the butter by melting it slowly over low heat. Skim off the surface foam and let the butter rest off the heat for a minute or two. Spoon the clear butter on top into a heavy 6 to 8 inch skillet and discard the milky solids at the bottom of the saucepan.

Melt the remaining ¼ pound plus 4 tablespoons of butter over moderate heat in heavy 3 or 4 quart saucepan. When the foam begins to subside, stir in the mace, nutmeg, cayenne pepper, and salt. Add the shrimp, turning them about with a spoon to coat them evenly.

Spoon the mixture into six 4 ounce individual baking dishes or custard cups, dividing the shrimp equally among them. Seal by pouring a thin layer of the clarified butter over each. Refrigerate the shrimp overnight or for at least 6 hours.

Potted shrimp are traditionally served with hot toast as a first course or at teatime. Good pre-old English dinner.

REAL COCONUT SHRIMP WITH APRICOT-HORSERADISH SAUCE

From "Miami Spice, the New Florida Cuisine."

1½ lb. jumbo shrimp
1 Tbsp. fresh lime juice
Salt and freshly ground pepper to
  taste
1 c. (about) flour
2 eggs, beaten

1½ c. freshly grated or very finely
  chopped fresh coconut*
3 to 4 Tbsp. clarified butter** or
  vegetable oil
Apricot-Horseradish Sauce (recipe
  follows)

Peel and devein shrimp, leaving tails intact. In mixing bowl, toss shrimp with lime juice, salt, and pepper. Marinate 5 minutes. Place flour in a shallow bowl, eggs in another shallow bowl, and coconut in a third. Just before serving, melt butter in large, heavy skillet. Dip each shrimp first in flour, shaking off excess, then in egg, then in coconut. Cook shrimp over medium heat until golden brown, about 1 minute per side. Drain on paper towels. Serve on doily-lined platter with Apricot-Horseradish Sauce for dipping. Serves 6 as an appetizer, 3 to 4 as an entree.

Apricot-Horseradish Sauce:

⅔ c. apricot jam
⅓ c. freshly grated or prepared
  white horseradish

1 Tbsp. fresh lime juice or to taste
Salt and freshly ground pepper to
  taste

Whisk together jam and horseradish until smooth. Whisk in lime juice, salt, and pepper. Serve immediately or refrigerate in glass jar with nonmetallic lid for several weeks. Makes 1 cup.

* To shell fresh coconut for grating: Punch in all 3 eyes of coconut, using screwdriver and hammer. Drain out liquid and reserve for drinking or mixing in cocktails, if desired. Wrap coconut in a towel and break it into 5 or 6 pieces by hitting it with a

hammer. Remove towel and set pieces on rack of oven preheated to 400°. Bake until meat begins to pull away from shell, 10 to 15 minutes. The same effect can be achieved by freezing coconut for a couple of hours. Pry meat away from shell and cut off brown skin. Coconut meat is now ready for grating or shaving into thin strips with vegetable peeler. One coconut yields 3 to 3½ cups grated flesh and ½ to 1 cup coconut water.

** To clarify butter: Melt butter over low heat in heavy saucepan without stirring. When completely melted, skim off the clear golden top liquid into a dish, leaving milk solids in the pan.

SHRIMP DIJON

Shrimp Dijon Butter:

1 lb. butter
1 Tbsp. fresh lemon juice
3 c. fine dry bread crumbs
2 Tbsp. chopped parsley

1 tsp. finely minced garlic
2 Tbsp. finely chopped shallots
1 Tbsp. Worcestershire sauce

Items needed:

1 recipe Shrimp Dijon Butter
4 jumbo shrimp (per person),
** cooked (80 to 96 shrimp)**
1 zig-zag cut lemon half per person
** (10 to 12 lemons)**

Parsley (for garnish)
Scallop shells for baking

Blend ingredients for Dijon butter together well. Form a roll approximately 2 inches in diameter and refrigerate. (May be frozen, also.)

To serve: Place shrimp on baking shells. Cut Dijon butter into 20 to 24 slices and place a slice of butter in the middle of each serving. Broil until butter is melted and shrimp is warm. Garnish with lemon half and parsley. Place shell on serving plates or serve at table for first course surrounded with napkin folded in the shape of a flower. Serves 20 to 24.

FAMOUS DILLED SHRIMP

1½ c. mayonnaise
⅓ c. lemon juice
¼ c. sugar
½ c. dairy sour cream
1 Bermuda onion, *thinly sliced*

2 Tbsp. dill
½ tsp. salt
2 lb. cooked, shelled, and deveined
** shrimp**

Mix all ingredients together, except shrimp. Stir cleaned and well drained shrimp into mixture. Cover and *place in refrigerator overnight.* Stir once before serving. Serve with small plates and colorful toothpicks. Serves 8.

Excellent for wedding receptions and fancy occasions. Make a lot because the demand is extremely high for shrimp prepared in this manner!

SPINACH BALLS

2 (10 oz.) pkg. frozen chopped
   spinach, thawed
4 eggs
¾ c. melted butter
1 white onion, grated or finely
   minced

2 c. herb flavored bread crumbs
½ c. finely grated Sevin cheese
¼ c. grated Parmesan cheese
1 clove garlic, minced

Squeeze and drain thawed spinach dry of liquid. Place in large mixing bowl and add all remaining ingredients. Blend well. Cover and refrigerate 2 to 3 hours.

Roll into 1 inch balls. Place on lightly greased cookie sheet and bake at 350° for 15 minutes. May be served alone or with a mustard dip. Yield: 50 appetizers.

MINI-BRONCO BURGERS

Use 1 regular loaf of bread. Cut into four bread rounds from each slice of bread.

Filling:

½ lb. ground round or extra lean
½ small can tomato paste
1 c. Cheddar cheese, shredded
¼ tsp. oregano
½ tsp. basil

Garlic salt to taste
Salt to taste
Red pepper flakes
1 Tbsp. dry minced onion

Combine all filling ingredients. Shape into meatballs and push each meatball with thumb onto each bread round. (Looks like a hamburger.) Place under broiler and cook until brown. Freeze up to 2 months. Thaw before placing under broiler. Watch carefully as burgers turn light brown quickly. Easily doubled!

BRANDIED CHEESE

In a bowl, stir together:

1 (8 oz.) pkg. cream cheese,
   softened

1 (8 oz.) ctn. dairy sour cream
3 Tbsp. brandy

Stir in 1½ cups shredded *Edam* or *Gouda* cheese (6 ounces). Turn into an 8 inch quiche dish or 2 smaller baking dishes (freeze one). Bake in a 350° oven about 30 minutes on cookie sheet until lightly browned. Place on serving platter and surround with 2 freshly sliced apples* and crackers. Top Brandied cheese with ¼ cup coarsely chopped walnuts. Serves 16.

Frozen cheese: Bring to room temperature and bake and serve as preceding.

* Use *red* apples and leave peel on.

FOUR CHEESE PUMPKIN

1 c. cottage cheese
1 (8 oz.) pkg. cream cheese,
    softened
2 c. (8 oz.) shredded Colby cheese
    (at room temperature)
1 c. (4 oz.) shredded Provolone
    cheese (at room temperature)

1 tsp. Worcestershire sauce
1 tsp. prepared mustard
Paprika
Green bell pepper
Assorted crackers

Using food processor or electric mixer, combine all cheeses, Worcestershire, and mustard. Process or mix until well blended. Wrap cheese mixture in plastic wrap; refrigerate until thoroughly chilled to blend flavors and for ease in handling. Shape into pumpkin; sprinkle with paprika. Use pieces of bell pepper to make stem. Keep refrigerated. Let stand at room temperature about 15 minutes before serving with assorted crackers. Yield: 8 cups.

HAWAIIAN CHEESE BALL

2 (8 oz.) pkg. cream cheese
1 (8 oz.) can crushed pineapple,
    drained well
2 c. pecans, chopped

2 Tbsp. chopped green onion
¼ c. chopped green pepper
1 Tbsp. seasoned salt

Soften cream cheese; add pineapple and remaining ingredients. Form into ball; roll in pecans. Wrap in plastic wrap and refrigerate until ready to serve. Makes 2 medium or 1 large ball. Serve with assortment of crackers. *Excellent.*

PACIFIC NORTHWEST SALMON BALL

1 lb. can red salmon
8 oz. cream cheese
1 Tbsp. lemon juice

1 tsp. prepared horseradish
¼ tsp. hickory liquid smoke
¼ c. chopped pecans

Drain and flake salmon after removing any skin or bones. Combine the salmon with the other ingredients, except pecans. Shape into ball. Refrigerate at least 3 hours. Roll ball in chopped pecans. Before serving place on platter and garnish with parsley and sliced fresh red pepper. Serve with crackers.

RUMAKI RUMBA

½ lb. sliced bacon (regular or
    turkey)
12 pitted dates
1 small can cubed or pineapple
    tidbits

½ c. brown sugar
2 tsp. curry powder

Cut bacon strips in halves or thirds. Wrap each date and piece of pineapple individually in bacon. Fasten with water soaked round toothpick. Place on broiler pan. Mix brown sugar and curry powder together. Broil the bacon wrapped appetizers for a minute or two, turn and sprinkle with sugar mixture. Broil until bacon is crisp! If oven preferred, bake approximately 10 minutes at 350°. Serve hot.

Option: Wrap sea scallops in bacon and broil with or without sauce. Serve immediately. Do not bake.

OLIVE AND CRAB MUSHROOMS

The California Olive Industry offers a make-ahead recipe ideal for entertaining. Assemble and refrigerate mushrooms in morning and bring to room temperature before broiling.

¾ c. California ripe olive wedges
¾ c. (6 oz. fresh, fresh-frozen/
   defrosted or canned)
   crabmeat
½ c. mayonnaise
½ c. shredded Cheddar cheese
⅓ c. (about 2 medium) chopped
   green onions

Dash of Worcestershire sauce (or to
   taste)
Dash of hot pepper sauce (or to
   taste)
24 to 36 small to medium
   mushrooms, cleaned and
   stemmed
6 Tbsp. butter or margarine, melted

Preheat broiler. Set aside 24 to 36 olive wedges for garnish. In a medium bowl, combine the remaining olives, crabmeat, mayonnaise, cheese, and green onions. Add a dash each of Worcestershire and hot pepper sauces or more to taste.

Dip the bottoms and sides of the mushroom caps into the melted butter. Using a teaspoon, fill each cap with some of the crab mixture. Garnish each cap with an olive wedge.

Transfer mushrooms to a broiler pan. Broil 3 to 4 minutes or until the filling is hot and bubbly. Makes 24 to 36 mushrooms.

SEAFOOD TARTLETS

1 loaf thin-sliced sandwich bread

6 Tbsp. butter, melted

Seafood Filling:

1 c. mayonnaise
⅓ c. grated Parmesan
⅓ c. shredded Swiss cheese
⅓ c. chopped onion

¼ tsp. Worcestershire
2 drops of Tabasco sauce
2 oz. cooked, small baby shrimp
2 oz. cooked crab or imitation crab

Preheat oven to 400°. Flatten pieces of bread with a rolling pin. Cut 2½ inch rounds with a cookie cutter.

Dip rounds into butter, coating both sides. Press into muffin tins that have holes 1½ inches across. Bake 10 minutes or until golden brown. Leave bread rounds in the pan after you take them from the oven.

Combine Seafood Filling ingredients while the bread is browning. Fill each tartlet and sprinkle with paprika. Place muffin tins under the broiler until the tartlets are golden and bubbly. Remove tartlets from pan and serve or cool and freeze them for later use. Cook frozen tartlets at 450° for 7 to 10 minutes until hot. Makes 32.

GRAPE SURPRISES

1 (8 oz.) pkg. cream cheese,
   softened
1 (8 oz.) pkg. sharp Cheddar cheese,
   shredded
½ c. butter, softened

1 Tbsp. prepared mustard
12 tsp. Worcestershire sauce
About 50 fresh seedless grapes
Paprika
Pecans or walnuts, chopped

Beat together cheeses, butter, mustard, and Worcestershire sauce. With damp hands, form mixture around individual grapes. Roll each ball in paprika and then chopped nuts. Chill and serve. Nice with a glass of wine.

BAMBINOS

4 doz. cracker rounds
2 oz. thinly sliced pepperoni
1 c. shredded Mozzarella cheese

¾ c. catsup
Dried oregano leaves

Heat oven to 400°. Spread rounds with catsup; top with pepperoni. Sprinkle cheese and oregano over pepperoni. Baked on ungreased cookie sheet for 3 to 4 minutes. Makes 4 dozen.

QUESADILLAS

3 c. shredded Monterey Jack cheese
   (12 oz.)
1 (4 oz.) can diced green chili
   peppers, drained

12 (7 or 8 inch) flour tortillas
1 recipe Green Chili Salsa (optional)

Place ¼ cup of cheese and about 1 teaspoon peppers over half of one tortilla. Fold in half, then in half again to form triangle. Place on baking sheet. Repeat with remaining ingredients. Overlap slightly on sheet if necessary.

Bake in 300° oven for 3 to 4 minutes or till cheese melts. Serve with salsa. Makes 12 appetizer servings.

Note: To make ahead, prepare quesadillas; chill, covered, till serving. Bake 2 to 3 extra minutes to melt cheese.

Nutrition information per serving: 171 calories, 9 g pro, 14 g carbo, 9 g fat, 25 mg chol, 236 mg sodium. U.S. RDA: 23% Vit. A. 27% calcium.

COLORFUL TORTILLA ROLL-UPS

2 (8 oz.) pkg. cream cheese,
   softened
6 oz. chopped ripe olives, drained
1 (7 oz.) can green chilies (seeds
   removed), drained and
   chopped

⅓ c. chopped green onion
1 c. grated Cheddar cheese
1 pkg. (about 8) flour tortillas

In large bowl, combine cream cheese, olives, chilies, onion, and Cheddar cheese. Spread about ½ cup of the cheese mixture to within ¼ inch of the edge of each tortilla. Roll tightly. Chill at least 2 hours, covered in plastic wrap. Trim ½ inch off

14

each end of tortillas. Cut tortillas into 8 pieces each. Lay cut tortillas on side as for pinwheels. Makes 64 pieces.

DURANGO NACHOS

1 (16 oz.) can Old El Paso fat free
  refried beans
¾ c. Old El Paso thick 'n chunky
  salsa

Tortilla chips
8 oz. (2 c.) shredded cheese
Old El Paso pickled jalapeno slices
  (if desired)

1. Combine refried beans and salsa; mix well.
2. Arrange tortilla chips in a single layer on large microwave-safe platter. Spread ½ of bean mixture on chips. Top with 1 cup cheese and desired amount of jalapeno slices.
3. Microwave on HIGH for 1½ to 3½ minutes or until cheese is melted, rotating plate ¼ turn halfway through cooking. Repeat with remaining ingredients. Makes 8 servings of nacho nachos.

OCTOBERFEST SAUSAGES

2 lb. Italian sausage or 1 lb. sweet
  and 1 lb. hot sausages
2 Tbsp. olive oil
1 (8 oz.) can tomato sauce
1 c. red wine

1 Tbsp. minced fresh parsley
½ tsp. dried basil
1 Tbsp. grated Romano cheese
Chopped parsley (for garnish)

Cut each sausage link into 4 pieces. Add oil to pan. Cook sausage on all sides. Remove sausage from pan and drain off oil. Add tomato sauce, half of wine, parsley, basil, and cheese to pan. Stir and simmer for half hour or more on low heat. Add rest of wine and bring liquids to boil, then add the cooked sausage and serve all in chafing dish. Sprinkle with chopped parsley. Serves 6.

Option: Refrigerate sausage overnight in wine sauce and arrange on platter with marinated artichoke hearts, black or green olives, cheese cubes, cherry tomatoes, green pepper strips, and sliced carrots. Serves a small group.

POLENTA TRIANGLES

3 c. cold water
1 c. coarse yellow corn meal
1 env. onion soup mix
1 (4 oz.) can mild chopped green
  chilies, drained

½ c. whole kernel corn
⅓ c. red pepper, roasted and finely
  chopped
½ c. sharp Cheddar cheese,
  shredded

In a 3 quart saucepan, bring water to a boil. With a wire whip, stir in corn meal and soup mix. Simmer, uncovered, stirring constantly, until thickened, 25 minutes. Stir in chilies, corn, and pepper. Spread into lightly greased 9 inch square baking pan; sprinkle with cheese. Let stand until firm, 20 minutes, and then cut into triangles. Serve at room temperature or heat until warm (5 minutes) in a 350° oven. Makes about 30 appetizers.

TROPICAL FRUIT BRIE QUESADILLAS

6 soft flour tortillas
1 (5 oz.) container spreadable Brie

Fruit Salsa (recipe follows)

Spread Brie between each of 2 tortillas until all tortillas are used. Warm stuffed tortillas on grill until cheese melts. Remove from heat and cut each tortilla into 4 or 6 wedges and place wedges on platter. Spoon Fruit Salsa onto each wedge; top with a fresh sprig of cilantro or edible flower such as a pansy and serve immediately.

Fruit Salsa:

3 c. fresh or canned mango,
   pineapple, and papaya, diced
⅓ c. fresh cilantro, shredded
⅓ c. red onion, diced

3 small fresh jalapeno peppers,
   seeded and minced
1 to 2 tsp. grated fresh ginger

Prepare salsa by dicing fruit and combining the fruit with shredded cilantro, diced red onion, and fresh jalapeno peppers, as well as ginger, lime juice, and salt and pepper to taste. The salsa can be prepared an hour in advance of serving. *Truly a beautiful appetizer!*

YAMPA VALLEY ZUCCHINI GARDEN

3 c. shredded, unpared zucchini
1 c. Bisquick baking mix
½ c. finely chopped onion
½ c. finely shredded carrot
½ c. grated Parmesan cheese
2 Tbsp. snipped parsley
2 tsp. seasoned salt

½ tsp. oregano
½ tsp. basil
Dash of pepper
2 cloves garlic, finely chopped
½ c. vegetable oil
4 eggs, beaten

Heat oven to 375°. Mix ingredients and spread into greased 9x13x2 inch pan. Bake until golden brown (about 25 minutes). Cut into small squares and serve. Makes approximately 4 dozen.

BASIL SUN DRIED TOMATO SLICES

1 (9 oz.) jar sun dried tomato spread
   (located in the fresh
   vegetable area of the grocery
   store)
1 (6 oz.) plastic container Kaukauna
   "fat free" cream cheese
   spread (such as roasted garlic
   and herb)

1 fresh baguette
1 small can sliced olives
1 bunch fresh basil

Just before company arrives, ¼ inch slice baguette. Spread with cream cheese spread. Top with sun dried tomato spread. Add one small leaf of fresh basil and a few olive slices. Place on serving tray. Makes as many as you slice.

GREEN VEGETABLES WITH TARRAGON CREAM

Enough young tender asparagus
   spears or green beans for
   group to be served
Fresh tarragon leaves

16 oz. sour cream
1 Tbsp. tarragon vinegar
Salt and pepper to taste

Make early in the day allowing time to mellow. Blanch the vegetables in boiling water. Cook just until tender (2 to 4 minutes). Plunge immediately into iced water; drain and chill. Strip tarragon leaves from stems and finely mince. Mix into sour cream; add vinegar, salt, and pepper. To serve, put cream in bowl and arrange vegetables neatly around the bowl. Guests will pick up a stem and dip into bowl.

RANCH OYSTER CRACKERS

Mix 1 ounce packet Hidden Valley Original Ranch dressing mix with ¼ cup oil. Pour over 12 ounces plain oyster crackers. Stir to coat. Bake 15 to 20 minutes at 250°F. Stir halfway through baking.

RANCH POTATO SKINS

Quarter 4 baked potatoes. Scoop out potatoes and combine with ¼ cup sour cream and 1 ounce package Hidden Valley Original Ranch dressing mix. Fill skins with mixture. Sprinkle with shredded Cheddar cheese. Bake 12 to 15 minutes at 375°.

Notes

Soups,
Salads

A HANDY SPICE AND HERB GUIDE

ALLSPICE-a pea-sized fruit that grows in Mexico, Jamaica, Central and South America. Its delicate flavor resembles a blend of cloves, cinnamon, and nutmeg. USES: (Whole) Pickles, meats, boiled fish, gravies; (Ground) Puddings, relishes, fruit preserves, baking.

BASIL-the dried leaves and stems of an herb grown in the United States and North Mediterranean area. Has an aromatic, leafy flavor. USES: For flavoring tomato dishes and tomato paste, turtle soup; also use in cooked peas, squash, snap beans; sprinkle chopped over lamb chops and poultry.

BAY LEAVES-the dried leaves of an evergreen grown in the eastern Mediterranean countries. Has a sweet, herbaceous floral spice note. USES: For pickling, stews, for spicing sauces and soup. Also use with a variety of meats and fish.

CARAWAY-the seed of a plant grown in the Netherlands. Flavor that combines the tastes of anise and dill. USES: For the cordial Kummel, baking breads; often added to sauerkraut, noodles, cheese spreads. Also adds zest to French fried potatoes, liver, canned asparagus.

CURRY POWDER-a ground blend of ginger, turmeric, fenugreek seed, as many as 16 to 20 spices. USES: For all Indian curry recipes such as lamb, chicken, and rice, eggs, vegetables, and curry puffs.

DILL-the small, dark seed of the dill plant grown in India, having a clean, aromatic taste. USES: Dill is a predominant seasoning in pickling recipes; also adds pleasing flavor to sauerkraut, potato salad, cooked macaroni, and green apple pie.

MACE-the dried covering around the nutmeg seed. Its flavor is similar to nutmeg, but with a fragrant, delicate difference. USES: (Whole) For pickling, fish, fish sauce, stewed fruit. (Ground) Delicious in baked goods, pastries, and doughnuts, adds unusual flavor to chocolate desserts.

MARJORAM-an herb of the mint family, grown in France and Chile. Has a minty-sweet flavor. USES: In beverages, jellies, and to flavor soups, stews, fish, sauces. Also excellent to sprinkle on lamb while roasting.

MSG (MONOSODIUM GLUTAMATE)-a vegetable protein derivative for raising the effectiveness of natural food flavors. USES: Small amounts, adjusted to individual taste, can be added to steaks, roasts, chops, seafoods, stews, soups, chowder, chop suey, and cooked vegetables.

OREGANO-a plant of the mint family and a species of marjoram of which the dried leaves are used to make an herb seasoning. USES: An excellent flavoring for any tomato dish, especially pizza, chili con carne, and Italian specialties.

PAPRIKA-a mild, sweet red pepper growing in Spain, Central Europe, and the United States. Slightly aromatic and prized for brilliant red color. USES: A colorful garnish for pale foods, and for seasoning Chicken Paprika, Hungarian Goulash, salad dressings.

POPPY-the seed of a flower grown in Holland. Has a rich fragrance and crunchy, nut-like flavor. USES: Excellent as a topping for breads, rolls, and cookies. Also delicious in buttered noodles.

ROSEMARY-an herb (like a curved pine needle) grown in France, Spain, and Portugal, and having a sweet fresh taste. USES: In lamb dishes, in soups, stews, and to sprinkle on beef before roasting.

SAGE-the leaf of a shrub grown in Greece, Yugoslavia, and Albania. Flavor is camphoraceous and minty. USES: For meat and poultry stuffing, sausages, meat loaf, hamburgers, stews, and salads.

THYME-the leaves and stems of a shrub grown in France and Spain. Has a strong, distinctive flavor. USES: For poultry seasoning, croquettes, fricassees, and fish dishes. Also tasty on fresh sliced tomatoes.

TURMERIC-a root of the ginger family, grown in India, Haiti, Jamaica, and Peru, having a mild, ginger-pepper flavor. USES: As a flavoring and coloring in prepared mustard and in combination with mustard as a flavoring for meats, dressings, salads.

SOUPS, SALADS

GINGERED CARROT VICHYSSOISE

A beautiful soup from Frog's files, with certainly more color and, to our minds, more character than the traditional vichyssoise. It seems just the thing to start off an elegant picnic, not to mention a special dinner.

1 c. thinly sliced leeks (about 2 large)
2 Tbsp. butter
¼ c. chopped onions
¾ lb. carrots, peeled and thinly sliced (about 3 medium)
2½ tsp. minced fresh ginger
½ lb. all-purpose potatoes, peeled and thinly sliced (about 1 medium)

½ tsp. salt
½ tsp. pepper
1 to 3 tsp. sugar if carrots themselves are not particularly sweet (optional)
1½ c. chicken stock
3 c. half & half
Minced chives or slivered candied ginger for garnish (optional)

Soak the sliced leeks in cold water to remove any grit, then rinse well under running water. Melt the butter in a medium-size saucepan. Add the drained leeks and onions and saute until wilted and translucent. Add the carrots, ginger, and potatoes. Saute and stir several minutes. Add the salt, pepper, optional sugar, and chicken stock. Cover and let simmer until the vegetables are very tender and can be easily mashed with a fork (about 10 to 15 minutes). Puree in a food processor or through a food mill and then strain through a fine sieve. Chill thoroughly. Blend in the half & half. To serve, ladle into chilled small soup bowls or cups. Garnish each serving, if desired, with minced fresh chives or slivers of candied ginger. Makes about 5 cups, serving 5 to 6.

COLD BUTTERMILK SHRIMP SOUP

1 qt. buttermilk
1 Tbsp. dry mustard
1 tsp. sage
1 tsp. sugar
½ to ¾ lb. cooked shrimp, chopped and chilled

1 cucumber, peeled, seeded, and chopped fine (save 6 slices for garnish)
2 Tbsp. chopped chives
Garlic to taste (optional)

Whisk together buttermilk, mustard, sage, and sugar. Add shrimp, cucumber, chives, and garlic to the whisked liquid. Chill 3 hours. Garnish each serving with ½ shrimp and 1 slice cucumber. Serves 6 cups. *Surprisingly good.*

LORI B.'S DILLED TOMATO SOUP

6 Tbsp. sweet butter
2 medium purple onions, peeled and sliced
1 qt. fresh or canned chicken stock
2 c. fresh tomatoes, peeled, seeded, and diced
2 cloves garlic, minced

2 Tbsp. fresh lemon juice
2 Tbsp. Dijon-style mustard
1 tsp. dill weed
1 Tbsp. horseradish
2 tsp. Worcestershire sauce
Salt and pepper to taste

Melt butter in a non-aluminum saucepan and saute onions over medium heat until translucent, about 8 minutes. Add chicken stock, tomatoes, garlic, and lemon juice. Heat to boiling. Lower heat and simmer for 30 minutes. Add mustard, dill weed, horseradish, and Worcestershire. Transfer in batches to blender or food processor fitted with a steel blade and process until pureed. A small sprig of fresh dill makes a lovely garnish.

GAZPACHO

Soup:

1 c. sliced hothouse cucumber
4 tomatoes, peeled and seeded
1 tsp. salt
1 tsp. red wine vinegar

4 Tbsp. fresh lime juice
2 cloves garlic, chopped
1 tsp. Worcestershire sauce
½ tsp. Tabasco

Garnish:

⅓ c. minced green bell pepper
⅓ c. minced celery
⅓ c. minced cucumber

1 Tbsp. chopped cilantro (fresh coriander)

1. Combine all the soup ingredients in a blender or food processor fitted with the steel blade and process to a smooth consistency.
2. Chill the soup until it is ice cold. After it is chilled, taste the soup for seasoning and adjust with more lime juice, Worcestershire, and Tabasco as needed. Garnish each serving with a sprinkling of bell pepper, celery, cucumber, and cilantro. Makes 4 servings.

FRESH TOMATO-BASIL SOUP

2 tsp. olive or vegetable oil
1 c. chopped onions
½ small garlic clove, mashed
6 large plum tomatoes, blanched, peeled, seeded, and chopped

1 c. canned ready-to-serve low-sodium chicken broth
2 Tbsp. chopped fresh basil
2 basil sprigs (garnish)

1. In 1½ quart nonstick saucepan, heat oil. Add onions and garlic and cook over medium-high heat until tender-crisp, about 2 minutes.
2. Stir in remaining ingredients and bring mixture to a boil. Reduce heat to low and let simmer, stirring occasionally, until flavors blend, about 15 minutes.
3. Pour soup into 2 soup bowls and garnish each portion with a basil sprig. Approximate total time: 30 minutes. Makes 2 servings, about 1¼ cups each.

Each serving provides: 1 fat, 4 vegetables, and 20 optional exchanges. Per serving: 114 calories, 4 g protein, 6 g fat, 14 g carbohydrate, 55 mg calcium, 41 mg sodium, 0 mg cholesterol, and 3 g dietary fiber.

LEMON SOUP WITH MINT

1 large potato, peeled and chopped
2¼ c. vegetable broth
½ c. water
3 Tbsp. lemon juice
Egg substitute equivalent to 1 egg

¾ c. plain nonfat yogurt
2 Tbsp. chopped mint
Salt and pepper to taste
Extra mint leaves or thinly sliced lemon (for garnish)

In a medium saucepan, simmer potato in broth and water until potato is tender, about 15 minutes. Puree potato broth and water mixture in a blender or food processor.

In a medium bowl, whisk together lemon juice and egg replacer. Gradually add 1 cup hot potato puree, whisking constantly.

Transfer all puree back into saucepan and cook gently until slightly thick, about 10 to 12 minutes. (Do not boil.) Remove from heat; cool.

Whisk in yogurt, mint, and salt and pepper. Chill. Garnish with mint leaves if desired. Serves 4.

STRAWBERRY WINE SOUP

2 c. sliced fresh strawberries
6 Tbsp. sugar
1 c. water
2 tsp. cornstarch mixed with 1 Tbsp.
    cold water
1 c. dry white wine

1 to 2 Tbsp. lemon juice
2 tsp. grated lemon peel
Cognac
Tiny lemon strips
¼ c. sour cream or nonfat yogurt
    (optional)

Combine strawberries, sugar, and water in pot; simmer until berries are soft.

Stir in cornstarch binder and cook and stir until thickened. Puree in blender. Add wine, lemon juice, and lemon peel. Chill and season to taste with additional lemon juice, wine, and cognac. Garnish with tiny lemon peel strips.

Optional: Puree with ¼ cup sour cream or nonfat yogurt. Serves 4.

BISQUE OF BUTTERNUT SQUASH WITH APPLE

1 small butternut squash (about 1
    lb., unpeeled), cut in half and
    seeded
2 tart green apples, peeled, cored,
    and coarsely chopped
1 medium onion, coarsely chopped
Pinch of rosemary
Pinch of marjoram

1 qt. chicken stock (or use rich
    canned chicken broth)
2 slices white bread, trimmed and
    cubed
1½ tsp. salt
¼ tsp. pepper
2 egg yolks
¼ c. heavy cream

Combine the squash halves, the chopped apples and onion, herbs, stock, bread cubes, salt, and pepper in a large heavy saucepan. Bring to a boil and simmer, uncovered, for about 45 minutes or until the vegetables are soft.

Scoop the flesh of the squash out; discard the skins and return the pulp to soup. Puree the soup to which you have returned the squash, in the blender until smooth. (You will probably have 2 blender loads.) Return the pureed soup to the saucepan.

In a small bowl, beat the egg yolks and cream together. Beat in a little of the hot soup, then stir back into the sauce. Heat, but do not boil, and serve immediately. Serves 4 to 6.

BROCCOLI-CHEDDAR SOUP

3 c. broccoli in ⅜ inch dice
¼ c. butter
1 c. chopped onions
1 tsp. minced garlic
2 Tbsp. flour
2 c. half & half
3 c. chicken broth

¾ lb. sharp Cheddar cheese, grated
½ tsp. nutmeg
¾ tsp. salt
½ tsp. pepper
2 Tbsp. Dijon mustard
¼ c. dry sherry (optional)

Blanch the broccoli in boiling, salted water; refresh under cold water. Drain and set aside. Melt the butter in a large saucepan; add the onions and saute until tender and translucent. Add the garlic and saute 30 seconds. Add the flour and cook and stir 2 minutes. Whisking hard, add the half & half and chicken broth. Bring the mixture to a boil. Reduce to a simmer and stir in the cheese. Add the seasonings, mustard, and sherry. Lower the heat to be sure soup doesn't boil again or it may curdle. Add the broccoli and heat through. Garnish with additional shredded Cheddar if desired. Makes 2 quarts.

Variations: Substitute cauliflower for the broccoli and garnish the soup with bits of red pepper and lots of minced parsley. If you prefer a smooth soup, puree the broccoli with some of the liquid and stir into the rest of the soup.

BASIC CHICKEN STOCK

In the restaurants, we will use 70 pounds of chicken backs, 140 quarts of water, 20 peeled and chunked onions, 5 bags of carrots in chunks, 5 bunches of parsley, 5 celery bunches in chunks, some thyme, bay leaves, and peppercorns for our chicken stock. We let it simmer over a very low flame all night.

For home purposes, however, try 6 to 7 pounds of chicken parts, 7 quarts of water, 2 onions, ½ bunch of celery, ½ bunch of parsley, ½ bag of carrots, 2 bay leaves, ½ teaspoon of thyme, and ½ teaspoon of peppercorns. Bring to a boil, then keep to a bare simmer about 3 hours. Strain and skim off the fat. Freeze or refrigerate as desired. This will make about 5 to 6 quarts.

RICH ASPARAGUS SOUP

Made in the style of a pureed vegetable soup, the addition of the bright green floating tips gives a bit of crunch and chopped tomato adds a colorful confetti effect.

½ c. (1 stick) unsalted butter
2 large yellow onions, coarsely
   chopped
4 large cloves garlic, coarsely
   chopped
1½ qt. chicken stock
3 lb. asparagus
1 bunch fresh parsley (stems
   removed), chopped (1 c.)
2 medium size carrots, peeled and
   cut into 1 inch pieces

8 fresh large basil leaves
1 Tbsp. dried tarragon
1 tsp. salt
1 tsp. freshly ground black pepper
Pinch of cayenne pepper
1 c. sour cream
1 ripe large tomato, seeded and cut
   into small dice

1. Melt the butter in a heavy, large saucepan over low heat. Add the onions and garlic and cook, uncovered, until wilted, about 25 minutes.

2. Add the stock and heat to boiling.

3. Trim the woody ends from the asparagus and cut the stalks into 1 inch pieces. Reserve the tips. Add the asparagus pieces, parsley, carrots, basil, tarragon, salt, pepper, and cayenne to the stock. Reduce heat to medium-low and simmer, covered, until the vegetables are tender, about 50 minutes.

4. Remove the soup from heat and let cool. Process in batches in a blender or a food processor fitted with a steel blade until smooth. Strain the soup through a medium-size sieve to remove woody fibers.

5 Return the strained soup to the pan; add the asparagus tips and simmer over medium heat until the tips are tender, about 10 minutes.

6. Ladle soup into soup bowls. Dollop each serving with sour cream and sprinkle with diced tomato. Makes 8 portions.

PUMPKIN AND LEEK SOUP

3 Tbsp. unsalted butter
6 leeks (white part only), well rinsed and chopped (about 2 c.)
2 garlic cloves, minced
4½ c. pumpkin in 2 inch cubes

4½ c. water
1½ c. milk or half & half
Salt and freshly ground black pepper
1 Tbsp. minced fresh chives

Melt the butter in a heavy saucepan. Add the leeks and saute slowly over low heat until they are tender but not brown, about 10 minutes. Stir in the garlic.

Add the pumpkin and water; cover and simmer until the pumpkin is tender, about 40 minutes. Allow the mixture to cool for 15 minutes, then puree in one or two batches in a food processor.

Return the puree to the casserole; add the milk or half & half and season to taste with salt and pepper. Reheat before serving. Sprinkle each serving with the chives. Serves 6 to 8.

LENTIL SOUP

2 hot and 4 sweet Italian link pork sausages (about 1 lb.)
¼ c. water
2 large onions, chopped medium fine (about 2 c.)
1 clove garlic, minced
4 medium carrots, sliced ⅛ inch thick (about 2½ c.)
1 large celery rib, coarsely chopped (about ¾ c.)

¼ c. parsley sprigs, minced
2 c. lentils, rinsed
28 oz. can peeled plum tomatoes, quartered (undrained)
2½ qt. water
1½ Tbsp. salt
¼ tsp. ground pepper
1 Tbsp. dried basil

In a covered saucepot (about 8 quarts), over low heat, cook sausage in the ¼ cup water until water evaporates. Brown sausage, uncovered, and drain on brown paper or paper towels; slice ½ inch thick and reserve. Pour off all but ¼ cup of the drippings, or if necessary, add enough olive oil to make that amount. Add onion and garlic and cook gently until onion is wilted. Stir in carrots, celery, parsley, lentils, tomatoes, the 2½ quarts water, salt, pepper, and basil. Bring to a boil over medium-low heat; simmer, covered, for about 3 minutes. Stir in sausage and simmer until lentils are tender and flavors are blended, about 20 minutes longer. Makes about 4 quarts. *Excellent!*

CHICKEN LIME SOUP

1 (3 to 3½ lb.) chicken
6 c. water
1 medium onion, quartered
1 stalk celery
Small bunch fresh cilantro (divided use)
6 whole peppercorns
1 tsp. salt
½ tsp. thyme
1 medium green pepper, diced

½ medium onion, diced
2 Tbsp. oil
1 (16 oz.) can whole tomatoes, drained, seeded, and diced
1½ tsp. freshly grated lime peel
Juice of 2 limes
¼ tsp. freshly ground black pepper
¼ tsp. salt (optional)
8 small corn tortillas
Oil for frying

Garnish:

Lime slices

Cilantro

Place chicken, water, quartered onion, celery, 3 cilantro sprigs, peppercorns, 1 teaspoon salt, and thyme in Dutch oven. Bring to boil; cover and simmer for 1 hour. Remove chicken and cool. Skin and bone chicken; cut into ½ inch cubes. Strain broth and discard vegetables.

In same Dutch oven, saute green pepper and chopped onion in oil. Add tomato pieces and cook a few more minutes. Add broth, grated lime peel, lime juice, and 3 tablespoons chopped cilantro. Bring to a boil; reduce heat and simmer, uncovered, for 30 minutes. Stir in chicken and pepper. Add salt to taste. Simmer 10 minutes longer.

Cut each tortilla in 8 wedges and fry in hot oil, stirring gently until crisp and lightly browned. Drain on paper towel. Place 8 wedges in each bowl and ladle soup over wedges. Garnish with thin lime slice and small sprigs of cilantro or serve from large glass bowl with tortilla wedges on the side. Makes 8 to 10 servings.

COUNTRY VEGETABLE SOUP

This is a hearty, traditional soup that is easily adapted to whatever produce is available throughout the year. Don't be put off by the length of preparation time needed. The beans soak without needing to be watched, and the soup simmers for almost all of two and a quarter hours.

1 lb. white beans, soaked in water overnight
1½ lb. smoked ham, cut into bite-size pieces
4 c. peeled and chopped onion
4 cloves garlic, peeled and minced
3 c. peeled and chopped fresh tomatoes or one 28 oz. can Italian plum tomatoes (with juice)
12 c. chicken stock
6 c. water

1½ bay leaves, crumbled
2 Tbsp. chopped fresh thyme or 2 tsp. dried
1 c. chopped parsley
4 stalks celery, chopped
4 carrots, peeled and sliced
3 medium zucchini, cut into bite-size pieces
1 Tbsp. salt
1 tsp. ground black pepper
Chopped parsley (for garnish)

Drain the soaked beans and place them in a 10 quart pot. Add the ham, onion, garlic, and tomatoes and heat over medium flame for 2 minutes. Add the chicken stock, water, bay leaves, thyme, and parsley. Bring to a boil. Simmer for about 1½ hours.

Add the celery and carrots and simmer for another 15 minutes. Add the zucchini, salt, and pepper and simmer for 10 minutes more. Garnish with parsley. Yield: 4 to 6 quarts. Preparation time: 2 hours 15 minutes (excluding soaking time).

MEXICAN SEAFOOD SOUP

1 qt. milk
5 medium potatoes, peeled and
    cooked
3 Tbsp. butter
1¼ c. grated Monterey Jack cheese
    (divided)
1 c. sour cream

1 tsp. chili powder
Seasoned salt and pepper to taste
1 c. minced clams and juice
2 to 3 c. cooked shrimp
1 Tbsp. chopped pimiento
¼ c. sherry
¼ c. minced scallions

Blend milk and potatoes in food processor in batches, making sure not to overprocess. Put in a large pot; add butter and bring to a simmer. Add 1 cup of cheese and stir until melted. Return small amount of soup to processor and blend with sour cream. Return to soup pot; add chili powder, salt, pepper, clams, shrimp, and pimientos and simmer for 5 minutes. Add sherry. Sprinkle with scallions and remaining cheese. Serve immediately. Makes 6 to 8 servings.

A hearty soup with wonderful Mexican flavor - most definitely a meal in itself. May be made ahead successfully if the seafood is added just before serving.

VEGETARIAN CHILI

⅓ c. olive oil
2 c. finely chopped onions
¾ c. chopped celery
1 c. chopped green peppers
1 c. chopped carrots
1 Tbsp. minced garlic
2 c. chopped mushrooms
¼ tsp. red pepper flakes
1 Tbsp. ground cumin
¾ tsp. dried basil
2 Tbsp. chili powder
¾ tsp. dried oregano
2 tsp. salt

½ tsp. pepper
2 c. tomato juice
¾ c. bulgur wheat
2 c. chopped tomatoes
2 c. (one 20 oz. can) undrained
    kidney beans
½ tsp. Tabasco sauce
2 Tbsp. lemon juice
3 Tbsp. tomato paste
1 Tbsp. Worcestershire sauce
¼ c. dry red wine
2 Tbsp. chopped, canned green
    chilies (or to taste)

Have ready all the ingredients. Heat oil in a large pot. Over high heat, add the onions, mushrooms, celery, green peppers, carrots, garlic, spices, salt, and pepper. Cook, stirring, for 1 to 2 minutes. Add the remaining ingredients. Bring to a boil, stirring. Reduce the heat and simmer for 20 minutes, uncovered. If too thick, the chili can be thinned with additional tomato juice.

PORTUGUESE BEAN SOUP

2 ham hocks
2 Portuguese sausage, sliced
3 qt. water
2 cans kidney beans *or* 1 pkg. red
    kidney beans, soaked
    overnight
1 onion, chopped in chunks

1 clove garlic, crushed
2 potatoes, cut in chunks
2 carrots, cubed
4 tomatoes, diced
Several sprigs parsley
Salt and pepper to taste

Put water in a Dutch oven or large saucepan. Add hocks and sausage. Cook
3 hours over low heat. Add beans, onion, garlic, potatoes, parsley, and tomatoes. Cook
1 hour. Serves 8.

FROGMORE STEW

8 hot smoked sausage links
    (approx. 2 pkg.)
12 ears freshly shucked corn
4 lb. large fresh shrimp (unpeeled)

¼ c. seafood boil (such as
    McCormick, Old Bay, or
    Zatarain's)
1 lemon

In a stock pot, combine the seafood boil and sliced lemon with 4 quarts water
and bring to boil. Add sausage cut into large pieces and boil 5 minutes. Add the corn,
cut into 3 or 4 pieces, and cook 5 minutes longer. Add the shrimp to the pot and cook
until pink and firm, about 3 minutes. Serves 8.

Great participatory meal. Fun for a crowd.

CORN CHOWDER

Although this is a year-round chowder, it is especially good in the summertime,
when it can be made with fresh sweet corn. With crusty French bread or a light
sandwich, it is a filling lunch.

1½ c. minced onion
5 Tbsp. butter
¼ tsp. sage
¾ tsp. whole cumin
¾ tsp. marjoram
⅓ c. flour
3 c. chicken stock or broth
½ c. Chablis
2 c. heavy cream

½ tsp. nutmeg
1 chopped green pepper
1 (12 oz.) can corn, drained, 1 (10
    oz.) pkg. frozen corn, or 1½ c.
    fresh corn
6 oz. Cheddar cheese, grated
2 Tbsp. chopped parsley
Tabasco and Worcestershire sauce
    to taste

Saute the onions in the butter until they are transparent. Add the herbs and stir
until they are fragrant. Add the flour and stir, cooking for 2 to 3 minutes over low heat.
Add the chicken stock and Chablis and whisk until the liquid thickens. Add the cream,
nutmeg, green pepper, and corn and simmer for 10 minutes (or 15 minutes if the
corn is fresh). Add the cheese and turn off the heat. Add the parsley, Tabasco, and
Worcestershire sauce. Serves 6 to 8.

SEAFOOD CHOWDER

½ (16 oz.) pkg. loose pack frozen
   cauliflower, broccoli, and
   carrots
¾ c. chicken stock
¼ c. sliced green onions
1 (12 oz.) can evaporated milk
2 tsp. cornstarch

1 c. water
4 oz. cream cheese, cut in 1 inch
   cubes
6 oz. seafood (shrimp, scallops, sea
   legs, if frozen, thawed)
Splash of white wine

In a large saucepan, combine vegetables, the ¾ cup chicken stock and green onion. Bring to boiling; reduce heat. Cook, covered, over low heat for 5 to 10 minutes or till vegetables are crisp-tender. Do not drain. Cut up any large pieces of vegetable. Stir in milk. Combine cornstarch and the 1 cup water; stir till smooth. Stir into vegetable mixture. Cook and stir till thickened and bubbly. Stir in cream cheese till melted. Add *undrained* thawed crabmeat; heat through. Serve with croutons. Makes 4 servings.

Per serving: 236 calories, 19 g protein, 22 g carbohydrate, and 8 g fat.

WHITE CHILI

1 lb. large white beans
6 c. chicken broth
2 cloves garlic, minced
2 medium onions, chopped
   (divided)
1 Tbsp. oil
2 (4 oz.) cans chopped green chilies

2 tsp. ground cumin
1½ tsp. dried oregano
¼ tsp. ground cloves
¼ tsp. cayenne pepper
4 c. diced, cooked chicken breasts
3 c. grated Monterey Jack cheese

Combine beans, chicken broth, garlic, and half of the onions in a large soup pot and bring to a boil. Reduce heat and simmer until beans are very soft, 3 hours or more. Add more chicken broth, if necessary. In a skillet, saute remaining onions in oil until tender. Add chilies and seasonings and mix thoroughly. Add to bean mixture. Add chicken and continue to simmer 1 hour. Serve topped with grated cheese. Makes 8 to 10 servings.

For a buffet, serve White Chili with some or all of the following condiments: Chopped tomatoes, chopped parsley, chopped ripe olives, guacamole, chopped scallions, sour cream, crumbled tortilla chips, or Salsa Cruda. Provide warm squares of Hearty Corn Bread.

CHICKEN TORTILLA SOUP

3 lb. chicken pieces (dark and light
   meat)

Flavor packet:

3½ qt. water
5 chicken bouillon cubes

1 tsp. celery seed
1 tsp. peppercorns

2 cloves garlic
1 jalapeno pepper

Tie these flavor packet ingredients in cheesecloth. Bring preceding ingredients to boil, then simmer until chicken is cooked. Debone chicken and remove all skin. Strain broth to remove fat particles. Also remove flavor packet.

Add the following ingredients:

1 (14.5 oz.) can chopped tomatoes
1 large onion, cut into 1 inch pieces
1 green pepper, cut into 1 inch
    pieces
3 fresh sprigs, cilantro

½ tsp. ground cumin
¼ tsp. cayenne pepper
½ tsp. white pepper
1 clove garlic, minced

Bring to boil and simmer 5 minutes.

Add:

1 c. regular rice, cooked   1 (10 oz.) pkg. frozen corn

Cook an additional 20 minutes. Ladle soup into bowls containing tortilla chips. Top with shredded Cheddar cheese. Pass fresh salsa for additional flavor. Serves 6 to 8.

HUNGARIAN MUSHROOM SOUP

One hour to prepare (approximately).

12 oz. fresh mushrooms, sliced
2 c. chopped onion
4 Tbsp. butter
3 Tbsp. flour
1 c. milk
1 to 2 tsp. dill weed
1 Tbsp. Hungarian paprika

1 Tbsp. tamari
1 tsp. salt
2 c. stock or water
2 tsp. fresh lemon juice
¼ c. fresh chopped parsley
Fresh ground black pepper to taste
½ c. sour cream

Saute the onions in 2 tablespoons butter. Salt lightly. A few minutes later, add mushrooms, 1 teaspoon dill, ½ cup stock or water, tamari, and paprika. Cover and simmer 15 minutes.

Melt remaining butter in a large saucepan. Whisk in flour and cook, whisking, a few minutes. Add milk. Cook, stirring frequently, over low heat, about 10 minutes, until thick. Stir in mushroom mixture and remaining stock. Cover and simmer 10 to 15 minutes. Just before serving, add salt, pepper, lemon juice, sour cream, and, if desired, extra dill. Serve garnished with parsley. Makes 4 rich servings.

STRAWBERRY AVOCADO SALAD

Salad:

1 head romaine lettuce, torn into
    bite-size pieces
1 avocado, seeded, peeled, and
    sliced

2 c. thickly sliced strawberries
1 can sliced water chestnuts,
    drained
½ c. pecan pieces

Balsamic Dressing:

2 Tbsp. balsamic vinegar
1 Tbsp. brown sugar
6 Tbsp. vegetable oil

1 Tbsp. finely chopped shallots
Salt and freshly ground pepper to
    taste

For salad: In large bowl, toss salad ingredients.

For dressing: In small bowl, whisk together vinegar and sugar. Gradually whisk in oil. Stir in finely chopped shallots. Add salt and pepper. Add enough dressing to salad to coat lightly.

SLIM STRAWBERRY CHEF'S SALAD

⅔ c. nonfat sour cream substitute
¼ c. red wine vinegar
2 scallions, sliced
2 to 3 tsp. hot sweet mustard
Salt and pepper to taste
Butter-lettuce leaves
2 pt. baskets strawberries, stemmed

2 c. assorted fresh fruit pieces
   (select from grapefruit
   segment, pineapple chunks,
   orange, and kiwi slices)
8 (1 oz.) slices lean turkey and/or
   ham
½ c. alfalfa sprouts

To make salad dressing, whisk together first 4 ingredients and season with salt and pepper; set aside.

To assemble salad, line four dinner plates with lettuce. Top with fruits, turkey, and sprouts, dividing equally. Serve with dressing on side. Serves 4.

GINGERED FRUIT SALAD

1 c. sliced strawberries
1 c. cantaloupe or honeydew melon
   balls
1 c. chopped fresh pineapple
½ c. seedless green grapes

1 medium nectarine, pitted and
   sliced
2 Tbsp. orange juice
1 tsp. grated ginger root
Mint leaves (optional)

Combine strawberries, melon, pineapple, grapes, nectarine, orange juice, and ginger root; toss gently. Cover and chill about 4 hours or till serving time. Garnish with mint leaves, if desired. Makes 4 servings.

TROPICAL FRUIT PLATE WITH FRESH BERRY SAUCE

½ c. fresh strawberries
½ c. fresh or frozen red raspberries
2 Tbsp. sugar
1 Tbsp. lemon juice

2 ripe kiwi fruits
1 ripe mango or papaya
1 small fresh pineapple
1 orange

For sauce, place strawberries, raspberries, sugar, and lemon juice in a blender container or food processor bowl. Cover and blend or process till smooth. Press mixture through a fine sieve to remove seeds. Cover and chill sauce.

Remove the thin brown skin from kiwi fruits using a small paring knife; slice fruits crosswise. For mango or papaya, use a sharp knife to remove peel; halve fruit. Cut mango flesh away from pit or spoon out seeds from papaya. Thinly slice mango or papaya lengthwise. For pineapple, twist off crown (leaves). Using a sharp knife, cut off peel and remove eyes (brown spots). Slice fruit crosswise; halve slices and cut out woody core. Peel orange and slice crosswise; halve slices, removing any seeds. Cover and chill all fruit till ready to serve.

To serve, arrange fruit on four plates. Spoon about 2 tablespoons sauce over fruit on each plate. Makes 4 servings.

SPINACH STRAWBERRY SALAD

1 bag spinach, washed and torn   1 pt. strawberries, sliced

Dressing - Mix and chill in a jar:

¼ c. sugar
¼ c. vinegar
2 tsp. sesame seeds
1 tsp. poppy seeds

1½ tsp. onion, minced
¼ tsp. Worcestershire sauce
4 tsp. paprika
½ c. vegetable oil

Let dressing warm to room temperature and shake well when ready to serve.

This is a pretty salad for a buffet.

SPINACH SALAD
(Tasty)

1 bunch fresh spinach, trimmed
1 c. pecans, coarsely chopped

12 oz. large curd cottage cheese,
    rinsed

Dressing:

1 c. sour cream
½ c. sugar
3 Tbsp. vinegar

1½ tsp. dry mustard
4 tsp. horseradish
¼ tsp. salt

Put nuts and cottage cheese over fresh spinach. Add dressing before serving; toss. Serves 6 to 8.

ITALIAN TOSSED SALAD

1 bunch red leaf lettuce
1 bunch romaine
1 can artichoke hearts (water
    packed)
1 small jar diced pimentos

3 oz. grated Parmesan cheese
1 small red onion, thinly sliced
1 pkg. Good Seasons salad
    dressing

Combine all, but add cheese and dressing 30 minutes before serving.

BOK CHOY SALAD

6 chicken breasts (boneless,
    skinless), cooked and sliced
4 Tbsp. sesame seeds, toasted
½ c. slivered almonds, toasted
6 green onions, chopped
1 head bok choy, separated,
    washed, patted dry, and
    chopped

1 pkg. Top Ramen chicken noodles
    (uncooked), broken apart
½ pouch fresh snow peas, parboiled

Toss preceding ingredients in large salad bowl. Top with dressing. Serves 6.

Dressing:

¼ c. honey
¼ c. canola oil
6 Tbsp. rice vinegar

½ tsp. salt
1 pkg. seasoning mix from the
    noodles

Prepare and refrigerate overnight.

Easily prepared, the deep green and white combination makes a festive presentation for a hot summer main dish.

RITZY RAMEN SALAD

Everyone will ask you what gives this terrific salad its extra crunch, then they'll ask for the recipe.

1 head cabbage, shredded
6 green onions, sliced
2 pkg. Ramen soup mix (oriental
    flavor)
½ c. slivered almonds, lightly
    toasted

½ c. sunflower seeds
1 bunch cilantro, chopped
6 chicken breast halves, cooked and
    cut into bite-size pieces

Dressing:

¾ c. vegetable oil
½ tsp. salt
6 Tbsp. rice wine vinegar
½ tsp. pepper

4 tsp. sugar
1 seasoning packet from one of the
    preceding Ramen pkg.

1. Combine cabbage and green onions in large bowl and set aside. Can be done the night before and covered.
2. Mix dressing ingredients and refrigerate.
3. Just before serving, crumble uncooked soup noodles. Toss cabbage and onions with the dressing and add almonds, sunflower seeds, cilantro, chicken, and noodles. Serves 8.

49TH STATE SALAD

1 c. celery, chopped
¼ c. onion, chopped
1 (6 oz.) can tuna, drained (1 c. diced
    chicken or salmon may be
    substituted)
1½ c. carrots, shredded
1 small can black olives, sliced

¾ c. salad dressing
½ tsp. prepared mustard
1 (2 or 3 oz.) can shoestring
    potatoes
1½ c. lettuce, shredded
2 hard-boiled eggs

Toss ingredients together with salad dressing. Chill. Just before serving, toss in shoestring potatoes and shredded lettuce. Serve on a lettuce leaf and garnish with sliced hard-boiled eggs. Serves 8.

SALAD PLATTER

1 Tbsp. Dijon mustard
2 Tbsp. red wine vinegar
3 Tbsp. olive oil
2 cloves garlic, minced
¼ c. parsley, minced
1 Tbsp. fresh (or ½ tsp. dried) basil, minced
½ tsp. oregano
Salt and pepper to taste
2 medium red onions, thinly sliced
1 lb. tiny red potatoes
½ lb. green beans, cut in 2 inch pieces
1 (10 oz.) pkg. frozen artichoke hearts
2 lemons, juiced
1 English cucumber, thinly sliced
2 heads leaf lettuce, washed
1 large celery heart, cut into spears
6 medium plum tomatoes, cut into wedges
1 can cooked white beans (cannellini, navy or Northern), drained
4 oz. small black olives

In a bowl, whisk together the mustard, vinegar, 5 tablespoons olive oil, garlic, parsley, basil, oregano, and salt and pepper to taste. Stir in red onions and set aside to marinate.

Cook the potatoes until tender. Slice and fan on a plate. Sprinkle with salt and pepper. Drizzle with 1 tablespoon olive oil and set aside. Cook green beans until al dente; cool.

Cook artichoke hearts according to package directions, adding half the lemon juice to cooking water. Drain, cool, and toss with remaining lemon juice.

Line platter with lettuce leaves. Lift onions from marinade and arrange with the vegetables in an attractive pattern. Just before serving, spoon leftover onion marinade over the vegetables.

CARROT ARTICHOKE SALAD

2 (6 oz.) jars artichoke hearts
2 (14 oz.) jars hearts of palm
1 sweet red pepper, cut in 2 inch slivers
⅓ c. olive oil
3 Tbsp. lemon juice
2 tsp. dried oregano
¼ tsp. salt
Pinch of pepper
5 c. grated carrots
1 clove garlic, minced
Salt and pepper to taste
2 Tbsp. chopped fresh parsley

Drain artichoke and palm hearts; rinse and pat dry. Cut hearts of palm diagonally in halves; halve lengthwise. In bowl, combine artichoke hearts, palm hearts, and red pepper. Stir together ¼ cup oil, 2 tablespoons of the lemon juice, oregano, salt, and pepper. Pour over artichoke mixture. (Can be made ahead and refrigerated up to 8 hours.)

In bowl, toss carrots, remaining oil, lemon juice, and garlic. Season with salt and pepper to taste. Mound artichoke mixture onto serving platter; surround with carrot mixture. Sprinkle with parsley.

LITE CAESAR SALAD

3 c. (¾ inch cubes) sourdough
  bread
Olive oil cooking spray
½ tsp. freshly ground pepper
⅓ c. freshly grated Parmesan
  cheese
3 Tbsp. fat-free chicken broth
1 Tbsp. minced fresh flat-leaf
  parsley
2 tsp. sherry vinegar

1 tsp. Dijon mustard
1 tsp. fresh thyme, minced
2 flat anchovy fillets, drained and
  mashed to paste
1 clove garlic, mashed to a paste
  with ¼ tsp. salt
1 Tbsp. olive oil
2 heads romaine lettuce, trimmed,
  cored, and shredded (10 c.)

Preheat oven to 350°F. In bowl, coat bread lightly with cooking spray; toss with ¼ teaspoon of the pepper. Bake on baking sheet 10 minutes, until golden; cool.

In small bowl, whisk 1 tablespoon of the cheese, the broth, parsley, vinegar, mustard, thyme, the anchovy and garlic pastes, and remaining pepper. Slowly pour in oil, whisking constantly, until thick.

In large serving bowl, toss lettuce with dressing, croutons, and half the remaining cheese. Top with leftover cheese. Makes 6 servings.

MEDITERRANEAN COUSCOUS SALAD

1¾ c. water
½ tsp. salt
1¼ c. couscous
⅓ c. chopped green onions
2 tomatoes, diced
1 c. diced Feta cheese
½ c. black olives, pitted and
  quartered

2 Tbsp. each chopped fresh mint
  and oregano
⅓ c. good quality olive oil
¼ c. fresh lemon juice
Pepper

In saucepan, bring water and salt to boil; and couscous and stir. Cover and remove from heat; let stand for 4 minutes. With fork, stir to separate grains.

In large bowl, combine couscous, green onions, tomatoes, Feta cheese, olives, mint, and oregano. Whisk together olive oil and lemon juice; pour over salad and toss to combine. Season with salt and pepper.

TABBOULEH SALAD WITH CHICKPEAS

1 c. bulgur
1½ c. boiling water
1½ tsp. salt
1 (19 oz.) can chickpeas, drained
  and rinsed
3 green onions, chopped
2 tomatoes, seeded and chopped
Half sweet red pepper, diced
Half sweet green pepper, diced

1 small English cucumber, seeded
  and chopped
1 c. chopped fresh parsley
¼ c. chopped fresh mint
⅓ c. olive oil
¼ c. lemon juice
1 clove garlic, minced
1 tsp. Dijon mustard
Salt and pepper to taste

In large bowl, cover bulgur with boiling water and salt; soak for 20 minutes. Drain, pressing out any excess water. Add chickpeas, green onions, tomatoes, peppers, cucumber, parsley, and mint.

In small bowl, whisk together oil, lemon juice, garlic, and mustard. Pour over bulgur mixture. Season with salt and pepper to taste. Cover and refrigerate overnight. Pack into individual containers or spoon into lettuce-lined pita pockets and wrap well.

PASTA SALAD WITH FETA DRESSING

2 c. medium pasta shells
1 Tbsp. olive oil
⅓ c. diced sweet pepper
¼ c. chopped green onions
¼ c. slivered black olives
¼ c. Feta cheese
3 Tbsp. white wine vinegar
2 Tbsp. minced, fresh parsley
1 clove garlic, minced

½ tsp. dried oregano
¼ tsp. salt
¼ tsp. pepper
⅓ c. olive oil
1 c. halved cherry tomatoes
½ c. coarsely chopped seeded cucumber
6 tender leaves of romaine lettuce

In pot of boiling, salted water, cook pasta shells until al dente. Drain. Rinse under cold running water and drain again. In bowl, combine pasta with 1 tablespoon olive oil. Add red pepper, onions, and olives.

In small bowl, mash Feta cheese with vinegar; blend in parsley, garlic, oregano, salt, and pepper. Whisk in ⅓ cup oil. Before serving, add tomatoes and cucumbers to pasta. Drizzle dressing over salad. Taste and adjust seasoning.

Line salad bowl with lettuce; mound with salad. Makes 4 servings.

ASPARAGUS-AND-TOMATO PASTA SALAD

2 c. diagonally sliced asparagus (about 1 lb.)
⅓ c. orange juice
3 Tbsp. white wine vinegar
2 Tbsp. water
1 Tbsp. olive oil
2 tsp. Dijon mustard
¼ tsp. freshly ground pepper
⅛ tsp. salt

2 c. cooked, small sea shell macaroni (about 1 c. uncooked pasta)
1½ c. quartered cherry tomatoes
1 c. diced yellow bell pepper
½ c. thinly sliced fresh basil leaves
⅓ c. chopped kalamata olives
¼ c. thinly sliced green onions
2 Tbsp. capers

Steam asparagus, covered, 2 minutes; drain and set aside. Combine orange juice and next 6 ingredients (orange juice through salt) in a large bowl; stir well with a wire whisk. Add asparagus, pasta, and remaining ingredients; toss well. Yield: 6 servings (serving size 1 cup).

PRESTO PESTO PASTA SALAD

1 red pepper, sliced julienne
1½ c. broccoli, steamed until bright
   green
3 c. cooked pasta (preferably a fat
   and stubby shape like wheels
   or rotini)

2 Tbsp. pesto
½ Tbsp. olive oil
⅛ tsp. salt
¼ tsp. freshly ground pepper

Toss together the bell pepper, broccoli, and pasta. Mix the pesto, oil, salt, and pepper in a small bowl. Pour over the pasta mixture and toss until evenly coated. Serves 4.

ITALIAN PASTA SUMMER SALAD

9 oz. refrigerated cheese and basil
   tortellini
5 to 7 oz. tri-color spiral pasta
1 can black pitted olives, drained
1 can green pimento stuffed olives,
   drained
1 small jar artichoke hearts in oil
1 small jar sweet roasted peppers,
   drained

1 can garbanzo beans, drained
1 small jar sun dried tomatoes in oil,
   drained
1 pkg. Good Seasons Italian
   dressing mix, prepared
⅔ c. salami, cut into mouth size
   pieces (optional)

Prepare pastas as directed; drain well. Mix all ingredients. Refrigerate day before. *Enjoy!* Excellent as side dish or main course. Keeps well when refrigerated. Serves 12 as side dish.

JUST CAN'T-BE-BEET BEEF SALAD

¾ lb. small red, striped, gold, or
   white beets or regular red
   beets
6 c. torn mixed greens
12 oz. boneless beef sirloin steak or
   loin steak (1 inch thick)

½ medium cucumber or yellow
   summer squash, halved
   lengthwise and sliced
1 c. enoki mushrooms
Creamy Dressing

For beets, cut off all but 1 inch of stems and roots; wash tops. Cook whole beets, covered, in boiling water in a medium saucepan till crisp-tender, allowing 15 to 20 minutes for small beets or 40 to 50 minutes for regular beets (If using beets of several colors, cook red ones separately.) Drain; cool slightly. Slip skins off beets; slice beets. Cover and chill till ready to use.

Grill meat, uncovered, directly over medium coals for 16 to 22 minutes for medium-rare to medium, turning once. Thinly slice steak.

To serve, arrange mixed greens on four dinner plates. Top with cooked beets, beef, cucumber or squash, and enoki mushrooms. Pass Cream Dressing. Makes 4 servings.

Creamy Dressing: Stir together ⅓ cup buttermilk, ⅓ cup fat-free mayonnaise dressing or salad dressing, 2 teaspoons fresh dill or ½ teaspoon dried dill weed, 1 teaspoon honey or sugar, and 1 teaspoon prepared horseradish in a small bowl. Cover and chill till serving time.

COPPER MOUNTAIN HOT TURKEY SALAD

¼ c. fat-free mayonnaise dressing
   or salad dressing
3 Tbsp. orange juice
1 tsp. honey
¼ tsp. dry mustard
2 turkey breast tenderloin steaks (8
   oz. total)

4 c. mixed salad greens
1 c. tiny red grapes or seedless red
   grapes
6 to 8 large strawberries
1 kiwi fruit, peeled and sliced
¼ cantaloupe, sliced or cubed (1 c.)

For dressing, stir together mayonnaise dressing or salad dressing, orange juice, honey, and mustard in a small bowl till combined. Remove 1 tablespoon of the dressing. Cover and chill the remaining dressing.

Brush turkey with reserved 1 tablespoon dressing. Grill turkey, uncovered, directly over medium coals for 15 to 18 minutes or till tender and no longer pink, turning once.

Meanwhile, arrange greens on two dinner plates. Arrange grapes, strawberries, kiwi fruit, and cantaloupe atop greens. Slice each turkey tenderloin crosswise into 5 or 6 pieces; place on fruit. Serve salad with the remaining chilled dressing. Store any leftover dressing in refrigerator for up to 1 week. Makes 2 servings.

The creamy orange-honey dressing doubles as a brush-on sauce for the grilled turkey.

THAI ORANGE CHICKEN SALAD

2 large carrots
2 sweet red peppers
1 tsp. sesame oil
3 green onions
2 cooked boneless chicken breasts
   (about 10 oz. total)

2 heads Boston lettuce
1½ c. bean sprouts
¾ c. fresh cilantro
2 sliced half oranges

Dressing:

4 cloves garlic
⅔ c. water
½ c. smooth peanut butter
⅓ c. rice vinegar

1 Tbsp. soy sauce
1½ tsp. granulated sugar
½ tsp. hot crushed pepper flakes

Using vegetable peeler, peel carrots into long strips. Slice peppers into thin rounds. In nonstick skillet, heat oil; cook carrots and red peppers over medium heat for 5 minutes or until tender crisp. Leave one inch of green at ends of onions; slice onions lengthwise into strips. Cut chicken into thin strips.

Dressing: In blender or food processor, process garlic until finely chopped; add water, peanut butter, vinegar, soy sauce, sugar, and hot pepper flakes. Process until smooth.

To assemble: Arrange lettuce leaves on 8 plates. Top with carrot mixture, bean sprouts, chicken, cilantro, and onions. Garnish with orange slices. Serve dressing on side. Makes 8 servings, about 205 calories each.

HOT CHICKEN SALAD

2 c. cooked chicken
2 Tbsp. onion, minced
1 c. celery, diced
2 Tbsp. lemon juice
⅔ c. mayonnaise
⅔ c. cream of chicken soup

⅔ c. slivered almonds
4 eggs, hard-boiled and diced
½ tsp. salt
½ tsp. pepper
2 c. Cheddar cheese, shredded
Potato chips

Mix ingredients down to cheese together well. Put in 9x13 inch baking dish. Sprinkle the cheese over top and crumble potato chips over all. Bake at 350° for 45 minutes or until bubbly.

MUSTARD-GLAZED CHICKEN SALAD

¼ c. peach preserves
¼ c. coarse grain brown mustard
¼ c. white wine vinegar
4 large skinless, boneless chicken
   breast halves (about 1 lb.
   total)
1 (10 oz.) pkg. Italian blend torn
   mixed salad greens or 12 c.
   lightly packed torn romaine and
   radicchio

1 large carrot, cut into matchstick
   size strips
1 c. sliced fresh mushrooms

For glaze, combine preserves, mustard, and vinegar in a small saucepan. Cook over low heat just till bubbly. Remove from heat; set aside.

Rinse chicken; pat dry with paper towels. Remove 3 tablespoons of the glaze and brush onto both sides of chicken. Stir 1 tablespoon water into remaining glaze; set aside.

Grill chicken on the rack of an uncovered grill directly over medium coals for 12 to 15 minutes or till chicken is tender and no longer pink, turning once halfway through grilling time.

To serve, arrange salad greens, carrot strips, and mushrooms on individual plates. Diagonally slice the chicken breast halves; reassemble breast halves over greens. Drizzle salad with reserved sauce. Makes 4 servings.

The three-ingredient glaze doubles as the dressing for the salad.

CHINESE CHICKEN SALAD

Salad:

3 chicken breasts
Garlic powder
Seasoned salt
1 head lettuce, shredded fine
4 green onions, chopped fine (tops
   also)

1 Tbsp. parsley or cilantro, chopped
½ c. blanched, slivered almonds,
   toasted and chopped
½ c. celery, sliced thin
1 small can sliced water chestnuts

Dressing:

½ c. cooking oil	1 tsp. MSG (optional)
½ c. white vinegar	1 Tbsp. sesame oil
¼ c. sugar	3 Tbsp. plum sauce
½ tsp. pepper	3 Tbsp. shoyu (soy sauce)
¼ tsp. salt	1 Tbsp. hoisin sauce (optional)

Topping:

1½ c. vegetable oil
1 pkg. won ton skins, sliced thin like
   noodles

Place all dressing ingredients in glass jar and shake well. For topping, deep-fry won tons in oil until puffy and light brown. Drain on paper towels and cool. To make salad, bone chicken breasts; sprinkle with garlic powder and seasoned salt and broil. Slice cooked chicken into thin strips. To assemble salad, toss lettuce, onions, parsley, almonds, celery, and chicken with dressing. Sprinkle fried won tons on top and serve. Serves 8.

Note: The following can be used in place of chicken: Roast beef, pork, veal, ham, sliced sandwich meat, canned tuna or salmon, drained and flaked. Refrigerate leftover dressing to use later.

FENNEL, PUMMELO, AND SHRIMP SALAD

1 pummelo or large white grapefruit	⅛ tsp. ground white pepper
1 orange	2 medium fennel bulbs, thinly sliced
Fresh orange juice	1 medium yellow onion, thinly sliced
1 Tbsp. salad oil	1 Tbsp. cooking oil
1 Tbsp. honey	24 medium shrimp in shells (about
1 Tbsp. lime juice	1 lb.)
1 Tbsp. lemon juice	Butter and red-leaf lettuce
2 cloves garlic, minced	

Section pummelo or grapefruit and orange over a small bowl, reserving juice. Add enough fresh orange juice to equal ¼ cup. Add 1 tablespoon oil, honey, lime juice, lemon juice, garlic, and white pepper to bowl. Whisk till well combined. Set dressing aside.

Cook fennel and onion in 1 tablespoon hot oil for 2 minutes. Let cool to room temperature. Shell and devein shrimp. Cook shrimp in boiling water 2 minutes or till just opaque. Do not overcook. Drain and cool.

Arrange butter lettuce and red-leaf lettuce on four plates. Place onion and fennel in center; arrange shrimp, orange, and pummelo or grapefruit sections atop. Drizzle with dressing. Makes 4 servings.

Grapefruit, lemon, and lime juices accent the flavor of fennel.

TOTE ALONG TUNA SALAD

2 c. cooked small pasta
½ c. chopped green onions
4 leaves leaf lettuce
1 (6 oz.) can flaked tuna, drained
1 large red pepper, seeded and
    chopped

1 c. cooked green beans, cut in ½
    inch slices, or peas, or cherry
    tomatoes, halved
2 Tbsp. chopped fresh parsley

Dressing:

2 Tbsp. lemon juice
2 Tbsp. red wine vinegar
1 Tbsp. Dijon mustard
1 clove garlic, minced
½ tsp. Worcestershire sauce

¼ tsp. dried oregano
¼ tsp. salt
Pinch of pepper
¾ c. olive or vegetable oil

Dressing: In small bowl, combine lemon juice, vinegar, mustard, garlic, Worcestershire, oregano, salt, and pepper. Gradually whisk in oil.

In large bowl, combine pasta with green onions. Stir in ¼ cup of the dressing, coating well. Line bottom of four 2 cup plastic containers with lettuce leaves. Over lettuce, layer ¼ each of the pasta, tuna, red pepper, green beans, tomatoes, and parsley. Top each cup with ¼ of the remaining dressing. Cover and refrigerate for up to 2 days. Makes 4 servings.

RED ONION SALAD WITH HONEY MUSTARD SAUCE

3 large red onions, sliced
½ chopped green onions

¼ c. chopped fresh parsley

Honey Mustard Sauce:

2 Tbsp. all-purpose flour
2 Tbsp. dry mustard
1 tsp. salt

½ c. white vinegar
¼ c. liquid honey
2 eggs

Honey Mustard Sauce: In top of double boiler, combine flour, mustard, and salt. In bowl, beat together 1 cup of water, vinegar, honey, and eggs. Beat into dry ingredients. Cook over boiling water, beating with electric mixer at low setting until mixture is consistency of thick cream. (Sauce can be made ahead and refrigerated for up to 1 week.)

Pour boiling water over onions in colander. Drain and refresh under cold water. Place in glass bowl with onions and parsley. Drizzle with ¼ of the sauce; toss gently. Makes 6 servings.

The dressing is wonderful tossed with coleslaw. This salad is ideal for a large buffet and excellent with cold meats.

POTATO SALAD WITH FRESH PEAS

5 unpeeled potatoes (about 2 lb.)
2 Tbsp. wine vinegar
2 Tbsp. vegetable oil
½ c. shelled peas (or thawed frozen
  petite peas)
¼ c. minced fresh parsley
¼ c. diced celery
¼ c. chopped green onions

¼ c. diced sweet pepper
⅓ c. mayonnaise
⅓ c. sour cream
1 Tbsp. Dijon mustard
¼ tsp. salt
¼ tsp. pepper
¼ tsp. celery seed
Fresh parsley sprigs

In pot of boiling water, cook potatoes until tender, but not mushy; drain. Cool, peel, and chop. Place in salad bowl. Sprinkle with vinegar and oil, tossing to coat evenly.

Meanwhile, cook peas, if using fresh, until tender. Drain. Add peas, parsley, celery, onions, and red pepper to potatoes, tossing gently.

In small bowl, stir together mayonnaise, sour cream, mustard, salt, pepper, and celery seed. Blend into potato salad. Garnish with parsley sprigs.

NEW-POTATO SALAD WITH BASIL AND SUN-DRIED TOMATOES

2½ lb. new potatoes
¼ c. oil drained from sun-dried
  tomatoes
6 Tbsp. vegetable oil
6 Tbsp. white wine vinegar
2 tsp. Dijon mustard
2 garlic cloves, crushed

1 tsp. salt
Pinch of freshly ground pepper
1 c. thinly sliced celery
¼ c. slivered fresh basil
⅔ c. thinly sliced green onions
¼ c. slivered, drained sun-dried
  tomatoes (packed in oil)

Scrub potatoes. Boil in salted water until just tender; drain and let cool. Meanwhile, prepare dressing. Place the ¼ cup oil from sun-dried tomatoes, vegetable oil, mustard, garlic, salt, and pepper in small bowl. Whisk until blended.

Peel and cut potatoes into ½ inch cubes. Place in large bowl and add half the dressing; mix lightly. Add celery, basil, green onions, sun-dried tomatoes, and remaining dressing; mix lightly. Cover and chill if not serving shortly. Bring to room temperature before serving.

POTATO AND TUNA SALAD WITH CAPERS AND DIJON DRESSING

2 medium potatoes
2 green onions, sliced
1 (6 oz.) can tuna
3 Tbsp. white wine vinegar
3 Tbsp. olive oil
2 Tbsp. finely chopped parsley or
  cilantro

2 Tbsp. drained capers
1 tsp. Dijon mustard
Salt and freshly ground pepper to
  taste

Cook unpeeled potatoes in boiling water until tender. Drain and cool. Peel and cube potatoes. Combine potatoes, green onions, and tuna in bowl. In separate bowl, whisk together vinegar, olive oil, parsley, capers, mustard, and salt and pepper. Pour over potato mixture and toss to coat. Serve at room temperature.

ASPEN-SALMON MOUSSE

1 env. unflavored gelatin
½ c. cold water
1 (15½ oz.) can salmon, drained, or
    2 (6½ to 7 oz.) cans tuna,
    drained
½ c. mayonnaise
2 Tbsp. green onions, chopped

2 Tbsp. dry sherry
2 Tbsp. lemon juice
2 tsp. fresh dill, chopped, or ¾ tsp.
    dried dill weed
½ tsp. salt
½ tsp. bottled hot pepper sauce
1 c. whipping cream

Garnish:

1 medium cucumber, sliced
1 medium lemon, sliced

Fresh dill (optional)

In small saucepan, sprinkle gelatin evenly over water; let stand 1 minute. Cook over low heat, stirring constantly, until gelatin is completely dissolved. Remove saucepan from heat; set aside.

In blender container or in food processor with steel blade attached, blend gelatin mixture with next 9 ingredients until smooth.

In medium bowl with mixer at medium-high speed, beat cream until soft peaks form. Gently fold whipped cream into salmon mixture. Pour into 6 cup mold; cover and refrigerate 4 to 5 hours or until set.

To serve, unmold mousse onto chilled plate. Garnish with cucumber, lemon slices, and fresh dill. Serves 6.

RED RASPBERRY-CRANBERRY SALAD

Try this with your next turkey feast.

2 (3 oz.) pkg. red raspberry gelatin
1½ c. boiling water
1 (10 oz.) ctn. frozen red raspberries
1 (10 oz.) pkg. frozen cranberry
    relish

½ c. ginger ale
Juice and grated rind of 1 lemon
½ c. slivered almonds (optional)

Dissolve gelatin in boiling water. Add frozen raspberries and cranberry relish and stir until melted and evenly blended (may need to cut frozen items into chunks) and gelatin is partially thickened. Stir in ginger ale and lemon rind and juice. Add almonds if desired. Pour into prepared mold and chill until set. Serves 8 to 12.

ROSY FRENCH DRESSING

1¼ c. vinegar
1 c. ketchup
¾ c. granulated sugar
⅔ c. dried onion flakes
4 tsp. dry mustard

1 Tbsp. celery seed
1 Tbsp. paprika
1 tsp. garlic powder
2¼ c. vegetable oil

In food processor or blender, whirl together vinegar, ketchup, sugar, onion flakes, mustard, celery seed, paprika, and garlic powder just until mixed. With machine running, gradually add oil. Store in refrigerator for up to 4 weeks.

Notes

Vegetables

EQUIVALENT CHART

3 tsp.	1 Tbsp.
2 Tbsp.	⅛ c.
4 Tbsp.	¼ c.
8 Tbsp.	½ c.
16 Tbsp.	1 c.
5 Tbsp. + 1 tsp.	⅓ c.
12 Tbsp.	¾ c.
4 oz.	½ c.
8 oz.	1 c.
16 oz.	1 lb.
1 oz.	2 Tbsp. fat or liquid
2 c.	1 pt.
2 pt.	1 qt.
1 qt.	4 c.
⅝ c.	½ c. + 2 Tbsp.
⅞ c.	¾ c. + 2 Tbsp.
1 jigger	1½ fl. oz. (3 Tbsp.)
8 to 10 egg whites	1 c.
12 to 14 egg yolks	1 c.
1 c. unwhipped cream	2 c. whipped
1 lb. shredded American cheese	4 c.
¼ lb. crumbled Bleu cheese	1 c.
1 lemon	3 Tbsp. juice
1 orange	⅓ c. juice
1 lb. unshelled walnuts	1½ to 1¾ c. shelled
2 c. fat	1 lb.
1 lb. butter	2 c. or 4 sticks
2 c. granulated sugar	1 lb.
3½-4 c. unsifted powdered sugar	1 lb.
2¼ c. packed brown sugar	1 lb.
4 c. sifted flour	1 lb.
4½ c. cake flour	1 lb.
3½ c. unsifted whole wheat flour	1 lb.
4 oz. (1 to 1¼ c.) uncooked macaroni	2¼ c. cooked
7 oz. spaghetti	4 c. cooked
4 oz. (1½ to 2 c.) uncooked noodles	2 c. cooked
28 saltine crackers	1 c. crumbs
4 slices bread	1 c. crumbs
14 square graham crackers	1 c. crumbs
22 vanilla wafers	1 c. crumbs

SUBSTITUTIONS FOR A MISSING INGREDIENT

1 square **chocolate** (1 ounce) = 3 or 4 tablespoons cocoa plus ½ tablespoon fat

1 tablespoon **cornstarch** (for thickening) = 2 tablespoons flour

1 cup sifted **all-purpose flour** = 1 cup plus 2 tablespoons sifted cake flour

1 cup sifted **cake flour** = 1 cup minus 2 tablespoons sifted all-purpose flour

1 teaspoon **baking powder** = ¼ teaspoon baking soda plus ½ teaspoon cream of tartar

1 cup **sour milk** = 1 cup sweet milk into which 1 tablespoon vinegar or lemon juice has been stirred

1 cup **sweet milk** = 1 cup sour milk or buttermilk plus ½ teaspoon baking soda

¾ cup **cracker crumbs** = 1 cup bread crumbs

1 cup **cream, sour, heavy** = ⅓ cup butter and ⅔ cup milk in any sour milk recipe

1 teaspoon **dried herbs** = 1 tablespoon fresh herbs

1 cup **whole milk** = ½ cup evaporated milk and ½ cup water or 1 cup reconstituted nonfat dry milk and 1 tablespoon butter

2 ounces **compressed yeast** = 3 (¼ ounce) packets of dry yeast

1 tablespoon **instant minced onion, rehydrated** = 1 small fresh onion

1 tablespoon **prepared mustard** = 1 teaspoon dry mustard

⅛ teaspoon **garlic powder** = 1 small pressed clove of garlic

1 lb. **whole dates** = 1½ cups, pitted and cut

3 medium **bananas** = 1 cup mashed

3 cups **dry corn flakes** = 1 cup crushed

10 **miniature marshmallows** = 1 large marshmallow

GENERAL OVEN CHART

Very slow oven	250° to 300°F.
Slow oven	300° to 325°F.
Moderate oven	325° to 375°F.
Medium hot oven	375° to 400°F.
Hot oven	400° to 450°F.
Very hot oven	450° to 500°F.

CONTENTS OF CANS

Of the different sizes of cans used by commercial canners, the most common are:

Size:	Average Contents
8 oz.	1 cup
Picnic	1¼ cups
No. 300	1¾ cups
No. 1 tall	2 cups
No. 303	2 cups
No. 2	2½ cups
No. 2½	3½ cups
No. 3	4 cups
No. 10	12 to 13 cups

VEGETABLES

NO-FAT CRISP COOKED ASPARAGUS

2 lb. asparagus
2 Tbsp. butter-flavor sprinkles

Freshly ground black pepper

Snap off and discard woody bases from fresh asparagus. Bias-slice into ⅛ inch thick slices.

Cook asparagus in a small amount of boiling water in a medium saucepan about 3 minutes or till crisp-tender. Drain; add butter-flavor sprinkles. Stir to mix and dissolve the sprinkles. Transfer to serving dish. Sprinkle with pepper. Makes 4 servings.

Microwave oven directions: Place asparagus and 2 tablespoons water in a microwave-safe casserole. Cover and cook on 100% power (HIGH) for 3 to 4 minutes or till just crisp-tender; drain. Add butter-flavor sprinkles and stir to mix. Serve as above.

ASPARAGUS WITH PARMESAN CHEESE AND BACON

3 Tbsp. butter
2 Tbsp. minced green onion
4 slices bacon, cooked, drained, and crumbled

⅓ c. grated Parmesan cheese
⅛ tsp. pepper
2 lb. medium asparagus, trimmed

Melt butter in a small skillet. Saute onion until tender, about 3 minutes. Remove from heat. Stir in bacon, cheese, and pepper.

Meanwhile, steam asparagus until tender, about 8 minutes. Drain. Place hot asparagus on serving dish. Sprinkle with cheese mixture. Serve immediately. Makes 6 servings.

ROASTED ASPARAGUS
(Lowfat, low-cal)

Preparation time: 5 minutes. Roast: 15 minutes. Heat: 5 minutes. Cost per serving: 42 cents. Planning tip: Can be made up through step 3 up to 1 day ahead.

2 lb. asparagus, woody stems
    broken off
1 Tbsp. olive oil (preferably extra-
    virgin)

½ tsp. salt
⅛ tsp. pepper
8 lemon wedges

1. Heat oven to 425°F. Have a 15½ x 10½ inch or larger jellyroll pan ready.
2. Put asparagus in pan. Drizzle with oil and sprinkle with salt and pepper. Turn until evenly coated, then arrange in a single layer.
3. Roast 10 to 15 minutes or until tender when pierced and tips start to brown. Serve immediately or cool in pan; cover and refrigerate.
4. To serve: Reheat in a 350°F. oven 5 minutes. Serve with lemon wedges.

ASPARAGUS CASSEROLE

5 Tbsp. butter or margarine
3 Tbsp. flour
¾ tsp. salt
2 (14 oz.) cans cut asparagus
¾ c. milk
1 c. grated American cheese

1⅓ c. bread crumbs
5 hard cooked eggs, sliced
1 (4 oz.) can sliced mushrooms,
  drained
1 Tbsp. parsley or flakes
2 Tbsp. chopped pimiento (optional)

Melt 3 tablespoons of the butter. Add flour and salt. Cook a few minutes over moderate heat, stirring. Drain asparagus. Reserve ¾ cup of the liquid. Gradually add this liquid and milk to the flour mixture. Cook over moderate heat, stirring until thickened. Add cheese and stir until cheese melts. Saute bread crumbs a few minutes with the remaining 2 tablespoons butter.

In a 2 quart buttered casserole (or a 2 quart shallow baking dish), layer half of each of the following ingredients in this order: Drain asparagus, sliced eggs, cheese sauce, mushrooms, and bread crumbs. (If using a shallow baking pan, use all the ingredients.) Repeat layers. Top with parsley and pimiento. Bake in preheated 350° oven for 30 minutes.

ARTICHOKE-SPINACH BAKE

1 (8½ oz.) can artichoke hearts,
  drained and quartered
2 (10 oz.) pkg. frozen chopped
  spinach, thawed and
  squeezed dry
8 oz. cream cheese

1 cube butter or margarine
8 slices bacon, cooked, drained,
  and crumbled
Parmesan cheese, freshly grated
Slivered almonds or pecans,
  toasted (for garnish)

Preheat oven to 350°. Cut artichokes into quarters; place in large bowl. Add spinach. Melt butter and cream cheese together in small saucepan. Cream cheese will be lumpy. Mix with vegetables and spoon into 8x8 inch baking dish. Sprinkle bacon on top. Sprinkle lavishly with Parmesan. Top with almonds or pecans if desired. Bake until bubbly, about 30 minutes. Preparation time is 20 minutes. Serves 4 to 6.

COLORFUL COLORADO BEANS

1 lb. bacon, chopped
1 lb. onions, chopped
1 clove garlic, finely minced
1 lb. hamburger (or sausage)
2 (15 oz.) cans red kidney beans,
  drained
1 (29 oz.) can baked beans

2 (15 oz.) cans baby lima beans,
  drained
4 Tbsp. vinegar
2 tsp. dry mustard
1 c. brown sugar, firmly packed
1 c. catsup
2 Tbsp. Worcestershire sauce

Fry bacon in large skillet until crisp. Remove from skillet. Pour off all but about 3 tablespoons bacon fat. Fry onions and garlic. Remove from skillet. Fry hamburger (or sausage) until done but not browned. Mix bacon, onion, garlic, hamburger (or sausage), and beans and place in a large deep greased baking dish (about 3 quarts or larger). Blend together well the last 5 ingredients and pour over bean mixture. Bake at 350° about 2 to 2½ hours. Serves 10 to 12.

44

SPEEDY BAKED BEANS

A fast bean bake when you consider the fact that the seasonings blend with the beans in minutes.

Vegetable cooking spray
2 (16 oz.) cans pork and beans
1 Tbsp. minced onion
2 Tbsp. molasses

2 Tbsp. catsup
¼ tsp. dry mustard
¼ tsp. chili powder

Coat inside of microwave-proof 1½ quart casserole with vegetable cooking spray according to directions. Stir together all ingredients in casserole until well mixed. Cover and microwave 10 minutes, stirring after 5 minutes. Makes 6 servings.

PINEAPPLE BEETS

¼ c. brown sugar
2 Tbsp. corn starch
¼ tsp. ginger
½ tsp. salt
1 (16 oz.) can sweetened pineapple
   chunks, drained (save juice)

⅓ c. vinegar
½ c. water
2 (16 oz.) cans beets (small, whole,
   or sliced), drained

Combine brown sugar, corn starch, ginger, and salt. Drain juice from pineapple and add juice to brown sugar mixture, then add vinegar and water. Cook until thick and bubbly. Stir in beets and pineapple. Serve warm or cold. Serves 8. *Great with ham dishes.*

BROCCOLI SOUFFLE

¼ c. butter or margarine
¼ c. flour
1¼ c. milk
½ c. Cheddar cheese, grated
5 eggs, separated

1½ tsp. salt
⅛ tsp. garlic powder
1½ c. cooked broccoli, chopped
2 Tbsp. lemon juice

Melt butter. Add flour and mix until smooth. Gradually add milk. Cook over low heat, stirring constantly, until thickened. Add cheese and continue to cook, stirring frequently, until melted. Remove from heat. Beat egg yolks well. Blend into cheese mixture with ½ teaspoon of salt. Add garlic powder, broccoli, and lemon juice. Sprinkle egg whites with remaining salt; beat until stiff. Fold egg whites into cheese sauce until blended. Turn into greased and dusted 1½ quart casserole. Place casserole in a pan containing about 1 inch hot water. Bake in a preheated 350° oven about 45 minutes or until firm. Yield: 6 servings.

DILLED FRESH BROCCOLI

1 large head broccoli, clean and
   break flower into small pieces
½ c. olive oil
½ c. vinegar

1 clove garlic, minced or pressed
1 Tbsp. dill weed
Salt and pepper to taste

Combine all ingredients into Ziploc bag so it can be turned. Turn several times. Marinate 24 hours.

BRAISED ONIONS WITH BRUSSELS SPROUTS

½ to ¾ lb. salt pork or bacon, diced
¼ c. butter or margarine
1 lb. small white onions, peeled
½ c. chicken broth

2 Tbsp. sugar
½ tsp. salt
2 (10 oz.) pkg. frozen Brussels
    sprouts

Fry salt pork until crisp. Drain and set aside. Melt butter in a skillet. Add the onions, chicken broth, sugar, and salt. Cover and cook the onions over low heat, stirring occasionally, until they are tender and most of the liquid is absorbed. Add sprouts. Cover and steam until sprouts are tender. Remove to a serving dish. Sprinkle with salt pork. Can be made ahead and reheated in the oven if desired. Yield: 8 servings.

CARROTS WITH BALSAMIC VINEGAR

5 or 6 medium carrots
¼ c. water
3 Tbsp. butter (divided)

Salt to taste
2 to 3 Tbsp. brown sugar
½ to 1 tsp. balsamic vinegar

Peel and slice carrots. Place in saucepan with water, 1 tablespoon butter, and salt. Cover tightly and simmer over low heat for 15 to 20 minutes or until just done. Carrots should have absorbed water. If not, drain. In small saucepan, combine brown sugar, 2 tablespoons butter, and vinegar. Cook until sugar dissolves. Pour over carrots and serve.

VAIL CARROTS AND LEEKS JULIENNE

10 medium carrots, peeled
4 leeks
½ c. butter
2 Tbsp. cold water

2 tsp. sugar
1 tsp. salt
½ tsp. freshly ground pepper

Cut carrots into julienne strips. Discard root ends and top 3 inches of leeks. Clean remaining leeks carefully and cut into julienne strips.

In large skillet, place ¼ cup butter, the vegetables, and remaining ingredients. Cover tightly with foil, pressing it down onto the vegetables. Cook for 10 to 15 minutes, stirring occasionally. When vegetables are tender-crisp, add remaining butter and adjust seasonings.

COINTREAU CARROTS

16 carrots or 1½ lb. peeled,
    diagonally thin sliced
4½ Tbsp. butter
1 Tbsp. lemon juice

3 Tbsp. Cointreau
3 Tbsp. minced parsley
1 (8 oz.) can mandarin oranges,
    drained

Saute carrots in butter over low heat until tender but slightly crisp. Add lemon juice and Cointreau and simmer until alcohol evaporates, about 1 minute. Toss with mandarin oranges and sprinkle with parsley just before serving. *Glamorous and perfect for holidays!*

46

MANITOU CARROTS

1½ lb. carrots, pared and thinly
    sliced
2 Tbsp. horseradish
½ c. mayonnaise
2 Tbsp. chopped onion
¼ tsp. salt
Dash of pepper

    Combine all ingredients and place in a 1½ quart casserole. Bake at 350° for 30 minutes. Serves 8 to 10.

CASTLE ROCK CHEESE AND CORN

1 (3 oz.) pkg. cream cheese
¼ c. milk
1 Tbsp. butter
½ tsp. onion salt
1 large (32 oz. or more) bag frozen
    cut corn

    Put cream cheese, milk, butter, and salt in a saucepan and stir until cheese is melted. Mix with corn; bake at 350° until corn is heated through, about 30 minutes. Serves 8 to 10.

SAN LUIS CORN PUDDING

2 c. corn
3 eggs, slightly beaten
2½ Tbsp. sugar
1½ Tbsp. melted butter
2 c. scalded milk
1 tsp. salt
⅛ tsp. pepper
2 Tbsp. flour

    Combine ingredients. Bake in buttered baking dish in slow oven (325°F.) until firm and golden on top, 40 to 45 minutes. *An old family favorite.*

EGGPLANT CREOLE

1 medium eggplant, diced
3 Tbsp. butter
3 Tbsp. flour
3 large tomatoes (2 c.), diced
1 green pepper, chopped
1 onion, chopped
1 tsp. salt
1 Tbsp. brown sugar
½ bay leaf
2 whole cloves
Shredded Cheddar cheese and/or
    buttered bread crumbs

    Cook eggplant 10 minutes in boiling, salted water. Drain and set aside in 3 quart casserole. Melt butter and add flour. To this mixture, add tomatoes, green pepper, onion, salt, brown sugar, bay leaf, and cloves. Pour this mixture over eggplant and top with desired shredded Cheddar cheese and/or buttered bread crumbs. Bake at 350° for 30 minutes. Serves 6.

GREEN BEANS WITH FRESH MUSHROOMS

1 lb. fresh green beans
1 onion, chopped
⅓ c. olive oil
½ lb. fresh mushrooms
2 Tbsp. chopped parsley
1 Tbsp. mint leaves, chopped
1 tsp. salt
Dash of pepper
½ c. water
2 to 3 Tbsp. fresh lemon juice

Remove ends and strings from beans; cut into 2 inch pieces or leave whole and cut lengthwise. Saute chopped onion in olive oil until soft; add sliced mushrooms and stir over moderate heat for 5 minutes. Add beans, parsley, mint, seasonings, and water. Cook slowly for 20 minutes or until desired tenderness. Watch carefully so beans won't scorch. Add lemon juice before removing from heat. Serves 4 to 6.

LA JUNTA MARINATED GREEN BEANS

2 Tbsp. wine vinegar
1 Tbsp. Worcestershire sauce
½ tsp. dry mustard

Dash of Tabasco sauce
1 medium can green beans

Mix all ingredients and marinate for a few hours. Heat and serve or serve cold.

MARVELOUS MUSHROOMS

1 lb. fresh mushrooms
⅓ c. soft butter
1 Tbsp. parsley, minced
1 Tbsp. onion, minced
1 Tbsp. Dijon mustard

1 tsp. salt
Pinch of cayenne
Pinch of nutmeg
1½ Tbsp. flour
1 c. heavy cream

Place mushrooms in a baking dish. Cream together butter, parsley, onion, mustard, salt, cayenne, nutmeg, and flour. Dot mushrooms with mixture and pour on the cream. Bake in a 350° oven for about an hour, uncovered. Stir once or twice during the baking. Serves 4 to 6.

HEARTS OF PALM AU COINTREAU

1 (14 oz.) can hearts of palm, cut
    into 1 inch slices
¼ lb. butter
1 Tbsp. chopped pimiento

¼ c. chopped, salted pecans (or
    more if you like)
1 Tbsp. Cointreau
Crisp chilled Bibb lettuce

Drain vegetable and saute in butter, together with pimento and pecans, until just heated through. Add Cointreau and stir to blend. Serve piping hot on chilled Bibb lettuce cups.

BLAKE STREET FRENCH PEAS

4 Tbsp. chopped onions
½ head Boston lettuce, shredded
1 Tbsp. butter

2 (10 oz.) frozen petite peas, cooked
    and drained
Salt and pepper to taste

Saute onions and lettuce in butter until lettuce wilts. Cook peas according to package. Drain and add to lettuce. Serve hot. Serves 6.

TANGY MUSTARD POTATOES

Preheat oven to 425°.

2 medium-large baking potatoes
3 Tbsp. good mustard
2 Tbsp. olive oil

3 Tbsp. freshly grated Parmesan
    cheese
Freshly ground pepper

Peel potatoes; cut into 4 sections lengthwise and then cut sections to French fry widths (about 10 pieces per potato). In separate dish, whisk together mustard, oil, and cheese. In plastic bag, combine all ingredients to coat potatoes with mustard mixture. Spread potato pieces on a lightly greased baking sheet. Grind pepper over potatoes. Bake in preheated 425° oven for 35 to 40 minutes or until brown. Serves 4.

Great with hamburgers and just as good with brunch eggs.

TUSCANY POTATOES

4 medium baking potatoes (1⅓ lb.)
1 (14½ oz.) can pasta-style chunky
    tomatoes
1 (15 oz.) can Great Northern beans,
    drained and rinsed
1 large zucchini, quartered
    lengthwise and sliced

½ tsp. dried rosemary, crushed
1 Tbsp. snipped fresh basil or 1 tsp.
    dried basil, crushed
¼ c. part-skim shredded Mozzarella
    cheese (1 oz.)
4 tsp. grated Parmesan cheese

Scrub potatoes; pat dry. Slice each potato lengthwise into 6 wedges. Place wedges on a baking sheet. Bake in a 425° oven about 30 minutes or till tender.

Meanwhile, combine *undrained* tomatoes, beans, zucchini, rosemary, and dried basil, if using, in medium saucepan. Heat to boiling. Reduce heat, cover, and simmer over medium-low heat about 10 minutes or till zucchini is crisp-tender. Stir in fresh basil, if using; heat through.

Arrange potatoes on serving plates. Top with tomato mixture. Sprinkle with Mozzarella and Parmesan cheeses. Makes 4 servings.

SKI COUNTRY HERBED POTATOES

1½ lb. new potatoes
4 tsp. margarine
1 Tbsp. minced fresh parsley

1 Tbsp. minced fresh chives
1 tsp. dried tarragon
Fresh black pepper

Peel potatoes and slice diagonally 1½ inches thick. Melt the margarine in a nonstick skillet over moderately high heat, then add potatoes and saute until golden brown, about 4 to 5 minutes. Lower heat, cover skillet, and cook for about 15 minutes, shaking skillet periodically to prevent sticking. Remove from heat and add herbs and pepper.

DO AHEAD SOUR CREAM POTATOES

10 medium size potatoes, peeled
    and cubed
1 (8 oz.) pkg. cream cheese

¼ to ½ c. sour cream
2 Tbsp. butter or margarine
Paprika or seasoned salt

Cook potatoes in salted water. Drain. Whip cream cheese and sour cream together in a large mixer bowl. Gradually add potatoes to cheese mixture and whip until smooth. Place in a large greased casserole. Top with butter and paprika or seasoned salt. Refrigerate.

To cook: Place in a preheated 350° oven for 30 minutes or until heated through. Yield: 12 servings.

ELEGANT SCALLOPED POTATOES

4 medium potatoes, peeled and
    sliced
1 (16 oz.) pkg. powdered alfredo
    sauce mix
2 Tbsp. butter
3 green onion and tops, minced
    finely

2 Tbsp. dry minced onions
2 c. milk
½ c. good white wine
¾ c. Romano or Parmesan cheese
Salt and pepper to taste

Thicken alfredo mix with 1 cup of the milk and 2 tablespoons butter. Mix in rest of milk, wine, and ½ cup cheese and stir thoroughly, stirring in salt, pepper, and onions. Layer in an 8x11 inch casserole dish, alternating potato slices and alfredo mixture. Top with remaining ¼ cup of cheese. Cover with foil and bake at 375° for 1 hour. Uncover and bake another 15 minutes.

GARLIC MASHED POTATOES

14 new potatoes, washed and
    cleaned
1 c. cream
¼ lb. butter

1 head garlic, broken into cloves
    (skin on)
1 Tbsp. olive oil
Salt and pepper to taste

Preheat oven to 350°. Place garlic cloves in a single layer in small shallow baking pan. Brush with the olive oil; turn to coat all sides of garlic. Bake until garlic is soft and golden, approximately 35 to 40 minutes. (Reserve and freeze unused garlic in freezer bags for other uses.) Place potatoes in large pot and boil until tender. Heat cream and butter in saucepan until hot. Remove skin from 6 garlic cloves and add to cream and butter mixture. Combine potatoes and cream mixture. Beat with electric mixer to consistency of mashed potatoes. Season with salt and pepper. Serve with main course of fish, chicken, or beef.

ROASTED STUFFED NEW POTATOES

22 very small red potatoes
½ c. lowfat large curd cottage
    cheese, or 4 oz. lowfat goat
    cheese
1 Tbsp. fresh lemon juice

½ tsp. salt
⅛ tsp. freshly ground pepper
1 large egg white, lightly beaten
2 tsp. chopped chives (plus chives
    for garnish)

Heat oven to 425°. On a baking sheet, roast potatoes until tender, turning 2 to 3 times, 20 to 25 minutes. Let cool. Halve 18 potatoes. Cut a sliver off bottom of each. Scoop flesh from potato halves into a bowl, leaving a shell ¼ inch thick. Peel remaining potatoes; add to potato flesh. Mash coarsely with a fork. Mix in cheese, lemon juice, salt, and pepper. Mix in egg white and chopped chives. Spoon filling into potatoes. Place on baking sheet. Bake until golden, 15 to 17 minutes. Garnish with remaining chives. Makes 36.

Option: Use chopped green or red pepper instead of chives and top with shredded Cheddar cheese.

SPINACH ROCKEFELLER

2 (10 oz.) pkg. frozen chopped
   spinach
½ c. butter or margarine
¾ c. fresh bread crumbs
2 medium onions, finely chopped
2 eggs
⅛ tsp. thyme

¼ tsp. monosodium glutamate
1 tsp. garlic powder
2 drops of Tabasco sauce
½ tsp. pepper
¼ c. Parmesan cheese
Salt to taste
10 tomato slices (1 inch thick)

Cook spinach and drain well. Add remaining ingredients, except tomato slices. Place in casserole and bake in a preheated 350° oven for 25 minutes. Ten minutes before spinach is done, place tomato slices on an ovenware platter and bake in oven along with spinach.

To serve: Place mounds of spinach on top of tomato slices, using an ice cream scoop or rounded spoon. Yield: 10 servings.

HIGH COUNTRY BOURBON SQUASH RINGS

2 large acorn squash, seeded and
   cut into ½ inch rings
⅓ c. bourbon

¼ c. butter, melted
2 Tbsp. brown sugar
¼ tsp. freshly grated nutmeg

Line baking dish with aluminum foil. Arrange squash rings in single layer on foil. Prick with fork. Brush rings generously with bourbon. Let stand 5 minutes to absorb liquor. Brush evenly with melted butter. Sprinkle with brown sugar and nutmeg. Bake until tender, about 20 minutes. Serves 8.

SAGUACHE-SAVORY SUCCOTASH

1 (1 lb.) can whole kernel corn,
   drained
1 (1 lb.) can French style green
   beans, drained
½ c. mayonnaise or salad dressing
½ c. green pepper, chopped

2 Tbsp. onion, chopped
½ c. sharp American cheese,
   shredded
½ c. celery, chopped
1 c. soft bread crumbs
2 Tbsp. melted butter or margarine

Combine all ingredients, except crumbs and butter. Place in 10 x 6 x 1½ inch baking dish. Combine crumbs and butter; sprinkle on top. Bake at 350° for 30 minutes or until crumbs are toasted. Serves 6 to 8.

SWEET POTATO DAUPHINOISE

2 lb. sweet potatoes
8 eggs
24 oz. whipping cream
½ tsp. salt

½ tsp. white pepper
½ tsp. nutmeg
3 oz. Parmesan cheese

Peel sweet potatoes and slice as thin as possible. Mix cream, eggs, and seasonings together. Grease a 9x12 inch pan lightly. Layer potatoes in pan and cover with custard mixture. Gently stir potatoes into custard. Sprinkle cheese on top. Bake at 300° for 2½ to 3 hours until golden brown. Test Dauphinoise by poking with a toothpick. If it comes out clean, it is done. Serves 10 to 12.

SWEET POTATOES IN ORANGE SHELLS

3 c. mashed sweet potatoes
½ c. brown sugar
¼ tsp. nutmeg
6 halves orange shell, rolled in
    sugar

2 egg yolks, slightly beaten
⅓ c. orange juice
2 Tbsp. butter
Salt and pepper to taste

Combine sweet potatoes, egg yolks, orange juice, sugar, salt, pepper, and nutmeg. Add butter and mix well. Spoon into orange shells. Sprinkle with more brown sugar and dot with butter. Bake at 350° for 15 to 20 minutes. Serves 6.

GREEK TOMATOES FOR TWO

3 small plum tomatoes (about 6 oz.),
    cut in halves
Vegetable cooking spray
1 Tbsp. dry bread crumbs

2 Tbsp. crumbled Feta cheese with
    basil and tomato
¼ tsp. dried oregano
⅛ tsp. pepper

Preheat toaster oven to 350°. Place tomato halves on toaster oven pan coated with cooking spray. Sprinkle bread crumbs over each tomato half, and top with cheese. Sprinkle with oregano and pepper. Bake at 350° for 20 minutes. Serve warm. Yield: 2 servings (serving size 3 tomato halves).

Note: To bake in a conventional oven, place tomato halves on a baking sheet. Bake at 350° for 25 minutes.

COPPER MOUNTAIN BACON STUFFED TOMATOES

8 strips bacon
2 Tbsp. chopped onion
4 medium size ripe tomatoes
⅓ c. Italian style dry bread crumbs
    (herb and cheese flavored)

⅓ c. grated Parmesan cheese
Salt and pepper
Butter

Dice bacon and fry to crisp. Drain and cook onion in bacon grease until limp. Remove and set aside. Scoop out insides of tomatoes, reserving pulp, leaving a firm shell about ½ inch thick. Lightly salt inside of shells and turn upside-down on rack to drain for a few minutes.

Chop tomato pulp, place in mixing bowl, and stir in bacon, onion, bread crumbs, and cheese. Mix well and taste for seasoning, adding salt and pepper.

Divide stuffing among the tomato shells. Place in small greased baking dish; dot with butter and sprinkle tops with additional Parmesan cheese. Bake in 350° oven about 20 minutes.

WESTERN SLOPE CANDIED TOMATOES

3 (28 oz.) cans whole tomatoes
2 medium onions, finely chopped
¾ c. sugar

½ c. butter
1 tsp. salt

Place all ingredients in deep 4 quart saucepan and boil gently for 30 minutes. Lower heat until mixture barely bubbles. Simmer, uncovered, for 6 to 8 hours. Do not stir while simmering, but shake saucepan occasionally to prevent sticking. You do not want tomatoes to break up while cooking.

Transfer tomatoes to buttered casserole and bake in 325° oven for 15 to 20 minutes or until browned on top. Makes about 25 and is delicious served with meat.

SUMMER TOMATO SAUCE WITH SPAGHETTI SQUASH

4 large ripe tomatoes, peeled, seeded, and coarsely chopped (3 c.)
1 large onion, sliced and separated into rings (1 c.)
1 Tbsp. olive oil
1 medium orange or red sweet pepper, cut into strips (1 c.)
1 medium green sweet pepper, cut into strips (1 c.)

2 Tbsp. chopped fresh oregano
¼ tsp. ground red pepper
1 (15 oz.) can small white beans, rinsed and drained
1 Tbsp. tomato paste
1 tsp. sugar
2 Tbsp. white wine vinegar
Hot cooked spaghetti squash
Shaved or grated Parmesan cheese

Drain tomatoes in a colander. Meanwhile, in a 3 quart saucepan, cook onion in hot oil, covered, over medium heat till almost tender. Add pepper strips, oregano, ground red pepper, and ½ teaspoon *salt*. Cook, covered, about 5 minutes or till peppers are crisp-tender. Stir in tomatoes, beans, tomato paste, and sugar; heat through. *Do not boil.* Stir in vinegar.

To serve, spoon sauce over spaghetti squash; top each serving with cheese. Makes 4½ cups squash (4 servings).

Note: To cook squash, halve one 2½ pound *spaghetti squash* lengthwise; remove seeds. Place halves, cut side down, in a microwave-safe dish with ¼ cup water. Microwave, covered on 100% power (HIGH) for 15 to 20 minutes or till tender, rearranging once. Scrape squash from shell with a fork.

SUMPTUOUS DRIED TOMATOES

Slice ripe tomatoes ½ inch thick. Dry in food dehydrator with thermostat set at 125° about 10 hours. Tomatoes should be soft with some crisp parts and no longer juicy, with a concentrated flavor. Do not dry completely. (If tomatoes are still too wet, continue drying overnight at 90°.)

Lay tomato slices on baking sheets and freeze till firm. Store in freezer bags in the freezer. Thaw before using. Be sure to use a food dehydrator with a thermostat. Any other type will not give good results.

TOMATO SORBET

⅓ c. boiling water
⅓ c. sugar
1½ to 2 lb. red or yellow tomatoes, cored and cut up

2 Tbsp. snipped fresh basil
Fresh basil leaves (optional)
Yellow cherry tomatoes (optional)

Pour boiling water over sugar in a small bowl; stir till sugar dissolves. Cover and chill. Place tomatoes, half at a time, in a blender container or food processor bowl. Cover and blend or process till slightly pureed. Press through food mill or sieve to remove skin and seeds. Measure 2 cups puree.

Combine sugar syrup, tomato puree, and 2 tablespoons basil. Freeze in ice cream freezer according to manufacturer's directions. Do not ripen. (Or, transfer to an 8x4x2 inch loaf dish. Cover and freeze for 2 to 3 hours or till almost firm. Break into small chunks. Transfer to a chilled bowl. Beat with an electric mixer till smooth but not melted. Return to pan, cover, and freeze till firm. Allow to stand at room temperature for 15 minutes before serving.) Garnish with fresh basil leaves and yellow cherry tomatoes, if desired. Makes about 6 servings.

Serve this savory sorbet as an appetizer while chicken or fish cook on the grill.

GREEK ISLE STEAMED VEGETABLE PLATTER WITH FETA

1¾ c. water
¾ c. brown rice
⅓ c. wild rice
1 tsp. dried fines herbes, crushed,
    or dried basil, crushed
⅛ tsp. pepper

2 c. bias-sliced carrots
1 c. halved baby zucchini
2 c. halved pea pods
1 medium tomato, cut into wedges
⅔ c. crumbled Feta cheese

For rice mixture, bring water to boiling in a medium saucepan. Stir in brown rice and wild rice. Reduce heat, cover, and simmer about 50 minutes or till rice is tender and liquid is absorbed. Stir fines herbes or basil and pepper into hot rice mixture. Keep warm.

Meanwhile, place carrots in a steamer basket over simmering water. Cover and steam for 5 minutes. Add zucchini; steam for 3 minutes. Add pea pods and tomato wedges. Cover and steam for 2 to 3 minutes more or till tender.

Spoon rice mixture onto a serving platter; top with steamed vegetables. Sprinkle with cheese. Cover platter with foil. Let stand for 3 minutes before serving to soften cheese. Makes 4 servings.

SWEET AND SOUR VEGETABLE DISH

1 can French style string beans
1 can English peas
2 green bell peppers, chopped
1 onion, chopped
1 c. celery, chopped

1 small jar pimentos, chopped
1 c. vinegar
1 c. sugar
1 tsp. salt

Drain peas and string beans. Add chopped ingredients, using a covered, round container. Heat 1 cup vinegar and 1 cup sugar until sugar dissolves. Add 1 teaspoon salt and pour over the vegetable mixture. Refrigerate overnight and serve cold. Serves 8.

A delicious crisp vegetable dish. Can easily be doubled or can be greatly enlarged to serve large crowds at luncheons and buffets. To serve 50 to 60, duplicate 7 times.

BAKED BANANAS AND YAMS

5 medium size bananas, peeled and
    cut into ½ inch slices
Juice of 2 lemons
3 c. yams (about 3 medium size),
    cooked and sliced
1 c. light brown sugar, firmly packed
¼ tsp. ground ginger
¼ tsp. pepper
2 Tbsp. nutmeats, chopped
1 Tbsp. sugar
½ tsp. salt
4 Tbsp. butter or margarine, melted

Cover banana slices with lemon juice to prevent discoloring. Arrange bananas and sweet potatoes in a greased 2 quart casserole. Sprinkle each layer with brown sugar, butter, ginger, pepper, and salt. Cover casserole and bake in a preheated 350° oven for 25 minutes or until bananas are soft. Uncover; sprinkle with nutmeats and the tablespoon of sugar. Return to the oven for 10 minutes. Yield: 8 servings.

ZUCCHINI ZANG PIE

¼ c. refrigerated or frozen egg
    product, thawed
¼ c. chopped onion
¼ c. grated Parmesan cheese
3 c. refrigerated, shredded hash
    brown potatoes (about ½ of
    20 oz. pkg.)
2 medium zucchini, thinly sliced (2½
    c.)
1 clove garlic, minced
1 tsp. cooking oil
3 oz. sliced reduced-fat Swiss
    cheese
¾ c. refrigerated or frozen egg
    product, thawed
¼ c. skim milk
2 tsp. snipped fresh oregano or ½
    tsp. dried oregano, crushed
¼ tsp. pepper
⅛ tsp. salt

Combine the ¼ cup egg product, onion, and Parmesan cheese in a large mixing bowl. Stir in potatoes. Transfer mixture to a greased 9 inch pie plate; pat mixture into the bottom and up the sides.

Bake, uncovered, in a 400° oven for 35 to 40 minutes or till golden. Cool slightly on a wire rack. Reduce oven temperature to 350°.

Cook zucchini and garlic in hot oil in a large skillet till zucchini is crisp-tender; cool slightly. Place cheese in bottom of crust, tearing to fit. Arrange zucchini mixture over cheese.

Combine the ¾ cup egg product, milk, oregano, pepper, and salt in a small mixing bowl. Pour over the zucchini mixture in the crust.

Bake in the 350° oven for 25 to 30 minutes or till filling appears set when gently shaken. Let stand for 10 minutes before serving. Makes 6 servings.

Notes

Egg, Cheese and Pasta

FREEZING CASSEROLES

Casserole cookery can mean carefree cooking when the dish can be prepared in large batches for more than one use. This will also be quite economical since you will be able to take advantage of less expensive vegetables when they are at peak seasons and meats on special sale.

Since many casseroles require time-consuming chopping and measuring, it is wise to fix an extra portion that can be cooked and frozen — to be used in the future when there isn't enough time to prepare a family meal or when unexpected guests arrive.

If you feel that you can't spare having the casserole dish in the freezer and out of daily use, just line the dish with heavy duty aluminum foil. Pour the mixture into the foil-lined dish and freeze solid. After the food is frozen, remove the foil from the casserole dish, peel off the food, wrap in freezer paper, fold tightly, seal with freezer tape and return to freezer.

DOs & DON'Ts

* DO label each container with the contents and the date it was put into the freezer. Always use frozen cooked foods within one to two months.

* DO avoid freezing a large recipe of casserole mixture until you try freezing a small amount. Some flavors tend to change during freezing.

* DO cook large turkeys and roasts. Remove large portions of meat from the bone and freeze for casseroles.

* DON'T overcook foods that are to be frozen. Food will finish cooking while being reheated.

* DON'T use too much salt and other seasonings. Some flavors tend to fade while others get stronger. It is better to add more seasonings later if necessary.

* DON'T freeze spaghetti, macaroni, or noodle mixtures. These tend to lose texture and become too soft when reheated.

* DON'T freeze potatoes. Don't freeze fried poultry or meats. Don't freeze cooked egg white.

* DON'T re-freeze thawed meats and poultry. Use thawed meat or poultry within twenty-four hours.

EGG, CHEESE AND PASTA

BACON AND DOUBLE CHEESE QUICHE

Paired with a tossed green salad, this full-flavored quiche makes an excellent lunch.

Thirty minutes preparation, 30 minutes chilling, and 45 minutes baking.

Crust:

1⅓ c. all-purpose flour
⅛ tsp. salt
½ c. (1 stick) chilled butter, cut into
    small pieces

2 to 3 Tbsp. cold water

Filling:

10 strips lean bacon
4 large eggs
1½ c. light cream
¼ tsp. dried thyme
⅛ tsp. white pepper

½ c. shredded Gruyere cheese
    (about 2 oz.)
½ c. shredded white Cheddar
    cheese (about 2 oz.)

To prepare the crust, in a large bowl, mix together the flour and salt. Using a pastry blender or 2 knives, cut in the butter until coarse crumbs form.

Add water, 1 tablespoon at a time, tossing with a fork, until a dough forms. Shape into a disk, wrap in plastic wrap, and chill in refrigerator for 30 minutes.

Preheat oven to 375°F. On a lightly floured surface, using a lightly floured rolling pin, roll the dough into 11 inch circle. Fit into 9 inch pie pan. Trim edge, leaving ¼ inch overhang. Fold under to form stand up edge. Prick dough with a fork. Line with foil and fill with pie weights or dried beans.

Bake for 10 minutes. Remove the foil and weights. Bake until lightly golden, about 5 minutes. Transfer to a wire rack to cool.

Meanwhile, prepare filling. In a medium skillet, cook the bacon over medium heat until crisp, 8 to 10 minutes. Transfer to a paper towel to drain.

In a small bowl, whisk together the eggs, cream, thyme, and pepper. Pour into crust. Crumble bacon. Sprinkle the egg mixture with the bacon, Gruyere cheese, and Cheddar cheese. Bake until golden and custard is set, about 30 minutes. Serve warm. Makes 8 servings.

MUSHROOM CRUST QUICHE
(A different twist!)

8 oz. fresh mushrooms, coarsely
    chopped
3 Tbsp. butter
½ c. crushed saltine crackers
½ c. sliced green onions
1 c. grated Swiss cheese

1 c. grated Monterey Jack cheese
1 c. small curd cottage cheese
3 eggs
¼ tsp. salt
¼ tsp. cayenne pepper
¼ tsp. paprika

Saute mushrooms in 2 tablespoons butter. Stir in cracker crumbs. turn into a 9 inch pie plate and press to form crust. Saute onions in 1 tablespoon butter. Spread onions, Swiss cheese, and Monterey Jack cheese over crust.

In a blender or food processor, combine cottage cheese, eggs, salt, and cayenne until smooth. Pour over cheese. Sprinkle with paprika. Bake at 350° for 25 to 30 minutes. Allow to stand 10 minutes before cutting. Serves 8.

GREEN CHILI QUICHE
(A simple supper!)

1 (9 inch) pastry shell, partially
    baked
8 oz. spicy pork sausage
1 (4 oz.) can diced green chilies,
    drained
3 eggs

1 c. heavy cream
¼ tsp. salt
¼ tsp. pepper
1 Tbsp. finely sliced green onion
4 oz. Monterey Jack cheese, grated

Prepare pastry. Brown sausage and drain well. Spread sausage over pastry. Spread chilies over sausage. Beat eggs and cream. Stir in salt, pepper, onion, and cheese. Pour over chilies. Bake at 375° for 30 to 40 minutes or until a knife inserted in the center comes out clean. Allow to stand 10 minutes before cutting. Serves 8.

PUFFED HERB SCRAMBLE

1 Tbsp. margarine
3 (8 oz.) ctn. refrigerated or frozen
    egg product, thawed
1 c. skim milk
½ c. all-purpose flour
2 Tbsp. grated Parmesan cheese
Nonstick spray coating

2 Tbsp. snipped fresh basil or
    parsley or 2 tsp. dried basil or
    parsley, crushed
¾ tsp. snipped thyme or ¼ tsp. dried
    thyme, crushed
⅛ tsp. salt
Dash of pepper

For puff, place margarine in a 10 inch ovenproof nonstick skillet. Place in a 400° oven for 3 to 5 minutes or till margarine melts. Meanwhile, combine ¾ cup of the egg product, ½ cup of the milk, flour, and Parmesan cheese in a medium bowl; beat till smooth. Tilt skillet to coat with melted margarine. Immediately pour egg product mixture into the hot skillet. Return to oven and bake about 25 minutes or till puffed and well browned.

Meanwhile for scramble, spray a large skillet with nonstick coating. Heat skillet over medium heat till hot. Combine remaining egg product, remaining milk, basil or parsley, thyme, salt, and pepper in a medium bowl. Pour into skillet. Cook, without stirring, till mixture begins to set on the bottom and around the edge.

Using a large spoon or spatula, lift and fold partially cooked eggs so uncooked portion flows underneath. Continue lifting and cooking over medium heat for 3 to 4 minutes or till eggs are cooked throughout but are still glossy and moist.

To serve, spoon egg mixture into puff. Cut into wedges. Makes 4 servings.

You'll need two skillets to prepare this brunch dish; one for baking the puff and one for scrambling the eggs.

SOUFFLE ROLL WITH CHICKEN-SPINACH FILLING

Souffle Filling:

3 Tbsp. butter
⅓ c. chopped onion
4 oz. fresh mushrooms, sliced
1 (10 oz.) pkg. frozen chopped
    spinach, thawed and
    squeezed dry

1 c. cooked, diced chicken
½ c. diced ham
1 (3 oz.) pkg. cream cheese
⅓ c. sour cream
1½ tsp. Dijon mustard

In a saucepan, melt butter. Saute onion and mushrooms for 2 minutes. Stir in remaining ingredients, cooking until cheese is melted. Season to taste. Set aside.

Souffle Roll:

6 Tbsp. butter
½ c. flour
2 c. milk
½ c. grated Parmesan cheese
½ c. grated mild Cheddar cheese

¼ tsp. salt
4 eggs (room temperature),
    separated
Paprika

Grease a 10x15 inch jellyroll pan. Line bottom with waxed paper. Grease and flour paper.

In a saucepan, melt butter; stir in flour and cook for 2 minutes. Add milk, whisking constantly. Stir until mixture comes to a boil and thickens. Add cheeses and salt, cooking until cheese is melted. Remove from heat. Cool slightly. Add egg yolks, mixing well.

In a large bowl, beat egg whites until stiff but not dry. Fold a dollop of whites into souffle base. Fold in remaining whites. Spread souffle evenly in prepared pan. Bake at 325° for 40 minutes or until golden brown.

When souffle is done, place another piece of greased waxed paper over souffle and cover with a flat baking sheet; invert. Remove pan and paper immediately. Spread filling evenly over top of entire souffle. Roll up lengthwise, using the waxed paper to support the roll. Roll onto platter, seam side down. Dust lightly with paprika. Serves 8.

"NEVER FAIL" CHEESE SOUFFLE

8 oz. sharp Cheddar cheese
10 slices buttered bread (crusts
    removed)
4 eggs

2 c. milk
1 tsp. salt
½ tsp. dry mustard

Put all ingredients into blender and process at high speed. (Because of the quantity, this will probably have to be done in two batches.) Bake in 1½ quart greased casserole at 350° for 1 hour. This may be made ahead of time or at the last minute. It never fails. Serves 8.

LAMAR CHEESE SOUFFLE

4 eggs
¼ c. butter (Imperial)
¼ c. all-purpose flour
½ tsp. salt

Dash of pepper
1 c. milk
2 c. shredded Cheddar cheese (8 oz.)

Separate the eggs and set aside. Melt butter; blend in flour, salt, and pepper. Add the milk all at once; cook until thickened, stirring all the time. Lower heat to simmer, adding cheese. When it is all melted, remove from heat. Beat egg whites until light and stiff, then beat yolks and add to cheese mixture. Gently fold into beaten whites. Pour into ungreased 2 quart souffle dish. Bake in 300° oven for 1 to 1¼ hours. Serve immediately. Serves 4.

DO-AHEAD SAUSAGE SOUFFLE

8 slices soft bread with crusts, diced
2 c. Cheddar cheese, shredded
1½ lb. sausage links, cooked and cut in thirds

4 eggs
2¾ c. milk
¾ tsp. dry mustard
1 can mushroom soup

Spread bread evenly in bottom of well greased baking dish, 8x11 inches. Sprinkle cheese evenly over top. Arrange sausage on top. Beat eggs with 2¼ cups of the milk. Pour over bread mixture. Mix together mustard and soup. Add remaining ½ cup milk. Mix well. Spoon on top of casserole. Cover tightly with foil. Refrigerate overnight. Place in cold oven. Set oven to 300°. Bake about 1½ hours or until puffy and brown. Serve immediately. Serves 8.

Use for Christmas morning breakfast. Great to bake while opening presents.

HAM, CORN, AND CHEESE SOUFFLE

Vegetable cooking spray
2 tsp. dry bread crumbs
1½ c. fresh corn kernels (about 2 large ears)
⅓ c. thinly sliced green onions
⅔ c. diced Maple-Glazed ham (about 3 oz.)
¼ c. all-purpose flour

¾ c. skim milk
½ c. (2 oz.) shredded reduced-fat sharp Cheddar cheese
¼ tsp. ground red pepper
2 egg yolks
4 egg whites
½ tsp. cream of tartar

Coat a 1½ quart souffle dish with cooking spray; sprinkle with bread crumbs. Set aside.

Coat a large nonstick skillet with cooking spray; place over medium-high heat until hot. Add corn and green onions; saute 5 minutes or until tender. Remove from heat and stir in ham; set aside.

Place the flour in a small saucepan. Gradually add milk, stirring with a wire whisk until blended. Cook over medium heat 3 minutes or until thickened, stirring constantly. Remove from heat; stir in cheese and pepper.

Beat egg yolks in a medium bowl at high speed of a mixer until thick and pale (about 5 minutes). Gradually add hot milk mixture to egg yolks, stirring constantly. Stir in the corn mixture and set aside.

Beat egg whites (at room temperature) and cream of tartar in a large bowl at high speed of a mixer until stiff peaks form. Gently stir ¼ of egg white mixture into corn mixture. Gently fold in remaining egg white mixture.

Pour mixture into prepared souffle dish. Bake at 325° for 1 hour or until puffed and golden. Serve immediately. Yield: 4 servings (serving size 1½ cups).

MEXICAN CHEESE PUFF

5 c. grated sharp Cheddar cheese
4 c. grated Monterey Jack cheese
2 medium tomatoes, seeded and
  chopped
1 (7 oz.) can diced green chilies
1 (2¼ oz.) can sliced black olives,
  drained
½ c. all-purpose flour

6 eggs, separated
1 (5.33 oz.) can evaporated milk
½ tsp. salt
½ tsp. dried oregano leaves,
  crumbled
¼ tsp. ground cumin
¼ tsp. freshly ground pepper
¼ tsp. cream of tartar

Preheat oven to 300°F. Butter 9x13 inch glass baking dish. Combine first 5 ingredients with 2 tablespoons flour and mix well. Spoon into dish. (Casserole can be prepared to this point and refrigerated until ready to serve.) Beat egg yolks in large mixing bowl. Gradually blend in remaining flour and milk and beat until smooth. Add salt, oregano, cumin, and pepper and mix well. Beat egg whites in medium bowl until foamy. Add cream of tartar and continue beating until stiff peaks form. Fold egg whites into yolk mixture, blending thoroughly. Spoon over cheese. Bake until top is golden brown and firm, about 1 hour. Let stand 15 minutes before serving. Makes 10 to 12 servings.

BRUNCH (OR DINNER) STRATA

12 slices French (or loaf) white
  bread, cubed after removal of
  crusts
¼ lb. Swiss cheese, sliced
½ lb. sharp Cheddar cheese, grated

1 lb. bacon, cut up and crisply fried
6 eggs
3 c. milk
½ tsp. salt

Spray 9x13 inch Pyrex baking dish with Pam. Distribute bread cubes on bottom of dish. Cover with Swiss cheese, then grated Cheddar and crumbled bacon. Mix eggs, milk, and salt. Pour into baking dish. Refrigerate overnight. Bake, uncovered, for 45 minutes at 350°. Test for doneness by inserting knife near center. If knife does not come out clean, continue cooking. The dish will, however, continue cooking for a few minutes after removal from oven.

Variations: In place of bacon use ½ pound ground pork sausage or Italian sausage, cooked and drained of fat on paper towel; ½ pound minced cooked ham; ¼ pound crabmeat; ½ pound chopped fresh spinach, well drained; a large yellow onion which has been chopped and sauteed, or any combination of the preceding.

Instead of white bread, particularly with sausage, try rye bread and add ¼ teaspoon caraway.

A little Worcestershire sauce or Tabasco may be added to taste.

Note: Bread will not be discernible in finished dish which will taste much like a crustless quiche.

HAM AND CHEESE STRATA

12 slices white bread
¾ lb. Cheddar cheese, shredded
1 (10 oz.) pkg. frozen broccoli,
  lightly cooked and well
  drained
¾ lb. ham, shredded
12 eggs, slightly beaten

1½ c. milk
2 Tbsp. instant onion
¾ tsp. salt
¼ tsp. dry mustard
¼ tsp. paprika
Parmesan cheese to sprinkle on top

With a large cutter, cut an entire hole from center of each slice of bread. Break scraps of bread and place in bottom of well buttered 9x13x2 inch baking dish. Place layer of cheese over bread, then layer of drained broccoli, then layer of ham. Arrange bread holes on top of ham. Combine the next 5 ingredients and beat with wire whip. Pour over bread and sprinkle with paprika. Cover and refrigerate overnight. Bake at 325° for 50 minutes and the last 5 minutes sprinkle with Parmesan cheese. Let stand 10 minutes before slicing. Serves 12.

FAMILY BRUNCH CASSEROLE

1½ lb. regular link sausage
8 slices bread, trimmed and cubed
¾ lb. grated Cheddar cheese
1 can mushrooms, drained
2 Tbsp. butter

4 eggs
2¼ c. milk
¾ tsp. dry mustard
1 can mushroom soup plus half of
  this can filled with milk

Fry sausage; drain and cut into 1 inch pieces. Arrange bread in buttered 8x12x2 inch pan. Cover bread with cheese; scatter sausage over cheese. Beat eggs, milk, and mustard and add drained mushrooms. Pour over the bread and cheese in pan. Cover and refrigerate overnight. Remove from refrigerator and let stand 1 hour. Dilute soup with the half can of milk; stir well and pour over casserole. Dot with 2 tablespoons of butter. Bake at 325° for 1 hour. Serves 8.

SOUTHWESTERN SAUSAGE AND CHEESE CASSEROLE

Layer in 13x9 inch greased pan:

2 (7 oz.) cans chopped green chiles
6 corn tortillas, cut in ½ inch strips

1 lb. sausage, cooked and drained
1 c. Monterey Jack cheese, grated

Beat together:

8 eggs
½ c. milk
½ tsp. pepper

½ tsp. salt
½ tsp. garlic powder
½ tsp. cumin

Pour over layers. Arrange 2 large sliced tomatoes on top. Sprinkle with paprika. Bake at 350° for 45 to 55 minutes. Serve with sour cream and salsa.

EGGS SUPREME
(Good potluck dish!)

¼ c. butter
¼ c. flour
1 c. sour cream
1 c. milk
¼ tsp. thyme
¼ tsp. marjoram
¼ tsp. sweet basil

¼ c. chopped fresh parsley
1 lb. sharp Cheddar cheese, grated
18 hard cooked eggs, sliced
1 lb. bacon, cooked and crumbled,
   or 1 lb. ham, cubed
1 c. seasoned stuffing mix

In a saucepan, melt butter; add flour and cook for 2 minutes. Add sour cream and milk; stir until thickened. Add herbs and cheese; cook until cheese has melted.

Arrange eggs, then bacon in a buttered 9x13 inch baking dish. Pour sauce over bacon and sprinkle with stuffing mix. Bake at 350° for 30 minutes. Serves 12.

EASY EGG BAKE
(Brunch)

2 Tbsp. (¼ stick) butter
10 eggs
½ c. sour cream
8 slices ham, chopped
6 green onions, chopped
5 slices American cheese, chopped
   (can use Cheddar or
   Monterey)

12 cherry tomatoes
1 (4 oz.) can butter mushrooms,
   drained
Salt and pepper

Melt butter in 2 quart baking dish. Combine all other ingredients. Beat and pour into dish. Bake 30 to 40 minutes until golden and puffy.

REUBEN BRUNCH CASSEROLE

10 slices rye bread, cut into ¾ inch
   cubes
1½ lb. cooked corned beef, coarsely
   shredded
2½ c. (10 oz.) Swiss cheese,
   shredded

6 eggs, lightly beaten
3 c. milk
¼ tsp. pepper

Arrange bread cubes in bottom of greased 9x13x2 inch glass baking dish. Top with corned beef. Beat eggs, milk, and pepper in bowl until well blended. Pour over corned beef and bread cubes. Cover with foil and refrigerate overnight. When ready to cook, preheat oven to 350°, then bake casserole 35 minutes or until bubbly.

BLACKHAWK EGG CASSEROLE

10 eggs
1 Tbsp. baking powder
16 oz. cottage cheese
½ c. butter, melted and cooled

½ c. flour
½ tsp. salt
1 lb. Monterey Jack cheese, grated
2 cans (4 oz.) chopped green chillies

Preparation time: 10 minutes + baking.

Beat eggs until lemon colored. Add baking powder, cottage cheese, butter, flour, salt, Monterey Jack cheese, and chillies. Blend well. Pour into greased 9x13 inch pan. Bake at 350° for 35 minutes or until set and browned on top. Yield: 10 to 12 servings.

You may use only 1 can of chillies for a less spicy dish.

GOURMET EGGS

¾ c. finely crushed cracker crumbs
3 Tbsp. melted butter
12 hard cooked eggs, peeled and
   sliced
12 slices crisp bacon, drained and
   crumbled
1 pt. dairy sour cream

2 Tbsp. light cream
1 tsp. instant minced onion
1 tsp. salt
¼ tsp. pepper
¼ tsp. seasoned salt
1 c. shredded Cheddar cheese
Bacon curls (optional)

Mix cracker crumbs with butter; sprinkle on bottom of baking dish (3 quart). Arrange egg slices over crumbs. Combine bacon, sour cream, light cream, and seasonings. Spoon over eggs; sprinkle with cheese. Bake at 350° for 20 minutes. Garnish with additional bacon curls if desired. Makes 5 to 6 servings.

EGGS BAKED WITH MUSHROOMS, LEEKS, AND PROSCIUTTO

These creamy eggs have a rich flavor and souffle-like texture. A good part of the recipe can be completed the day before.

1 stick (8 Tbsp.) unsalted butter
5 c. leek julienne (white and 1 inch
   of pale green part, about 5)
½ lb. fresh mushrooms, stemmed
   and sliced
½ lb. paper thin slices prosciutto,
   cut into ¼ inch wide strips
5 c. whipping cream

12 large eggs
1 tsp. freshly grated nutmeg
1 tsp. salt
Freshly ground pepper
2½ c. freshly grated Gruyere cheese
   (about 8 oz.)
Minced fresh parsley

Using 1 tablespoon butter for each, butter two 3 quart shallow baking dishes. Melt remaining 6 tablespoons butter in heavy, large skillet over medium heat. Add leeks and saute until softened, about 8 minutes. Add mushrooms and saute 5 minutes. Add prosciutto and saute 2 minutes. Spread half of mixture over bottom of each dish. (Can be prepared 1 day ahead. Cover and refrigerate.) Preheat oven to 375°F.

Whisk cream, eggs, nutmeg, salt, and pepper in large bowl. Stir in 2 cups cheese. Pour over vegetable mixture in baking dishes. Stir to mix vegetables with cream. Sprinkle remaining cheese over. Bake at 375° until knife inserted in centers comes out clean and tops are golden brown, about 30 minutes. Cool 10 minutes. Sprinkle with parsley and serve. Makes 12 servings.

CREAM OF HAM AND EGGS

2 cans cream of mushroom soup
   (undiluted)
5 slices American cheese
1 (¾ inch) slice ham, diced into
   cubes

6 hard-boiled eggs, cut into 8
   wedges
2 jars marinated artichoke hearts

Combine all ingredients and heat thoroughly. Serve on English muffins. Serves 8.

HAM-DEVILED EGGS IN SHRIMP SAUCE

12 hard-boiled eggs
1 (2¼ oz.) can deviled ham
3 Tbsp. mayonnaise

½ tsp. mustard
¼ tsp. curry powder

Shrimp Sauce:

2 Tbsp. butter
2 Tbsp. flour
1 can cream of shrimp soup
1 soup can milk (1⅓ c.)

8 oz. Cheddar or American cheese,
    shredded
Toast points or English muffins

Cut boiled eggs in halves. Remove yolks and mash, then mix with ham, mayonnaise, mustard, and curry. Refill egg whites and place in baking dish.

Shrimp Sauce: In saucepan, melt butter and blend in flour. Stir in soup. Add milk all at once. Cook and stir until thick and bubbly. Add cheese; stir to melt. Cover eggs with sauce. Bake at 350° for 20 minutes. Serve on toast points or muffins. Serves 6.

POTATO OMELET-FRITTATA

3 large potatoes, peeled and sliced
    thin
3 Tbsp. olive oil
1 onion, finely chopped

½ bell pepper, finely chopped
7 eggs, well beaten
Salt and pepper to taste
2 Tbsp. grated Italian cheese

Put olive oil into large (10 inch) frying pan and heat. Saute onion and bell pepper, then add potatoes and saute until golden brown, but *not* well done. Sprinkle with salt and pepper. Mix cheese with eggs and pour this over the potatoes, lifting potatoes so that eggs can reach bottom of pan. Make sure potatoes are covered with eggs. When eggs are cooked and top is solid, turn the frittata to other side to finish cooking. Serves 4 to 6.

EGG SALAD
(Butter adds flavor and richness)

12 eggs, hard cooked
6 Tbsp. butter, softened
½ c. mayonnaise (or enough to
    moisten salad)
1 tsp. Dijon mustard

1 c. celery, finely chopped
½ c. minced onion
½ c. chopped dill pickle
Salt and pepper to taste

Cut eggs in halves and separate yolks from the whites. Mash yolks with the softened butter. Chop whites and add to yolk mixture with remaining ingredients.

LUSCIOUS LOWFAT LASAGNA

1 (8 oz.) pkg. lasagna noodles
2 tsp. olive oil
2 onions, chopped
3 cloves garlic, minced
8 oz. extra-lean ground beef
28 oz. can crushed tomatoes
¼ c. thawed orange juice
   concentrate

½ and ¼ tsp. salt
½ tsp. cinnamon
½ tsp. freshly ground black pepper
¼ c. flour
2½ c. lowfat milk (1%)
1 lb. shredded nonfat Mozzarella
   cheese (about 4 to 5 c.)
½ c. grated Parmesan cheese

Heat water for boiling. Cook the noodles until tender. Drain. Rinse in cold water and lay on foiled counter, separating the noodles. Heat oil in nonstick skillet and add the onions and garlic. Stir frequently until onions are tender. Add beef and cook until beef is no longer pink. Add tomatoes, juice concentrate, basil, salt, pepper, and cinnamon. Cook until sauce thickens slightly, about 6 minutes. Keep warm.

Preheat the oven to 450°. Over medium heat, prepare white sauce. Whisk the milk into the flour in pan. Bring to boil and add the remaining salt. Whisk until thickened, about 5 minutes.

Spread ¼ to ½ cup sauce in bottom of 9x13x2 inch baking pan. Layer 3 noodles on top and spoon ¼ of the remaining meat sauce, ⅓ of the white sauce, and 1 cup of the Mozzarella over. Repeat twice with the remaining noodles, meat sauce, white sauce, and Mozzarella. Lay the remaining noodles on top. Spread the remaining meat sauce over; sprinkle casserole with the remaining cup of Mozzarella and Parmesan cheeses. Bake for 15 minutes or until sauce bubbles and cheese melts. If time permits, make a day ahead. Serves 8.

WESTERN HILLS MEXICAN LASAGNA

2 lb. ground beef
1 medium onion, chopped
2 (16 oz.) cans stewed tomatoes
1 small can tomato sauce

1 pkg. taco seasoning mix
1 small can chopped chilies
1 pkg. soft corn tortillas
Cheddar cheese, grated

Brown meat and onion; add taco seasoning and add tomatoes and chilies. Simmer 35 minutes. Layer in 13x9 inch dish with tortillas. Start with sauce. Top with grated cheese. Bake 30 minutes at 350°. Freezes well. Cheese topping could be a mix of Cheddar and Jack cheese.

MEATLESS SPAGHETTI SUPPER

4 Tbsp. olive oil
2 to 3 cloves garlic
1 (16 oz.) can peeled tomatoes
1 tsp. dried basil

1 tsp. sugar
Salt to taste
1 lb. spaghetti (thin or regular)
4 Tbsp. grated Parmesan

Heat the olive oil in a skillet. When hot, add garlic until blanched. Next, add the tomatoes, basil, sugar, and salt. Stir until blended. Lower heat and cook gently for 30 minutes, stirring frequently. Put cooked spaghetti (don't overcook) in a large serving bowl; cover with sauce. Sprinkle with at least 4 heaping tablespoons grated Parmesan cheese. Mix well and serve. Serves 4.

SPINACH LINGUINE WITH GOAT CHEESE

3 Tbsp. olive oil
1 bunch green onions, sliced
4 plum tomatoes, chopped
1 red bell pepper, chopped
6 oil-packed sun-dried tomatoes, drained and chopped
2 garlic cloves, minced

¼ tsp. dried oregano, crumbled
1 Tbsp. chopped fresh parsley
1 Tbsp. chopped fresh basil
Salt and pepper
8 oz. spinach linguine, freshly cooked
4 oz. soft goat cheese, sliced

Heat oil in heavy skillet over medium heat. Add next 6 ingredients and saute until onions are tender, about 15 minutes. Stir in parsley and basil. Season with salt and pepper. Add pasta; toss thoroughly. Divide pasta between 2 plates. Top each with half of goat cheese. Serves 2.

FETTUCINE WITH SPINACH-RICOTTA SAUCE

3 Tbsp. olive oil
1 medium onion, chopped
3 large garlic cloves, minced
1 Tbsp. all-purpose flour
2 c. milk (do not use lowfat or no-fat)
1 (10 oz.) pkg. frozen chopped spinach, thawed and well drained
1 c. Ricotta cheese
⅓ c. freshly grated Parmesan cheese

10 oil-packed sun-dried tomatoes, drained and cut into thin strips
3 Tbsp. chopped fresh basil
¼ tsp. ground nutmeg
Salt and pepper
1 lb. fettucine
⅓ c. minced onions
⅓ c. toasted pine nuts
Freshly grated Parmesan cheese

Heat oil in medium saucepan over medium heat. Add onion and cook until translucent. Add garlic. Cook 1 minute. Stir in flour and cook 1 minute. Gradually whisk in milk and cook until sauce is smooth and bubbling, stirring constantly. Mix in spinach, Ricotta, ⅓ cup Parmesan, sun-dried tomatoes, basil, and nutmeg. Season to taste with salt and pepper. Simmer until heated through, stirring occasionally. Meanwhile, cook fettucine al dente. Transfer pasta to a platter. Spoon sauce over. Garnish with green onion and pine nuts. Sprinkle with Parmesan. Serves 4.

COLLEGIATE PEAKS PENNE WITH SPICY RED SAUCE

⅓ c. olive oil
6 garlic cloves, slightly crushed
1 (16 oz.) can whole tomatoes (undrained)
½ c. chopped fresh parsley

¼ tsp. dried crushed red pepper
Salt and pepper
½ lb. penne pasta, freshly cooked
Freshly grated Parmesan cheese

Cook oil and garlic in heavy, large skillet over medium-high heat until garlic begins to sizzle. Stir in tomatoes with liquid, ¼ cup parsley, and dried red pepper, breaking up tomatoes with spoon. Season with salt and pepper. Reduce heat to medium-low. Cover partially and cook until tomatoes are thick, stirring sauce occasionally for about an hour and 15 minutes. Discard garlic. Mix in remaining parsley. Pour sauce over pasta and toss well. Sprinkle with Parmesan.

SPINACH-FETA SHELLS WITH MINTED TOMATO SAUCE

12 jumbo pasta shells
1 (10 oz.) pkg. frozen chopped spinach, thawed and well drained
½ c. crumbled Feta cheese (about 2 oz.)
½ c. fat-free Ricotta cheese
¼ c. toasted, chopped walnuts or almonds
1 slightly beaten egg white
⅛ tsp. ground cinnamon

⅛ tsp. pepper
1 (14½ oz.) can low-sodium tomatoes, cut up
2 Tbsp. reduced-sodium tomato paste
1 Tbsp. snipped fresh mint or 1 tsp. dried mint, crushed
1 tsp. sugar
¼ tsp. garlic powder
¼ c. shredded reduced-fat Mozzarella cheese (1 oz.)

Cook pasta shells according to package directions. Drain; set aside.

For filling, combine the chopped spinach, Feta cheese, Ricotta, walnuts or almonds, egg white, cinnamon, and pepper in a medium mixing bowl. Stir to mix. Set aside.

For sauce, combine *undrained* tomatoes, tomato paste, mint, sugar, and garlic powder. Stuff each shell with 2 *slightly rounded tablespoons* of the spinach filling. Place in an ungreased 2 quart square baking dish. Spoon sauce over shells. Bake, covered, in a 350° oven for 30 to 35 minutes or till heated through. Sprinkle with Mozzarella. Bake, uncovered, 2 to 3 minutes more till melted. Makes 6 main dish servings.

Toasting the walnuts or almonds for the filling gives more flavor from a small amount of nuts.

BUTTERFLY PASTA AND BASIL

2½ c. cooked bow tie pasta
1 c. fresh spinach, julienned
1 red bell pepper, julienned
1 scallion, minced

2 Tbsp. lemon juice
1 Tbsp. olive oil
1 clove garlic, minced
2 Tbsp. fresh basil, minced

Combine the pasta, spinach, red bell pepper, and scallion. Whisk together the lemon juice, olive oil, garlic, and basil. Pour over pasta mixture. Serve warm or at room temperature. Serves 4.

FETTUCINE WITH HOT RED PEPPER SAUCE

1 Tbsp. dried crushed red chile pepper
2 medium red peppers, chopped
4 Tbsp. olive oil
3 large cloves garlic, crushed
1 medium tomato, peeled and chopped

¾ tsp. dried oregano
½ tsp. dried basil
⅛ tsp. freshly ground pepper
4 Tbsp. red wine vinegar
1 lb. cooked fettucine

Saute garlic in the olive oil until soft. Add the crushed red chili and saute 5 minutes. Add the red peppers and saute until softened. Add the tomato, oregano, basil, pepper, and vinegar and heat through. Toss with the cooked pasta. Serves 4.

FOOTHILLS CAPPELLINI POMODORA

20 oz. Roma tomatoes
4 oz. olive oil
2 cloves garlic, chopped fine
2 Tbsp. Fontina (basil in oil)

2 tsp. salt
1 tsp. black pepper
1 lb. pkg. angel hair pasta, cooked
   al dente

    Chop tomatoes fine. Combine tomatoes, olive oil, chopped garlic, Fontina, salt, and pepper. Blend thoroughly and let set at least 3 hours to blend flavors. Mix gently with cooked angel hair pasta and heat. Serve with Parmesan cheese.

PEPPERY PASTA AND FETA CHEESE

2 Tbsp. olive oil
1 large red bell pepper, diced
1 large green bell pepper, diced
6 large garlic cloves, chopped
1 c. or 6 oz. jar thinly sliced stemmed
   pepperoncini
½ c. chopped fresh basil or 2 Tbsp.
   dried basil

1 (28 oz.) can Italian plum tomatoes
   and juice
1 lb. bow tie pasta, freshly cooked
8 oz. Feta cheese, coarsely
   crumbled

    Heat oil in heavy Dutch oven over medium high heat. Add both bell peppers and garlic. Saute until peppers soften, about 4 minutes. Mix in pepperoncini and basil and then tomatoes. Simmer until sauce reduces slightly, breaking up tomatoes with back of spoon, about 5 minutes. Add pasta and mix until sauce coats the pasta. Add Feta and toss mixture to blend. Yields 3 to 4 servings.

LOWFAT FETTUCINE ALFREDO

1 (12 oz.) pkg. fettucine noodles or
   linguine, cooked al dente with
   salt
1 Tbsp. flour
¼ tsp. pepper

¼ tsp. nutmeg
2 c. milk
½ c. freshly grated Parmesan
   cheese
1 Tbsp. parsley, chopped

    Combine flour, pepper, and nutmeg. Whisk into milk. Cook slowly until slightly thick, stirring constantly. Add cheese and parsley. Toss with drained pasta. Serve. Yields 2 to 3 servings.

CHERRY CREEK SCALLOP ASPARAGUS PASTA

2 small cloves garlic
1 Tbsp. butter
2 Tbsp. olive oil
2 Tbsp. parsley, chopped
½ c. mushrooms, chopped
1 lb. fresh bay scallops
2 Tbsp. dry white wine

1 c. blanched asparagus, cut into 1
   inch pieces
Juice from lemon wedge
½ lb. spaghetti noodles
4 Tbsp. light alfredo sauce
Freshly grated Parmesan cheese

    Cook spaghetti in salted water. While spaghetti is cooking, mince garlic and saute in butter and oil. Add mushrooms and saute until brown. Add parsley, lemon juice, scallops, and wine to garlic and mushrooms. Saute 4 or 5 minutes until scallops turn a solid white. Drain spaghetti; add scallops, alfredo sauce, and prepared asparagus. Other vegetables may be used instead of asparagus.

SCALLOPS AND ANGEL HAIR PASTA

3 Tbsp. chopped onion
1 clove garlic, minced
2 Tbsp. butter or margarine
4 sliced mushrooms
¾ lb. bay scallops or equivalent of
   large
¼ c. white wine

¼ c. skim milk
1 Tbsp. Dijon mustard
½ tsp. tarragon
Salt and pepper to taste
⅓ c. Mozzarella cheese
Chopped parsley
Angel hair pasta

Saute onion and garlic in butter. Add mushrooms and bay scallops. Saute 3 to 4 minutes. Add wine, skim milk, mustard, tarragon, and salt and pepper. Saute 2 to 3 minutes or until slightly thickened. Pour over cooked angel hair pasta. Add Mozzarella cheese and parsley on top.

PLATTE RIVER ALBACORE FETTUCINI

4 c. broccoli florets or 10 oz. pkg.
   frozen cut broccoli
½ lb. fettucini
1 (12 oz.) can or 2 (6⅛ oz.) cans solid
   white albacore in water

1 c. lowfat Ricotta cheese
⅓ c. grated Parmesan cheese
½ c. lowfat milk
½ tsp. garlic salt
½ tsp. Italian seasonings

Cook broccoli in water until crisp tender. Remove with slotted spoon in serving bowl. Add fettucini in same pot and cook until tender. Drain and add to broccoli. Mix in drained albacore. Combine remaining ingredients in same pot. Stir until smooth and heated through. Serve with salt and pepper and pour over cooked pasta and serve.

RIGATONI WITH SHRIMP AND FETA

5 Tbsp. olive oil
1¼ lb. medium shrimp, peeled and
   deveined
¼ tsp. red pepper flakes
1 clove garlic, chopped
½ c. dry white wine
2 c. fresh tomatoes, peeled and
   cubed

⅓ c. chopped fresh basil
1 tsp. dried oregano
Salt
Freshly ground pepper
6 oz. crumbled Feta cheese
12 oz. rigatoni

Preheat oven to 400°. Heat 3 tablespoons of olive oil in a skillet. Saute shrimp just till they turn pink. Stir in red pepper flakes. Transfer shrimp and juices to a baking dish. Add remaining oil to skillet. Briefly saute garlic. Add wine and cook 2 minutes over high heat. Stir in tomatoes, basil, oregano, and salt and pepper. Simmer, uncovered, for 10 minutes. Sprinkle the Feta cheese over shrimp. Spoon tomato sauce over all. Cover dish and bake for 10 minutes.

Cook rigatoni. Drain and transfer to serving bowl. Add shrimp tomato mixture and gently mix with noodles. Serve immediately.

FOUR PEPPERS AND SALMON OVER PASTA

¼ lb. rotini (or a short nubby pasta),
    cooked al dente
1 red bell pepper
1 green bell pepper
1 clove garlic, chopped
1 Tbsp. canola oil
1 Tbsp. olive oil

½ lb. fresh poached salmon, flaked
1 Tbsp. green peppercorns packed
    in water or vinegar
⅛ tsp. salt
¼ tsp. freshly ground pepper
2 Tbsp. chopped fresh parsley

    Remove seeds and membranes from peppers. Julienne into uniform pieces. Saute garlic in canola oil until golden. Add the bell peppers and saute until they wilt. Stir in olive oil, salmon, peppercorns, salt, and pepper. Add pasta and continue to heat until the salmon warms through. Toss in parsley and serve immediately. Serves 4.

SEA SALAD WITH PASTA

2 c. uncooked sea shell pasta in
    various colors
8 oz. crabmeat (real or imitation)
1 pt. cherry tomatoes, cut in halves
1 red bell pepper, seeded and diced
2 zucchini, julienned

3 green onions with tops, diced
2 c. broccoli florets
1⅓ c. reduced calorie Ranch
    dressing
6 large lettuce leaves

    Cook pasta al dente. Drain; rinse in cold water and drain. Set aside to cool. Add chilled crabmeat, tomatoes, red pepper, zucchini, green onions, and broccoli florets to cooled pasta in a large serving bowl. Add dressing and toss gently. Chill at least 1 hour. Serve on lettuce. Serves 6.

STEEL CITY BROCCOLI AND GARLIC PASTA

2 tsp. olive oil
2 large cloves garlic, minced
2 Tbsp. onion, chopped
2 Tbsp. white wine
½ c. chicken stock

2 c. broccoli, chopped
½ lb. linguine, cooked al dente
4 tsp. freshly grated Parmesan
    cheese

    Heat oil in nonstick pan. Add garlic and onion and saute over low heat until onion becomes translucent. Add wine, stock, and broccoli. Cover and cook until the broccoli turns bright green. Toss in the pasta and cook until heated through and broccoli is tender. Season with salt and pepper. Turn out onto a dish and sprinkle with cheese. Serves 2 or 3.

ROTINI WITH BROCCOLI, PEPPERS WITH ONIONS

1 lb. rotini pasta
8 oz. mushrooms, sliced
1 c. broccoli florets
1 green pepper, seeded and diced
1 red bell pepper, seeded and diced
2 green onions (including tops),
    diced
½ c. olive oil

¼ c. red wine vinegar
¾ tsp. salt
¼ tsp. pepper
¼ c. chopped fresh parsley
1 tsp. dried tarragon or dried
    oregano (or 1 Tbsp. either
    herb, fresh)
16 cherry tomatoes, halved

Cook pasta al dente. While pasta is cooking, place nonstick skillet over medium heat and saute mushrooms in a little water until mushrooms are tender and give up their liquid, about 5 minutes. Drain and set aside. Steam broccoli until bright green. Rinse under cold water; drain. Drain pasta and let cool about 5 minutes. Mix pasta, mushrooms, broccoli, green and red peppers, and onions in a large serving bowl.

In a covered jar, combine oil, vinegar, salt, pepper, parsley, and tarragon or oregano; shake well. Pour over pasta mixture and toss well. Chill 3 hours before serving; add tomatoes just before serving. Makes 12 cups. Serves 6.

TOMATO PASTA WITH SAUSAGE AND SHRIMP

Serves 6. Cooking time: 30 minutes.

1 lb. hot Italian bulk sausage, chopped
½ lb. penne round pasta
4 to 6 medium garlic cloves, minced
1 shallot, minced
½ tsp. dried thyme leaves

1 (16 oz.) can chopped tomatoes (with juice)
2 bay leaves
⅓ c. heavy cream
24 to 29 large raw shrimp in shell
Salt and pepper to taste

Peel shrimp; cut in halves lengthwise, leaving end intact to keep together. Cook penne. Brown sausage and drain, saving 1 tablespoon grease to saute garlic, shallot, and thyme in. Saute, then add tomatoes with juice, cream, and bay leaves. Add sausage. Gently simmer 10 minutes. Add shrimp and cook on low just until shrimp curls. Season with salt and pepper. Sprinkle liberally with Parmesan and freshly ground pepper. May be made ahead, warming and adding shrimp just before serving. Serves 6. *Excellent and a man pleaser!*

FRESH TOMATO FETTUCCINE

5 medium size ripe tomatoes, diced
1 medium red onion, chopped
1 to 2 cloves garlic, minced
¾ c. shredded fresh basil
1 c. chopped parsley

⅓ c. coarsely crumbled Feta cheese
3 Tbsp. extra virgin olive oil
2 Tbsp. balsamic vinegar
Salt and pepper to taste
1 lb. fettuccine

Combine all, except fettuccine. Cook fettuccine al dente and add tomatoes. May be topped with olive but is pretty without. Serve warm, cold, or at room temperature. Serves 8.

Hint: The basil and parsley can be put in food chopper for a very short spin and come out looking just right.

ROTINI WITH RATATOUILLE
(Low cost, lowfat, low-cal)

The salting eliminates the slightly bitter taste sometimes found in eggplants, especially those that are old or overripe.

1 medium eggplant (1 lb.), trimmed and cut in ½ inch pieces
1½ tsp. salt
1 Tbsp. olive oil
1 medium (8 oz.) zucchini, quartered lengthwise, then cut crosswise in ¼ inch thick pieces
2 small onions, thinly sliced

½ medium green bell pepper, cut in ¼ inch pieces
½ Tbsp. finely chopped garlic
1 (14 to 15 oz.) can crushed tomatoes or half a 28 oz. can (1½ c.)
1 c. water
¼ tsp. freshly ground pepper
1 lb. rotini or cut fusilli (pasta twists)

1. Put eggplant in a colander; sprinkle with 1 teaspoon of the salt and toss to mix. Let drain at least 20 minutes. Pat dry with paper towels.

2. Meanwhile, heat 1 teaspoon of the oil in a large nonstick skillet over medium heat. Add zucchini and cook about 5 minutes, stirring occasionally, until edges are browned. Transfer with a slotted spoon to a plate.

3. Bring a large pot of lightly salted water to boil over high heat.

4. Meanwhile, heat remaining 2 teaspoons oil in the skillet over medium heat. Add eggplant and cook about 6 minutes, stirring occasionally until browned. Add onions, bell pepper, and garlic. Reduce heat to medium-low and cook, stirring often, 8 minutes or until soft. Stir in tomatoes, water, remaining salt, and pepper. Cook, partially covered, until thickened, about 15 minutes. Stir in zucchini.

5. Meanwhile, add pasta to boiling water and cook according to package directions.

6. Drain pasta and put into a warmed large serving bowl. Add eggplant mixture; toss to mix well. Serves 6.

PENNE WITH CREAMY ONIONS AND PEAS
(Low cost)

Preparation: 8 minutes. Cook: 18 minutes. Cost per serving: 50 cents.

1 lb. penne or ziti pasta
6 strips (about 6 oz.) bacon
1½ c. finely chopped onions
1 Tbsp. minced garlic

2 c. frozen green peas
⅓ c. water
1 c. milk
⅔ c. grated Parmesan cheese

1. Bring a large pot of lightly salted water to boil. Add pasta and cook according to package directions.

2. Meanwhile cook bacon in a large nonstick skillet until crisp. Drain on paper towels; when cool, crumble bacon.

3. Discard all but 2 tablespoons fat in skillet. Add onions and garlic and cook over medium heat 4 to 5 minutes, stirring often, until onions are translucent.

4. Stir in peas and the water, cover, reduce heat, and simmer 5 to 7 minutes, until peas are hot. Stir in milk; cook 1 to 2 minutes to heat through.

5. Drain pasta and put into a warmed large serving bowl. Add pea mixture. Sprinkle with cheese and crumbled bacon. Toss to mix well. Serves 6.

PENNE WITH TOMATO AND RICOTTA

1 lb. penne, cooked
2 Tbsp. olive oil
1 medium onion
2 large cloves garlic, minced
½ c. (4 oz.) pancetta, chopped
½ c. dry wine (red or white)
1 (28 oz.) can Italian plum tomatoes, crushed

Salt and pepper
Pinch of red pepper
1 c. Ricotta
½ c. grated Romano or Parmesan cheese
Chopped parsley for garnish

Saute onion in olive oil. Add garlic and cook 1 minute. Separately cook pancetta. Drain; add onion. Add wine and cook until boiling. Add tomatoes, salt, pepper, and red pepper. Simmer 15 to 20 minutes. Pour sauce over penne. Do not stir. Spoon in Ricotta and add cheese. Freezes well.

GOAT CHEESE PASTA SALAD WITH TOMATOES AND BASIL

8 oz. fusilli pasta
8 Tbsp. olive oil
4 Tbsp. sherry wine vinegar
2 Tbsp. balsamic vinegar
¼ tsp. dried, crushed red pepper
¼ tsp. salt
4 large plum tomatoes, seeded and chopped
4 green onions, thinly sliced
18 kalamata olives, pitted (Greek olives)

4 oz. salami, chopped (optional)
11 oz. soft goat cheese, cut into chunks
½ c. packed fresh basil leaves, cut into thin strips
Salt and pepper
Red leaf lettuce
Fresh basil leaves

Cook pasta until just tender. Rinse under cold water. Drain well. Transfer to large bowl. Toss with 2 tablespoons oil. Cover and refrigerate until cold.

Combine both vinegars, crushed red pepper, and salt in a small bowl. Gradually whisk in remaining 6 tablespoons oil. Pour dressing over pasta. Add tomatoes, green onions, olives, and salami and toss to coat. Add goat cheese and basil; toss to combine. Season with salt and pepper. Line platter with lettuce leaves. Mound salad in center. Garnish with basil leaves. Serves 4.

ACINI DE PEPE WITH WILD RICE IN HERB BUTTER

2½ c. cooked acini
½ c. cooked wild rice
¾ lb. fresh mushrooms, sliced
3 Tbsp. butter
½ Tbsp. dried basil

½ tsp. oregano
½ tsp. dried thyme
1 Tbsp. chopped shallots
½ tsp. salt
½ tsp. fresh cracked pepper

Cook the acini and wild rice separately, according to package directions. Melt butter over medium heat; saute mushrooms and add the herbs, shallots, salt, and pepper and cook for 1 minute. Add the acini and wild rice; toss to blend and heat thoroughly. This dish can be prepared a day ahead and reheated in the microwave oven.

POLENTA WITH SUNNY TOMATOES

18 cherry tomatoes, cut in halves
    widthwise or 1 jar sun-dried
    tomatoes in oil, well drained
1½ c. quick-cooking polenta or
    yellow corn meal
Nonstick vegetable oil spray
½ tsp. olive oil
1 small clove garlic, minced

1 medium shallot, minced
½ c. plus, lowfat Ricotta cheese
1 tsp. freshly grated Parmesan
    cheese
½ tsp. chopped fresh rosemary
1 Tbsp. chopped cilantro parsley
½ tsp. chopped fresh thyme

Bring 4½ cups water to a boil; add 1 teaspoon salt. Add polenta in a thin stream; whisk until thickened. Reduce heat to low; cook, stirring occasionally, for 5 minutes. Spray a large baking pan with vegetable oil spray. Spread polenta in pan ¼ inch thick. Cover and refrigerate for 30 minutes. Heat oil over low heat; cook garlic and shallots until translucent. Place in a bowl; add Ricotta cheese, Parmesan cheese, rosemary, cilantro parsley, and remaining salt and pepper. Cut polenta into 36 squares.

In nonstick skillet, brown polenta squares, about 2 minutes per side, in as many batches as necessary. Spread 1 teaspoon of Ricotta mixture on each polenta square; top with a tomato. Sprinkle with chopped thyme. Makes 36 pieces.

Option: Prepare a tomato/sausage mixture to place on top of Ricotta cheese mixture and top with chopped fresh basil.

UNUSUAL LIGHT EGG NOODLES

1 c. refrigerated or frozen egg
    product, thawed
¼ c. all-purpose flour
¼ c. water

⅛ tsp. salt
Nonstick spray coating
Cooking oil (optional)

Combine egg product, flour, water, and salt in a bowl. Beat with a wire whisk or rotary beater till well combined.

Spray a 6 inch skillet with nonstick coating; heat over medium heat. Remove from heat and spoon 2 *tablespoons* batter into pan. Tilt pan to evenly coat bottom of skillet. Cook over medium heat about 1 minute or till lightly browned. Invert pan over paper towels to remove crepe. Repeat with remaining batter, brushing pan very lightly with cooking oil, if necessary. Cool crepes completely. Stack about *half* of the crepes and roll up. Slice into ¼ inch wide strips; fluff with fingers to separate. Repeat with remaining crepes.

To serve, place hot food on top of noodles. Makes 4 servings.

Notes

Fish and Chicken

GRILLING TIPS

1. To clean the grilling surface, heat grill for five minutes, then brush with a wire brush to loosen debris.
2. When cooking meats without sauce, oil the grill with one to two tablespoons of vegetable or olive oil to prevent meat from sticking.
3. Trim cuts of meat of all excess fat before grilling, leaving ¼ inch around the edges.
4. Ribs will cook better when simmered for approximately one hour in water before grilling. This process removes fat from the ribs, and will prevent flare-ups on the grill.
5. Cuts of beef and lamb for outdoor grilling should be a minimum of 1½ inches thick, but not more than three inches thick, to retain pink inside after the surface sears.
6. When marinating small cuts of meat, allow three hours per inch of thickness in refrigerator. For larger cuts of meat, allow one to two days in the refrigerator, depending on the size of the cut. Turn the meat occasionally to distribute the marinade.
7. Always marinate in a noncorrosive container, such as glass, porcelain, glazed earthenware or stainless steel.
8. Use tongs to turn meat and fish. Piercing the food will let the juices escape.
9. When using bamboo skewers for kabobs, soak them in water for at least 30 minutes before use to prevent them from burning.
10. Cutting into meat to check for doneness will let the juices escape. Instead of cutting, touch the meat. If it is firm to the touch, then it is well done. If it feels very soft, it is still raw. If it feels soft to the touch but springs back, it is medium rare. (Be careful not to burn yourself.)
11. Chicken with bones can be baked in an oven for 15 to 20 minutes, covered, at 300° before grilling. Alternatively, parboil for about five minutes (with or without skin). This keeps grilling time down and prevents chicken from drying out.
12. Remove skin, clean and parboil chicken. Cover with barbecue sauce or other marinade and freeze in an appropriate quantity for your meal. This gets the mess and work behind you and allows the marinade to be absorbed. Thaw when you are ready to grill.
13. Chicken cutlets can be grilled quickly over high heat. Do not overcook! Use a grilling basket if pieces are small.
14. To test chicken for doneness, light meat should be white and the juice translucent, not pink; dark meat juices should be clear.
15. It is difficult to keep fish from sticking to the grill. Thicker cuts and fish steaks work best. The easiest solution is a grilling basket, sprayed with Pam.
16. Fish is done if opaque throughout. Do not overcook!
17. Hard vegetables, such as cauliflower, broccoli, and small onions, should be parboiled approximately 1½ minutes before putting on skewers. Soft vegetables, such as cherry tomatoes and mushrooms, can be boiled for 30-45 seconds.
18. One inch cross sections of corn on the cob make a nice addition to kabobs.
19. Marinate sliced eggplant or zucchini in Italian dressing overnight then grill as desired.
20. Do not mix items on a kabob that require different cooking times, such as steak and mushrooms. Segregate items on separate skewers to adjust times. It is not as pretty, but it avoids a cooking disaster.
21. Be creative with marinades, but do not forget old stand-bys such a bottle of Catalina dressing for chicken or a mixture of Italian dressing (one bottle) and tomato paste (large can) for beef kabobs. All you need for fish is some tamari sauce (similar to soy sauce) and a few drops of oil.

FISH AND CHICKEN

ORANGE ROUGHY

1 lb. orange roughy
1 egg, beaten
¼ c. oil
1 tsp. seasoned salt
1 tsp. paprika

¼ c. wheat germ
¼ c. Parmesan cheese
1 tsp. tarragon
¼ c. lemon juice

Mix together tarragon, seasonings, wheat germ, and Parmesan on waxed paper. Dip filets into egg, then into dry mixture. Brown on both sides in oil until fish is cooked. Pour on lemon juice. Serve with asparagus and brown and wild rice.

FILET VERONIQUE

1 lb. frozen sole filets (or fresh)
¼ lb. seedless green grapes
1 tsp. dried parsley
¼ tsp. tarragon
½ clove garlic, minced

¾ c. white wine
1½ Tbsp. butter
1 Tbsp. flour
2 Tbsp. orange juice
Salt and lime juice to taste

Thaw filets and sprinkle lightly with salt and lime juice. Arrange with grapes in lightly greased skillet. Sprinkle with parsley, tarragon, and garlic. Add wine and simmer for 12 to 15 minutes until filets flake easily and look milky white rather than transparent. Remove from heat, but keep warm on separate platter.

In original skillet, melt butter with remaining juices and blend in flour until smooth. Add orange juice and cook, stirring until mixture thickens. Add more wine if necessary. Pour sauce over filets. Makes 3 to 4 servings.

SOLE FILETS WITH GRAPES

2 lb. sole or other thin fish filets,
  thawed (if frozen)
Salt and pepper to taste
2 c. seedless green grapes
2 Tbsp. butter or margarine
½ c. chopped onion
½ c. dry white wine

¾ c. half & half cream
1 egg yolk, beaten
1 Tbsp. flour
¼ tsp. salt (or to taste)
Dash of nutmeg
Paprika to taste

Sprinkle both sides of fish with salt and pepper. Roll filets and secure with picks. Melt butter in 10 inch skillet over moderate heat. Add onion. Cook until onion is soft. Add fish rolls, seam sides down, and wine. Cover and simmer for 8 minutes or until fish flakes easily when tested with fork. Remove fish and place in shallow baking dish. Remove picks. Keep fish warm.

In a bowl, combine cream, egg yolk, flour, salt, and nutmeg. Mix until smooth. Gradually add cream mixture to poaching liquid and cook over medium heat, stirring constantly, until sauce thickens. Add grapes and pour sauce over fish. Sprinkle with paprika and broil about 5 inches from source of heat for 4 to 5 minutes or until lightly browned. Makes 6 servings.

Suggested accompaniments: Vegetable salad, pasta, rice or potatoes, Pino Blanc wine.

FILET OF SOLE WITH CRABMEAT AU MONBLASON

2 c. dry white wine
1 (8 oz.) bottle clam juice
3 sprigs fresh parsley
1 bay leaf
½ tsp. thyme
½ lb. mushrooms, sliced
5 Tbsp. sweet butter
3 Tbsp. flour

2 Tbsp. brandy
1 c. Swiss Gruyere cheese, grated
¼ c. cream sherry
12 oz. crabmeat (fresh or canned)
½ c. heavy cream
Salt and freshly ground black
    pepper to taste
1½ lb. filet of grey sole

Simmer the wine until reduced to 1 cup, measuring for accuracy. Add the clam juice, parsley, bay leaf, and thyme to wine. Simmer for 15 minutes and then strain the liquid.

Saute the sliced mushrooms in 2 tablespoons of the butter. Stir in the flour and cook gently until slightly browned. Stir in the brandy. Gradually add the wine and clam juice to make a smooth, slightly thickened sauce.

Add the sauteed mushrooms, ½ cup of the cheese, cream sherry, crabmeat, and cream. Mix well and season with the salt and pepper. Spread half of the sauce in the bottom of a 9x13 inch flat Pyrex dish or in 2 smaller ones. Place the filets over the sauce and cover with remaining sauce. Cover evenly with remaining cheese. Bake in preheated 400° oven for 20 minutes. Glaze under the broiler for 7 to 8 minutes until a golden crust is formed. Do not overcook. Serves 4 to 6.

COD AU GRATIN

1 lb. cod filets
2 Tbsp. butter
1 can cream of shrimp soup
½ tsp. curry powder

¼ c. grated Parmesan cheese
Paprika
Pepper
1 c. baby shrimp

Butter a baking dish with half the butter. Put the filets in a single layer and dot with remaining butter. Cover with baby shrimp. In a saucepan, mix soup, curry powder, and pepper. Heat slowly, just to mix thoroughly. Pour over fish. Sprinkle with Parmesan cheese and paprika. Bake at 400° until hot and bubbly, 30 to 40 minutes. Cover the baking dish with foil during the last 15 minutes of baking to prevent fish from drying out. Serves 2.

ALASKA HALIBUT BAKE

½ c. sour cream
¼ pkg. onion soup mix
Halibut for 4
3 tsp. Parmesan cheese

1 tsp. chopped parsley
¼ tsp. paprika
3 Tbsp. melted butter or oil
½ c. bread or cracker crumbs

Combine soup mix and sour cream. Mix bread crumbs, cheese, paprika, and parsley. Dip fish in sour cream mix and roll in bread crumbs. Pour butter or oil over fish. Bake at 350° for 15 to 20 minutes. Save extra sour cream and onion soup mix for halibut dip. Serves 4.

SCALLOPS AND DILL STIR-FRY

A tasty low calorie dish - about 188 calories per serving!

1 Tbsp. lemon juice or 2 Tbsp. dry white wine
¼ tsp. dill weed
1 clove garlic, crushed
Dash of nutmeg
Salt and pepper
2 Tbsp. butter

¼ lb. fresh mushrooms, thickly sliced
1 green or red pepper, cut in 1 inch pieces
1 (8 oz.) can scallops, rinsed and drained

Stir together juice or wine and seasonings. Melt butter; when hot, add mushrooms and stir-fry for 1 minute. Add green or red pepper, scallops, and juice mixture. Stir-fry over medium heat for 2 minutes. Taste and add more nutmeg if necessary. Yield: 2 to 3 servings.

SEVICHE OF SEA SCALLOPS WITH FRESH ARTICHOKES

8 to 10 large fresh sea scallops
1 fresh lime
Salt and white pepper
½ Tbsp. minced shallots or scallions
2 Tbsp. minced fresh parsley

2 Tbsp. flour
2 or 3 lemons
2 or 3 large fine artichokes
1 tsp. Dijon-type mustard
1 Tbsp. raw egg white
4 to 5 Tbsp. light olive oil

For decoration:

Watercress or shredded romaine

Sliced tomatoes or cherry tomatoes

The scallops: Wash and drain the scallops to remove possible sand. Dipping a sharp knife in cold water for each cut, slice them crosswise (across the grain) into pieces ³⁄₁₆ inch (¾ cm) thick. Toss in a bowl with the juice of the lime, a sprinkling of salt and pepper, the shallots or scallions, and the parsley. Cover and marinate (let set) in the refrigerator for half an hour or until serving time.

The artichokes: To make a *blanc* or cooking liquid that will keep the artichokes white, place the flour in a medium-size saucepan; gradually beat in 1 cup (¼ liter) cold water. Stir in 2 more cups (½ liter) water, a tablespoon of lemon juice, and 1½ teaspoons salt; bring to the boil, stirring, then remove from heat. One by one, break stems off artichokes and bend leaves back upon themselves all around to snap them off the base until you come to the bulge at the top of the artichoke bottom. Cut off crown of leaves at this point and trim base all around to remove greenish parts - rubbing frequently with cut lemon to prevent darkening. Drop each as done into the cooking water. Simmer 30 to 40 minutes until tender when pierced with a knife and leave in cooking water until ready to serve.

Will keep 2 to 3 days under refrigeration. Wash under cold water, scoop out chokes with a teaspoon and cut into ³⁄₁₆ inch (¾ cm) slices going from top to bottom. Fold gently in a bowl with the following dressing.

Vinaigrette Liee (lightly thickened French dressing): For about ⅓ cup dressing, beat ½ teaspoon salt with 1½ tablespoons lemon juice and the teaspoon of mustard. Beat in the egg white and then, by dribbles, the oil. Taste carefully for seasoning, adding pepper to taste - dressing should not be too strong or it will mask the taste of the artichokes.

Assembling: Line individual small plates or shells with watercress or shredded romaine, then arrange slices of artichoke interspersed with tomato, for instance, around the edges of the dishes, and a rosette of scallop slices in the middle, with a central dot of tomato for accent. Cover with plastic wrap and refrigerate until serving time. May be prepared up to an hour ahead. Makes 4 servings.

BAY SCALLOPS IN GARLIC BUTTER SAUCE

⅛ tsp. lemon zest, freshly grated
2 Tbsp. fresh parsley leaves,
   minced
1 clove garlic, minced

2 Tbsp. butter
¾ lb. bay scallops
¼ c. dry white wine

In a small bowl, toss together the lemon zest and the parsley. Reserve this mixture. In a heavy skillet, cook the garlic in the butter over moderately low heat, stirring occasionally, for 1 minute. Increase the heat to high and cook the garlic, stirring until it is pale golden in color. Add the scallops, patted dry. Cook them, stirring occasionally, for 1½ to 2 minutes or until they are just firm. Transfer with a slotted spoon to a platter. Add the wine to the pan juices and boil the mixture, stirring until it is reduced to about ¼ cup. Season the sauce with salt and pepper to taste. Spoon the sauce over the scallops and sprinkle the scallops with the reserved parsley mixture. Serve with Italian bread. Serves 2.

SALMON FILETS

4 (6 to 8 oz.) salmon filets
2 Tbsp. butter or margarine
½ tsp. Worcestershire sauce
Mrs. Dash seasoning

Dill
Ground pepper
Onion chips
Paprika

Wrap salmon, which has been sprinkled with seasonings, in foil that has been brushed with margarine. Broil on gas grill or in oven 10 to 12 minutes till flaky. Cooking time varies depending on thickness of filets. Serve with lemon wedges. Serves 4.

SEAFOOD AND ARTICHOKE CASSEROLE

½ lb. fresh mushrooms, sliced
6 Tbsp. butter
1½ lb. cooked shrimp, shelled, and
   deveined (or same quantity of
   crabmeat or a combination of
   shrimp and crab)
1 (13 oz.) can artichoke hearts,
   chopped

¼ c. flour
1½ c. light cream or evaporated milk
½ c. dry sherry
1 Tbsp. Worcestershire sauce
Salt and pepper to taste
¼ tsp. paprika
½ c. Parmesan cheese, freshly
   grated

Preheat oven to 350°. Saute mushrooms in 2 tablespoons of butter until soft. Layer a 3 quart casserole with mushrooms, seafood, and artichoke hearts, ending with mushrooms on top.

In a saucepan, melt remaining butter until foamy. Add flour and cook, stirring, for 3 minutes over medium heat. Add cream, stirring until sauce is well-blended and thickened. Add the sherry, Worcestershire sauce, salt, pepper, and paprika. Pour sauce over the casserole and sprinkle with grated Parmesan. Bake 30 to 40 minutes until bubbling hot and lightly browned. Serve with rice. Can be prepared a day ahead. Serves 6.

EGGPLANT WITH SEAFOOD CASSEROLE

1 medium eggplant, peeled, diced, and cooked
½ c. butter
1 medium onion
½ bell pepper, chopped
½ bunch green onions, chopped
2 cloves garlic
1 c. Italian bread crumbs
1 egg, slightly beaten
1 (6½ oz.) can crabmeat, drained
1 tsp. salt
Red and black pepper to taste

Put eggplant into large bowl and mash. Saute onions, bell pepper, and garlic until soft. Add to the eggplant mixture. Add bread crumbs and mix well. Add crabmeat and mix. Season to taste. Add eggs by gently mixing and pour mixture into greased casserole. Bake 25 minutes at 325°. Serves 3 to 4.

Eggplant can be halved and parboiled first, then scoop out eggplant, saving halves for stuffing. Place mixture in eggplant halves; sprinkle with bread crumbs and bake as preceding.

SHRIMP AND WILD RICE CASSEROLE

¼ c. green peppers, thinly sliced (optional)
½ c. onion, thinly sliced
½ c. mushrooms, thinly sliced
¼ c. butter
1 Tbsp. Worcestershire sauce
Tabasco
2 c. cooked wild rice
1 lb. cooked shrimp
2 c. thin cream sauce (using chicken broth instead of milk)

Saute the onion, green peppers, and mushrooms in butter until soft. Add the seasonings, rice, shrimp, and cream sauce. Place in a buttered casserole and bake at 300° until thoroughly heated. Serves 6.

ANOTHER SHRIMP AND RICE BAKE

1½ c. rice (uncooked)
8 oz. fresh baby shrimp or 2 (4 oz.) pkg. frozen baby shrimp
1 c. sour cream
3 oz. Blue cheese, crumbled
1 tsp. Worcestershire sauce or A.1. Steak Sauce

Cook rice and spread into 6 individual casseroles or 1 large one. Arrange washed shrimp over rice. Combine sour cream, Blue cheese, and Worcestershire sauce and spoon over shrimp, making sure all edges are sealed. Cover and bake at 350° for 25 minutes. Makes 6 individual servings.

In large casserole it serves 4 with generous second helpings.

SHRIMP AND CRAB NEW ORLEANS

2 cans crabmeat, drained with
   cartilage removed
2 cans shrimp, rinsed and drained
   (or frozen)
1 medium green pepper, chopped
1 medium onion, chopped
1 c. celery, chopped
2 hard cooked eggs, chopped

1 c. mayonnaise
1 tsp. Worcestershire
½ tsp. salt
⅛ tsp. pepper
¼ c. slivered almonds
2 Tbsp. butter, melted
1 c. dry bread crumbs

Heat oven to 350°F. Mix all ingredients, except bread crumbs, butter, and almonds. Pour into greased 1¼ quart casserole or 9x13 inch casserole. Toss bread crumbs and butter. Sprinkle over casserole. Bake 30 minutes; sprinkle with almonds. Bake another 10 minutes. Perfect ladies' lunch. May add water chestnuts if desired.

GINGER TUNA

3 (7 oz.) cans solid white tuna
½ c. green onions, chopped
1 tsp. margarine
½ c. carrots, thinly sliced on
   diagonal

3 tsp. slivered ginger (fresh or
   candied)
2 c. sour cream (or sour cream
   substitute)
Salt and pepper to taste

Drain liquid from tuna into skillet. Add margarine and onions and heat to wilt. Break tuna into pan in large pieces. Add remaining ingredients. Add pepper to taste. Heat gently. Serve over cooked rice or pasta. Serves 6 to 8.

LIMON TUNA CASHEW CASSEROLE

1 c. celery, chopped
1 can mushroom soup
¼ c. onion, chopped
¾ c. whole cashews

1 can albacore solid white tuna
⅓ c. milk
1 large can Chinese noodles

Grease flat Pyrex baking dish and line with noodles, saving half for topping. Mix remaining ingredients and place on top of noodles. Cover the casserole with reserved noodles and bake 30 minutes at 350°. Garnish with lemon slices. Serves 4 to 6.

BAUR'S DEVILED CRAB

6 Tbsp. flour
¼ c. butter
½ tsp. Worcestershire sauce
½ tsp. celery seed
½ lb. crabmeat, flaked

1 c. light cream
1 egg yolk, slightly beaten
½ tsp. salt
Salt and pepper to taste
Fine and coarse bread crumbs

Make a smooth paste of flour and cream. Heat slowly until warm. Add butter. Cook until thick, stirring constantly. Add some of the mixture to egg yolk. Stir into remaining hot mixture. Add remaining ingredients. Chill 2 or 3 hours. Shape into individual mounds of crabmeat. Roll mounds in the fine bread crumbs, then egg yolks, then coarse bread crumbs. Allow to warm up, then deep-fry.

Baur's of old Denver served this with coleslaw.

BEER BATTER FOR SHRIMP

1 (12 oz.) can beer
1½ to 2 c. flour
1 Tbsp. salt

1 Tbsp. paprika
Pepper

Combine all ingredients and beat with wire whisk until frothy. Batter may be used immediately or stored in refrigerator for several days.

CARIBBEAN SHRIMP

2 Tbsp. instant minced onion
2 Tbsp. butter or margarine
1 c. chopped green bell pepper
1 (14½ oz.) can whole tomatoes
1 bay leaf
½ tsp. sugar

¼ tsp. ground allspice
¼ tsp. salt
⅛ tsp. ground red pepper
1 lb. medium shrimp, shelled and
    deveined
1 Tbsp. fresh lime or lemon juice

In a cup, combine onion with 2 tablespoons water; set aside to soften, about 10 minutes.

In a large skillet, heat butter until hot. Add green pepper and reserved onion; cook and stir until almost crisp-tender, about 3 minutes.

Add tomatoes, bay leaf, sugar, allspice, salt, and ground red pepper, breaking up tomatoes with a spoon. Bring to a boil; reduce heat and simmer, uncovered, until slightly thickened, about 20 minutes.

Add shrimp; cook and stir until pink, 3 to 5 minutes. Stir in lime juice. Remove bay leaf before serving. Serve over steamed rice if desired. Makes 4 servings.

SHRIMP WITH MUSHROOMS

1½ Tbsp. margarine
½ tsp. salt
¼ tsp. pepper
¼ tsp. Worcestershire sauce
Dash of paprika
¾ lb. mushrooms, peeled and sliced
1 Tbsp. shallot, chopped fine
2 tsp. parsley, chopped fine

3 tsp. green pepper, chopped
2 Tbsp. grated Cheddar cheese
2 Tbsp. flour
¾ c. milk
1 lb. shrimp, deveined and boiled in
    court bouillon, about 3
    minutes, or until shrimp is pink
Bread crumbs, buttered

Melt butter in saucepan. Add salt, pepper, Worcestershire sauce, paprika, mushrooms, and shallot. Add flour and stir until smooth. Add milk, green pepper, and shrimp. Cook until thickened. Pour into buttered casserole or ramekins. Cover with buttered bread crumbs and grated cheese. Bake 20 minutes at 400°. Serves 4.

SHRIMP WITH WALNUTS

3 lb. large raw shrimp
1 c. walnut halves
½ c. soy sauce
¼ c. oil
1½ Tbsp. sugar
2 Tbsp. minced onion

½ c. dry sherry
2 tsp. dark sesame oil
8 small dried chili peppers
2 to 3 Tbsp. minced fresh ginger
1½ bunches green onions
Peanut oil

Peel and devein shrimp under cold water; set aside in colander to drain. Toast walnuts at 250° for 15 minutes; set aside. Combine remaining ingredients, except green onions and peanut oil, in a large bowl. Add the shrimp and mix well with marinade. Let marinate for 30 minutes or up to 1½ hours in refrigerator. Slice onions, including green tops, on the diagonal into 1½ inch pieces; set aside. Heat a small amount of peanut oil in wok or skillet over medium heat. With slotted spoon, add shrimp to pan, reserving marinade. Stir-fry for 2 to 3 minutes until shrimp curl and turn pink. Transfer to warm serving platter. Pour the marinade and warm walnuts into any pan juices that may have accumulated; turn heat to medium high and stir constantly until liquid is reduced to a syrup. Add shrimp back to pan with green onions. Stir well to coat with sauce. Serve immediately with rice. Yield: 6 servings.

SEAFOOD PAN ROAST

2 tsp. butter
Salt and white pepper to taste
⅛ tsp. celery seed
¼ tsp. paprika
Couple dashes of Tabasco and
    Worcestershire sauce
Squeeze of fresh lemon juice
2 oz. white wine

4 Tbsp. spicy cocktail sauce
12 oz. clam broth (canned)
12 oz. whipping cream
4 oz. raw, peeled, shrimp
4 oz. scallops
4 oz. crabmeat
Chopped cilantro (for garnish)

Place butter, seasonings, and cocktail sauce in the top portion of a double boiler. Add wine and clam juice and place over boiling water. Cover and bring to a boil. Add seafood and cook just until done. Add whipping cream and heat through, but do not boil. Garnish with chopped cilantro and serve with French bread. Serves 2.

CHINESE CASSEROLE

1 (3 oz.) can Chinese noodles
1 c. celery, diced finely
¼ onion, minced
1 c. whole cashews
1 can mushroom soup

¼ c. water
¼ c. pimento
1 can mandarin oranges
1 can tuna (or chicken)

Combine all ingredients, except half of noodles. Spread in casserole dish and sprinkle remaining noodles on top. Bake at 350° for 50 minutes.

SALMON CAKES

Make sure your poaching liquid is only at a simmer before adding the salmon. Cook gently for 10 minutes per inch of thickness. When forming the cakes, handle them gently so they don't get too dense.

Poaching Liquid:

4 c. water
1 c. dry white wine
4 sprigs celery leaves

6 sprigs parsley
6 whole peppercorns
1 tsp. coarse salt

Additional ingredients:

1 lb. salmon filets
1¼ c. bread crumbs
1 Tbsp. chopped fresh thyme leaves
   or 1 tsp. dried thyme
1 tsp. dried oregano
½ tsp. dry mustard
Pinch of cayenne pepper
Salt and pepper to taste
1 c. prepared mayonnaise
½ c. finely diced onion

½ c. diced (¼ inch) celery
1 Tbsp. drained tiny capers,
   coarsely chopped
1 Tbsp. chopped parsley
1 tsp. Worcestershire sauce
1 large egg, lightly beaten
2 Tbsp. canola oil (or more if
   necessary)
Sheila's Tartar Sauce (see recipe)

1. To poach the salmon, place the water, wine, celery leaves, parsley sprigs, peppercorns, and salt in a large saucepan. Bring to a boil and reduce the heat to a simmer. Add the salmon and simmer for 10 minutes or until cooked through and the salmon flakes easily with a fork. Carefully remove salmon from the poaching liquid with a slotted spatula and set aside to cool. When cool enough to handle, remove the skin and bones and flake salmon into a large bowl. Set aside.

2. Combine ¼ cup of the bread crumbs, thyme, oregano, mustard, cayenne, and salt and pepper in a small bowl. Add to the salmon along with the mayonnaise, onion, celery, capers, parsley, Worcestershire sauce, and egg. Toss to combine.

3. Place the remaining cup of bread crumbs in a shallow dish. Form the salmon mixture into 10 patties, 2½ inches across and ¾ inch thick. Carefully dredge the patties in the crumbs. Remove to a plate and cover. Refrigerate for 1 hour.

4. Heat the oil in a nonstick skillet over medium heat. Cook the salmon cakes about 3 minutes per side or until golden brown. Drain the cakes on a paper towel. Serve topped with Tartar Sauce.

Tartar Sauce:

1 c. reduced-calorie mayonnaise
1 tsp. Dijon-style mustard
1 tsp. finely grated lemon zest
1 Tsp. fresh lemon juice
Dash of Tabasco sauce
2 Tbsp. drained pickle relish

2 Tbsp. chopped flat-leaf parsley
2 Tbsp. finely minced shallots
1 Tbsp. drained tiny capers
Salt and freshly ground black
   pepper

Combine the mayonnaise, mustard, lemon zest, lemon juice, Tabasco, and relish in a bowl. Stir in the parsley, shallots, capers, salt, and pepper to taste. Refrigerate, covered, for at least 1 hour before serving for flavors to blend. Makes 1¼ cups, 2 tablespoons per serving.

CRAB CAKES

1 lb. fresh lump crabmeat (2 c.),
  picked over and patted dry
1 c. fresh bread crumbs (about 3
  slices fresh or day-old bread)
¼ c. reduced-fat mayonnaise
1 large egg white, lightly beaten with
  a fork
2 Tbsp. fresh lemon juice
1 scallion, trimmed and finely
  chopped

⅓ c. finely diced red or green bell
  pepper
1 Tbsp. chopped fresh parsley
1 tsp. Old Bay seasoning
¼ tsp. freshly ground black pepper
¼ to ½ tsp. Tabasco sauce
½ c. fine dry bread crumbs
1 tsp. vegetable oil (preferably
  canola oil)
Lemon wedges for garnish

Preheat oven to 450°. In a large bowl, stir together crabmeat, fresh bread crumbs, mayonnaise, egg white, lemon juice, scallions, bell peppers, parsley, Old Bay seasoning, pepper, and Tabasco.

Put the dry bread crumbs in a shallow dish. Form the crab mixture into six ½ inch thick patties. (The mixture will be very soft.) Dredge the patties in the dry bread crumbs, reshaping as necessary.

Brush oil evenly over the bottom of a heavy ovenproof skillet. Heat the skillet over medium-high heat. Add the crab cakes and cook until the undersides of the cakes are golden, about 1 minute. Carefully turn the crab cakes over and transfer the skillet to the oven. (If you do not have an ovenproof skillet, transfer the crab patties to a baking sheet.) Bake for 10 to 12 minutes or until heated through. Serve with lemon wedges. Makes 6 servings.

CRAB IMPERIAL

1 lb. crabmeat
1 Tbsp. pimento, finely chopped, or
  red bell pepper and green
  pepper
1 Tbsp. Worcestershire sauce
¼ tsp. salt
1 tsp. Old Bay seasoning

2 Tbsp. parsley, chopped
1 Tbsp. baking powder
1 egg, beaten
2 Tbsp. mayonnaise
1 egg yolk
2 Tbsp. mayonnaise
Crushed crackers

Pick crabmeat from shells gently. Add pimento (or bell peppers), Worcestershire sauce, salt, Old Bay seasoning, and parsley to crabmeat. Blend together 1 egg, 2 tablespoons mayonnaise, and baking powder and add to crab mixture with just enough crushed crackers to bind mixture together. Fill shells or small Pyrex dishes with mixture and top with mixture of 1 egg yolk and 2 tablespoons mayonnaise. Bake at 450° for 6 to 10 minutes or until golden brown. Serves 6.

ALMOND AND CRAB CASSEROLE

1 can crabmeat
1 c. shrimp, cooked
2 cans cream of mushroom soup
1 c. celery, finely chopped

¼ c. onion, minced
1 c. La Choy noodles
1 (2 oz.) pkg. chopped almonds

Combine crab, shrimp, soup, celery, onions, and noodles. Put in greased casserole and sprinkle almonds over mixture. Bake at 375° for 25 minutes or until brown. Serves 6.

BUDGET CRABMEAT SOUFFLE

1 (1 lb.) pkg. imitation crabmeat,
    thawed and shredded
½ c. milk
2 c. soft bread crumbs
1 heaping tsp. grated onion

1 Tbsp. minced parsley
¼ tsp. cayenne pepper
½ tsp. salt
1 tsp. Worcestershire sauce
1 c. mayonnaise

Mix all ingredients well. Bake in greased casserole for 15 minutes at 400°.

SALMON-CRAB TERRINE WITH BASIL CREAM SAUCE

1 (1 lb.) salmon filet
3 Tbsp. brandy
2 Tbsp. fresh lemon juice
1 Tbsp. safflower oil
1 Tbsp. minced shallot
1 tsp. salt
½ tsp. freshly ground white pepper
¼ tsp. Worcestershire sauce

1 lb. snow crabmeat
½ c. whipping cream
2 (8 oz.) pkg. frozen asparagus
    spears, thawed and drained
1⅓ c. bread crumbs
2 egg yolks
9 large romaine lettuce leaves,
    cored and blanched

Basil Cream Sauce:

3 Tbsp. butter
1 Tbsp. minced shallot
2 c. fresh basil leaves (or spinach)
1 c. whipping cream

¼ tsp. freshly grated nutmeg
¼ tsp. salt
⅛ tsp. freshly ground white pepper

Cut 12 (1 inch) cubes from salmon filet. Tear or pull remaining salmon into pieces. Combine brandy, lemon juice, safflower oil, shallot, salt, pepper, and Worcestershire sauce in large nonmetal bowl. Add salmon cubes and pieces and refrigerate for 1 hour.

Remove salmon cubes from marinade and set aside. Transfer salmon pieces and marinade to processor. Add crabmeat and whipping cream and puree until smooth. Taste and adjust seasoning. Remove salmon mixture from processor and set aside. Add asparagus spears, bread crumbs, and egg yolks to work bowl and puree.

Oil an 8x3x2 inch loaf pan. Line with blanched romaine leaves right side out. Allow excess to hang over sides of pan. Divide salmon mixture in half; spread half of asparagus mixture over salmon. Arrange marinated salmon cubes atop asparagus. Cover with remaining asparagus. Top with remaining salmon mixture. Fold excess leaves over top. Cover with pieces of buttered waxed paper. Fill shallow large baking dish with hot water. Bake terrine 1 hour in preheated 350° oven.

Meanwhile, prepare sauce: Melt butter in medium skillet over medium heat. Add shallot and cook until softened but not brown, about 3 minutes. Add basil and cook until wilted, about 1 minute. Add whipping cream, nutmeg, salt, and pepper. Increase heat to high and bring to a boil. Reduce heat to medium and cook, stirring occasionally, until sauce is reduced by ⅓, about 15 minutes. Transfer to processor and puree until smooth (use sauce immediately, do not reheat).

Unmold terrine onto platter and cut into 1 inch thick slices. Top each with sauce. Terrine can be prepared several days in advance and can be served either warm or chilled.

This is a beautiful do-ahead gourmet first course. Looks complicated but worth the effort.

CASINO-CLAM SOUFFLE

1 (7 oz.) can minced clams, drained
   (reserve juice)
Milk
3 Tbsp. butter
3 Tbsp. flour
1 egg, beaten

1 Tbsp. minced onion
1 Tbsp. minced parsley
Salt to taste
6 Tbsp. butter, melted
1½ c. bread crumbs

Add enough milk to reserved clam juice to make 1½ cups liquid. To make white sauce, melt 3 tablespoons butter and stir in flour. Add clam juice and milk mixture. Heat to boiling, stirring constantly. Boil and stir 1 minute. Remove from heat and cool thoroughly. Beat in egg, onion, parsley, and clams with wire whisk. Add salt. Place in 1 quart greased baking dish. Mix melted butter with bread crumbs and sprinkle over top. Bake at 350° for 30 minutes. Serves 4.

WILD AND BROWN RICE WITH OYSTERS

Brown lightly in ½ cup butter ½ cup minced onion and 2 cups celery. Stir in 3 tablespoons flour, ¼ cup milk, 3 cups hot drained, boiled wild rice,* ½ teaspoon salt, ¼ teaspoon sage, ⅛ teaspoon thyme, and pepper. Place in 11x7 inch oblong dish. Dip in ¼ cup butter (melted), 1 pint or 2 small cans small oysters, then in ½ cup cracker or bread crumbs; arrange over top of rice. Sprinkle with remaining crumbs and butter. Place in broiler just low enough to keep from burning, 10 minutes. Serves 6.

* I use MJB brown and wild rice mix and omit the last 4 ingredients.

CHICKEN ROLLATINE

2½ Tbsp. butter
2 large cloves garlic, chopped
1 sweet red pepper, diced
4 green onions, finely chopped
4 whole boneless, skinned chicken
   breasts (2½ lb.)
½ tsp. salt

½ tsp. black pepper
½ lb. Mozzarella, shredded
¼ c. flour
3 eggs, beaten
1 c. Italian style bread crumbs
⅓ c. chopped fresh parsley
½ c. oil

Heat butter in saucepan. Add garlic, red pepper, and green onion; saute 5 minutes. Let cool. Split chicken breasts; place between sheets of plastic wrap. Pound paper-thin. Season chicken with salt and pepper. Combine Mozzarella and red pepper mixture in small bowl. Place 2 tablespoons mixture in center of each chicken circle. Fold sides over to form a bundle. Turn flap side down on metal baking pan. Freeze 20 minutes to hold together for frying. Place flour, eggs, and crumbs mixed with parsley in 3 separate pans. Dip bundles in flour, then eggs and crumbs to coat. (Can prepare several hours in advance and refrigerate.) Heat half the oil in skillet. Working in batches, fry bundles in 1 to 2 minutes per side until lightly browned. Place on baking pan. Bake in 350° oven for 20 to 25 minutes or until cooked through and a nice light brown color. Serve with a white pasta, carrots, and a green vegetable salad. Serves 8.

GRILLED CHICKEN AND PASTA

4 chicken breast filets
Lemon pepper
Olive oil
1 c. blanched asparagus, sliced
   diagonally

½ c. sliced mushrooms
1 red bell pepper, cubed and
   blanched
¼ c. sliced black olives
8 oz. rotini, cooked

Sauce:

3 c. chicken broth
2 Tbsp. Parmesan or Romano
   cheese

2 Tbsp. cornstarch
2 Tbsp. chopped fresh basil
1 Tbsp. garlic, chopped

Mix sauce ingredients and bring to boil; simmer about 45 minutes to reduce to 2 cups. Season boneless skinless chicken breasts with lemon pepper; broil or grill. Do not overcook. Slice into bite-size pieces. Stir-fry asparagus, pepper, and mushrooms until tender and add the prepared pasta and olives. Mix all: Chicken, prepared sauce, and vegetable-pasta together. Add additional cheese to taste. Garnish with fresh basil leaves. Serve with green salad. Serves 4.

CHICKEN A LA KING A LA THE DENVER TEA ROOM

2 sticks butter
1½ c. flour
8 c. chicken stock
1 c. half & half
1 lb. cooked, skinned, diced chicken
1 large red bell pepper, cut in ¼ inch
   strips

1 large green bell pepper, cut in ¼
   inch strips
½ lb. mushrooms, sliced and
   sauteed in 1 Tbsp. butter
Salt and pepper to taste
Baked puff pastry shell

Melt butter in large saucepan. Whisk in flour, cooking over moderate heat a few minutes, still whisking. Gradually add chicken stock. Cook over moderate heat, whisking until thickened. Whisk in half & half. Cook over low heat about 25 minutes. Add more chicken stock to reach desired consistency. Add remaining ingredients, cooking over low heat about 20 minutes. Serve in pastry shell. Makes 8 servings.

CHICKEN QUICHE

The lemon flavored pastry makes this special.

Filling:

2 whole chicken breasts, skinned,
   boned, and cut into 1 inch
   cubes
1½ tsp. salt (divided)
⅛ tsp. white pepper
¼ c. corn oil
1 large onion, thinly sliced and
   separated into rings
1 large, firm tomato, peeled, seeded,
   and cut into cubes and
   drained

3 large eggs
¾ c. milk
¾ c. light cream
4½ to 5 oz. Gruyere cheese, cut into
   small cubes
¼ c. freshly grated Parmesan
   cheese
Pinch of ground nutmeg
1 tsp. butter, cut into small pieces

Add ½ teaspoon of the salt and pepper to chicken. Heat corn oil and saute chicken slowly, 5 to 6 minutes. Remove chicken; add onion rings and cook until nearly tender. Add tomato; cover and cook 7 minutes or until moisture evaporates. Beat eggs; add milk, cream, cheeses, nutmeg, and remaining teaspoon salt. Arrange onion, tomato, and chicken on bottom of pastry shell. Pour in egg mixture and dot with butter. Bake in a preheated 375° oven for 35 to 40 minutes. Check by inserting knife 3 inches from edge. If the knife comes out clean it is done.

Lemon Pastry Shell (10 inch):

1½ c. sifted flour	**1 heaping tsp. shortening**
½ tsp. salt	**Grated rind and juice of ½ lemon**
9 Tbsp. butter	**Scant ¼ c. ice water**

Sift flour and salt; cut in butter and shortening until crumbly. Add lemon rind, juice, and ice water. Mix lightly. Form a ball and roll out on lightly floured board. Roll 1½ inches larger than 10 inch pie pan. Trim to 1 inch beyond pan. Roll edge under. Form into rim and flute. Bake at 425° for 10 minutes for partially baked shell for Chicken Quiche.

Sauce:

10 small mushrooms, chopped	**½ c. light cream**
3 Tbsp. butter	**2 Tbsp. chutney, chopped**
Salt and pepper to taste	**1 c. sour cream**
2 Tbsp. flour	**¼ c. dry sherry**

Saute mushrooms in butter. Add salt and pepper to taste. Add flour and blend. Stirring constantly, add cream and cook until sauce is thickened. Add chutney, sour cream, and sherry. Cook until heated thoroughly. Serve over quiche. Serves 8.

APRICOT-GLAZED CORNISH HENS

¾ c. apricot preserves	**2 Tbsp. butter or margarine, melted**
2 tsp. orange rind, grated	**1 (6 oz.) pkg. long grain and wild**
2 Tbsp. orange juice	**rice mix**
4 Cornish hens	**2⅓ c. chicken broth**
¼ tsp. paprika	**½ c. green onions, sliced**
½ c. cashews	

Combine apricot preserves, orange rind, and orange juice. Set aside. Remove giblets from hens; reserve for other uses. Rinse hens with cold water and pat dry. Close cavities and secure with wooden picks; truss. Sprinkle with paprika. Place hens, breast side up, in a lightly greased roasting pan. Bake at 350° for 1¼ to 1½ hours, basting frequently with about ½ cup apricot mixture during the last 30 minutes.

Saute cashews in butter in a large skillet until cashews are golden. Drain cashews and set aside, reserving butter in skillet. Saute green onions in same skillet until tender. Add rice mix and prepare according to package directions, substituting chicken broth for water and omitting salt. Arrange Cornish hens on serving platter; brush with remaining apricot mixture. Serve with rice. Serves 4.

WESTERN SLOPE PEACH-STUFFED CHICKEN BREAST

6 whole chicken breasts, boned and
    skinned (about 7 oz. each)
1½ tsp. salt
⅛ tsp. pepper
3 fresh peaches, peeled and diced
⅓ c. onion, chopped
½ c. coarsely chopped cashews
½ tsp. grated ginger

⅛ tsp. freshly ground nutmeg
3 Tbsp. unsalted butter, melted
Flour for dredging
1 egg, lightly beaten
1 c. corn flake crumbs
1 c. fresh bread crumbs
1 tsp. paprika
Peach Sauce (recipe follows)

Preheat oven to 375°. Place each chicken breast on a sheet of waxed paper and flatten to ¼ inch using a meat mallet or rolling pin. Sprinkle 1 teaspoon salt and the pepper over inside of the breasts. Set aside. Combine the peaches, onions, cashews, nutmeg, and ginger, stirring well. Place ¼ cup filling in the center of each breast. Fold side of chicken over filling and secure with a toothpick.

Melt the butter in a 13x9x2 inch pan. Combine the corn flake crumbs and bread crumbs with paprika and salt to taste. Dredge each breast in flour, then dip in egg. Roll each breast in crumb mixture. Place breasts, top side down, in the pan. Bake in preheated oven for 25 minutes. Turn and bake for 20 minutes more. Serve topped with fresh peach sauce. Serves 6.

CHICKEN POCKETS

1 box stuffing mix
1¼ c. water
8 tsp. butter
4 boneless chicken breasts
Paprika to taste
Sage to taste

Pepper to taste
2 Granny Smith apples, quartered
    and cored
4 pieces foil, sprayed on one side
    with Pam cooking spray

Mix stuffing and water. Let stand 5 minutes. Put 2 teaspoons butter on foil. Top with ¾ cup stuffing mixture and breast. Sprinkle with paprika, sage, and pepper. Tuck 2 apple quarters alongside. Fold foil to seal and place on cookie sheet. Bake 25 minutes or until chicken is cooked at 450°. Serves 4.

MADEIRA CHICKEN AND SHRIMP

3 (4 lb.) broiler fryers, cut up, or 16
    to 20 chicken breasts and
    thighs on the bone
Salt and pepper
2 Tbsp. butter or margarine
2½ Tbsp. vegetable oil
20 whole mushrooms
1 (16 oz.) bag frozen whole onions,
    thawed
2 Tbsp. sugar
4 cloves garlic, crushed

1 c. beef broth
¾ c. red wine vinegar
½ c. dry Madeira wine
1 tsp. dried tarragon
1 tsp. thyme
1 Tbsp. plus 1 tsp. tomato paste
1 (¾ oz.) pkg. brown gravy mix
20 medium shrimp, shelled with tail
    left on and deveined
Parsley (for garnish)

Preheat oven to 350°. Dry chicken well and sprinkle with salt and pepper. In a large, heavy saucepan, melt 2 tablespoons butter or margarine and oil. Over moderately high heat, saute chicken pieces a few at a time until brown on all sides. Remove them to an ovenproof casserole. Saute whole mushrooms in same saucepan until lightly browned. Remove and add to chicken. Add onions to saucepan; sprinkle with sugar and saute over moderate heat, stirring until glazed and lightly browned. If too dry, add an additional tablespoon of oil. Stir in garlic, beef broth, vinegar, Madeira, tarragon, thyme, tomato paste, and brown gravy mix. Bring to a boil, stirring constantly, scraping up any brown bits that stick to the bottom of the pan. Pour over chicken and mushrooms in casserole. Cover and bake at 350° for 45 minutes.

If serving immediately, add shrimp, cover, and continue to bake an additional 15 minutes. May be refrigerated up to 2 days, or it may be frozen. If preparing ahead, bring to room temperature; bake, covered, at 350° for 25 minutes or until heated through. Add shrimp, cover, and bake 15 minutes longer or until shrimp turn pink. With slotted spoon, remove chicken, shrimp, onions, and mushrooms to serving platter. Spoon desired amount of sauce over all. Garnish with parsley. Serves 8 to 10.

SOUR CREAM CURRY CHICKEN

4 whole chicken breasts, split, skinned, and boned
3 tsp. curry powder
3 tsp. salt
6 Tbsp. Dijon mustard

Garlic powder to taste
1 c. butter
1 c. honey
16 oz. sour cream

Melt together butter, honey, curry powder, salt, garlic powder, and Dijon mustard. Place chicken in a single layer in large baking dish. Pour sauce over chicken. Bake at 350° for 1¼ hours, turning occasionally. Remove chicken to heated platter and keep warm. Stir sour cream into sauce. Return chicken to baking dish. Bake another 10 minutes. Serve over hot cooked rice or egg noodles. Serves 6 to 8.

CHICKEN IN ORANGE SAUCE

2 split breasts of chicken, skinned (4 pieces)
¼ tsp. salt
2 Tbsp. oil
2 Tbsp. flour

¼ tsp. cinnamon
Dash of ginger
¼ tsp. salt
1½ c. orange juice
⅓ c. seedless raisins

Preheat oven to 350°. Season chicken pieces with ¼ teaspoon salt. In a large skillet, lightly brown chicken in oil. Arrange chicken in flat baking dish. Add flour, cinnamon, ginger, and ¼ teaspoon salt to drippings in the skillet to make a smooth paste. Add orange juice and raisins to the skillet. Stir until thickened and boiling. Pour mixture over chicken. Cover and bake for 25 minutes. Uncover and continue baking another 30 minutes. Serves 4.

MEXICAN CHICKEN

1 or 2 large chickens
1 can cream of chicken soup
1 can cream of mushroom soup
1 can Ro-Tel tomatoes
1 c. sweet milk

1 c. chicken broth
1 large onion, sliced
1 bag Doritos chips
½ lb. grated sharp Cheddar cheese

Boil chicken; remove meat and cut up. Mix soups, tomatoes, milk, and onion; crumble Doritos. Place in layers; cover with cheese and bake for 1 hour.

DELLA ROBBIA CHICKEN

Use 1 whole chicken or 4 chicken breasts, deboned and cooked 1 hour in oven.

Sauce:

1 (8 oz.) bottle Russian dressing
1 (12 oz.) jar chili sauce
1 small onion, chopped

1 (16 oz.) can dark sweet pitted
   cherries, drained
1 (16 oz.) can peach halves, drained

Combine all sauce ingredients, except peaches, and pour mixture over the chicken. Bake at 350° for 45 minutes. The peaches should be placed on the chicken the last 10 minutes of cooking. Serves 4 to 6.

LOUISVILLE LEMON CHICKEN

4 chicken breasts, washed and
   drained
3 egg whites, beaten until frothy
Whole wheat flour
¾ c. sugar or honey

½ c. chicken broth or bouillon
1 Tbsp. corn starch
2 Tbsp. water
Juice and grated rind of 1 lemon

Toss chicken in egg whites and coat with flour. Fry breasts in vegetable oil until brown. Drain. Combine remaining ingredients in pan and bring to boil. Cover chicken with sauce and cook 45 minutes at 350°.

CANTONESE CHICKEN

1 chicken, cut up
1 c. barbecue sauce
1 c. brown sugar

1 large can sliced pineapple
   (reserve juice)
Salt and pepper

Place pieces of chicken in a casserole. Season with salt and pepper. Mix together barbecue sauce, brown sugar, and reserved pineapple juice. Pour mixture over chicken and bake at 350° for 1½ hours. Put slices of pineapple on top of chicken during the last 15 minutes of cooking time.

CHICKEN CURRY IN PAPAYA

⅓ c. butter or margarine
2 Tbsp. minced onion
1 stalk celery, chopped
1 apple, diced (tart apples are best)
5 Tbsp. all-purpose flour
1 Tbsp. curry powder
¼ tsp. garlic powder
½ tsp. dry mustard
1 tsp. salt

1 bay leaf
3 whole cloves
3 c. chicken broth
3 to 4 c. cooked chicken, cut bite-
   size pieces
¼ c. milk or cream or half & half
2 Tbsp. chopped chutney
3 papayas

In a 3 quart saucepan, melt butter. Add onion, celery, and apple and cook about 10 minutes, stirring occasionally. Mix together flour, curry powder, garlic powder, mustard, and salt. Add to apple mixture along with bay leaf and cloves. Gradually stir in chicken stock and cook, stirring, until sauce thickens. Reduce heat and simmer 30 minutes. Add chicken, milk, and chutney and cook 5 minutes longer. Cut 3 papayas in halves. Carefully remove all the seeds (be sure not to miss one). Fill with curried

1413-96

chicken. Arrange in baking dish and bake in a 350° oven for 10 to 15 minutes. Serve rice as a side dish.

Shrimp Curry: Follow preceding recipe adding 3 cups shrimp that have been cooked, shelled, and deveined in place of the chicken.

Note: Avocados may be used instead of papayas.

HAWAIIAN CHICKEN

8 chicken breasts
½ c. flour
⅓ c. salad oil

1 tsp. salt
¼ tsp. pepper

Sauce:

1 (20 oz.) can sliced pineapple, drained (reserve syrup)
1 c. sugar
2 Tbsp. cornstarch
¾ c. cider vinegar

1 Tbsp. soy sauce
¼ tsp. ginger
1 chicken bouillon cube
1 large green pepper, cut into ¼ inch rings

Preheat oven to 350°. Wash chicken; pat dry and coat with flour. Heat oil in skillet; add chicken and brown on all sides. Place browned chicken in baking dish and sprinkle with salt and pepper.

To make sauce, pour syrup from pineapple into 2 cup measure and add enough water to make 1½ cups liquid. Pour into saucepan and add rest of sauce ingredients, except pineapple and green pepper. Bring to boil, stirring constantly. Boil for 2 minutes. Pour over chicken and bake 30 minutes. Add pineapple and green pepper slices and bake 45 minutes more. Spoon sauce over chicken while baking. Use extra sauce as topping for rice pilaf.

TERIYAKI CHICKEN

2½ Tbsp. soy sauce
½ tsp. minced ginger
5 tsp. honey
1 Tbsp. sherry

1 Tbsp. white wine vinegar
1 clove garlic, mashed
1 lb. boneless chicken breast

Combine first 6 ingredients. Marinate chicken for about 20 minutes. Broil chicken 6 inches from heat for 5 minutes. Baste, turn over, and broil 8 minutes more. Reduce marinade to half and add to chicken.

CHICKEN AND PORK FAJITAS WITH SALSA

4 chicken breast halves, skinned and boned
2 lb. boneless pork loin, trimmed of fat
½ c. olive or vegetable oil
6 Tbsp. fresh lime juice
3 tsp. ground cumin
2 large garlic cloves, mashed
¼ tsp. salt

1 jalapeno pepper, chopped (optional)
8 flour tortillas
6 oz. grated Monterey Jack cheese
Tomato Avocado Salad (in salad section)
Salsa (in appetizer section)
6 oz. shredded Monterey Jack cheese

Cut chicken and pork into ¼ inch slices. Combine oil, lime juice, cumin, garlic, salt, and jalapeno in medium bowl. Add chicken and pork and mix well. Cover and refrigerate 1 hour or more, tossing occasionally with fork. Let stand at room temperature and marinate 1 more hour prior to cooking. Drain, keeping marinade for basting. Heat tortillas in foil in low oven.

Prepare barbecue grill with very hot coals. When the fire is ready, position the rack 5 to 6 inches from coals. Cover the grill with a layer of heavy-duty foil. Puncture the foil to make plenty of ventilation holes. Place the chicken and pork on the foil; baste with the marinade and grill with cover on until lightly browned, about 3 minutes per side.

To assemble each fajita, spoon tomato avocado salad down center of each tortilla. Arrange chicken or pork slices on top. Cover with salsa and grated cheese. Fold up bottom of tortilla slightly and then fold in sides. Serve immediately. Serves 8.

HORSERADISH-CRUSTED CHICKEN BREAST

Chicken:

6 (about 6 oz.) boneless, skinless chicken breasts	½ c. toasted, chopped hazelnuts
1½ c. grated Asiago cheese (about 4½ oz.)	2 Tbsp. minced onion (or shallot)
¾ c. sliced sun-dried tomatoes	2 Tbsp. canola oil
¾ c. plain dry bread crumbs	1½ Tbsp. prepared horseradish
	1 Tbsp. minced parsley
	2 Tbsp. melted butter

Mushroom Sauce:

4 Tbsp. butter	2 c. chicken stock
3 Tbsp. minced onion	½ c. toasted, chopped hazelnuts
4 c. sliced shiitake or crimini mushrooms (about 10 oz.)	1 Tbsp. prepared horseradish
1 c. dry red wine	2 tsp. honey
	3 c. lightly cooked spinach

Heat oven to 400°. On a clean surface, pound chicken breasts flat. Mix cheese and sun-dried tomatoes in a bowl and divide evenly among chicken breasts. Roll up each and secure with a food pick. Place on a lightly greased baking sheet, seam side down.

Combine bread crumbs, nuts, onion, oil, horseradish, and parsley in a bowl. Spread ¼ cup mixture evenly over tops of chicken. Drizzle with melted butter. Bake until cooked through, 20 to 25 minutes.

Meanwhile, for Mushroom Sauce, heat 1 tablespoon of the butter in a 10 or 12 inch skillet; add onion and cook 1 minute. Add mushrooms and cook 3 to 4 more minutes. Add wine and cook until reduced by half; add 1½ cups of the chicken stock and reduce by half. Add remaining chicken stock, hazelnuts, horseradish, and honey and simmer until slightly thickened, about 10 minutes. Swirl in remaining 3 tablespoons butter. Keep warm. Remove breasts from oven and slice. Serve each portion over ½ cup spinach and top each with Mushroom Sauce. Makes 6 servings.

STUFFED CHICKEN PARMESAN

1 c. boiling water
8 sun-dried tomatoes (packed
   without oil)
1 Tbsp. water
2 egg whites
⅔ c. dry Italian seasoned bread
   crumbs
⅓ c. all-purpose flour
¼ c. (1 oz.) grated fresh Parmesan
   cheese

¼ tsp. pepper
4 (4 oz.) skinned, boned chicken
   breast halves
4 very thin slices fresh Parmesan
   cheese (about ½ oz.)
2 tsp. capers
Vegetable cooking spray
2 c. hot cooked angel hair (about 8
   oz. uncooked pasta)
Chunky Tomato Sauce

Combine boiling water and sun-dried tomatoes in a bowl; let stand 30 minutes or until softened. Drain tomatoes and set aside.

Combine 1 tablespoon water and egg whites in a shallow bowl; stir well and set aside. Combine bread crumbs, flour, grated cheese, and pepper in a shallow dish; stir well and set aside.

Cut a horizontal slit through thickest portion of each chicken breast half to form a pocket. Stuff 2 sun-dried tomatoes, 1 slice of cheese, and ½ teaspoon capers into each pocket and close opening with a wooden pick. Dip each breast half in egg white mixture; dredge in bread crumb mixture.

Preheat oven to 400°. Place chicken on a baking sheet coated with cooking spray. Lightly coat chicken with cooking spray and bake at 400° for 15 minutes. Turn chicken over and lightly coat with cooking spray. Bake an additional 10 minutes or until done. Discard wooden picks.

Place ½ cup pasta on each of 4 plates and top with stuffed chicken. Spoon ¾ cup Chunky Tomato Sauce over each serving. Yield: 4 servings.

Chunky Tomato Sauce:

1 Tbsp. olive oil
1 c. chopped onion
2 garlic cloves, minced
6 c. coarsely chopped tomato
   (about 3 lb.)
⅓ c. tomato paste

2 Tbsp. balsamic vinegar
1 tsp. sugar
¼ tsp. salt
¼ tsp. black pepper
¼ tsp. crushed red pepper
¼ c. chopped fresh basil

Heat oil in a large nonstick skillet over medium heat. Add onion and garlic; saute 5 minutes or until tender. Add tomato and next 6 ingredients (tomato through crushed red pepper); stir well. Reduce heat and simmer, uncovered, 15 minutes. Remove from heat; stir in basil. Yield: 5 cups (serving size 1¼ cups).

Note: Substitute 3 (14.5 ounce) cans diced tomatoes, undrained, for 6 cups chopped tomato if desired.

QUICK AND EASY CASSOULET

1 Tbsp. oil
1 lb. or more chicken breasts, cut
    in pieces
1 large onion, cut into thin wedges
3 stalks celery, thinly sliced
1 lb. fully cooked, smoked turkey
    sausage, cut in 1 inch chunks
1 can Northern navy beans
    (undrained)

1 can white kidney beans
    (undrained)
1 (15 oz.) can stewed tomatoes
4 to 5 fresh carrots, cut up and diced
¼ tsp. dried thyme
1 to 2 c. dry white wine or chicken
    broth

In Dutch oven, heat oil over medium heat. Brown chicken 10 minutes, turning as needed. Remove and set aside. Add onion and celery to pan and cook until tender. Stir in chicken, sausage, tomatoes, carrots, and thyme. Bring to a boil. Add 1 cup wine and cook, covered, over low heat or bake in 350° oven 30 to 40 minutes, until chicken is done. Add more wine as needed to keep moist. Add beans during last 15 to 20 minutes. Serves 8.

This is a good company, easy dinner! Serve in bowls with a nice green salad, hard rolls, and a great dessert! One of our favorites!

CHICKEN WITH WINE AND CHEESE

1 stick margarine
4 Tbsp. flour
1 tsp. salt
½ tsp. pepper

6 chicken breasts, split
⅔ c. sherry
¾ c. Parmesan cheese, freshly
    grated

Preheat oven to 350°. Melt margarine in 9x12x2 inch baking pan. Meanwhile, place flour, salt, and pepper in paper bag. Drop chicken in bag and shake. Put pieces in margarine and turn till coated with margarine. Place in baking dish, skin side up. Bake 30 minutes. Pour sherry over all and sprinkle with cheese. After 20 minutes, baste again. Cook an additional 20 minutes. Cover after adding wine and cheese.

OVEN FRIED CHICKEN

2½ c. potato chips, crushed
Garlic powder or garlic salt
Dash of pepper

¾ c. butter or margarine, melted
8 skinless, boneless chicken
    breasts

Mix crushed chips with garlic powder and shake well. Dip chicken breasts in most of melted butter. Place in a shallow baking dish. Pour remaining butter and chips over chicken. Bake, uncovered, at 350° to 375° for 1 hour. Do not turn chicken.

TWICE AROUND TURKEY

8 oz. seasoned stuffing (3½ c.)
3 c. turkey or chicken, cooked and
    cubed
½ c. butter or margarine
½ c. flour

¼ tsp. salt
Pepper
4 c. turkey drippings or chicken
    broth
6 eggs, slightly beaten

1413-96

Make stuffing according to recipe on package. Grease 9x13 inch pan; spread stuffing on bottom and turkey on top. In a large saucepan, melt butter; blend in flour and seasonings. Add drippings/broth and cook, stirring until it thickens. Stir some of hot mixture into eggs and add to sauce. Pour over the turkey and stuffing. With a spoon work the sauce down into turkey/stuffing in about 9 places. Bake at 325° for 40 to 45 minutes. Let stand 5 minutes before serving. Cut and serve with sauce.

Sauce:

1 can condensed cream of
   mushroom soup
¼ c. white wine or milk

1 c. sour cream
¼ c. pimiento, chopped

Combine ingredients; heat slowly until hot.

TURKEY ALMANDINE

1½ c. (¾ lb.) butter (divided)
6 onions, finely chopped
1 lb. mushrooms, sliced
1¼ c. flour
1 tsp. salt
¼ tsp. pepper
1½ tsp. curry powder
1½ tsp. dry mustard
Dash of cayenne

6 c. chicken broth
2 c. light cream
2 c. sliced, blanched almonds,
   toasted
3 qt. cooked turkey, boned, cut in
   pieces (10 lb. turkey)
1 c. sherry
Chopped parsley

Melt 6 tablespoons butter in Dutch oven. Saute onions until golden. Add mushrooms and saute for about 4 minutes. Remove onions and mushrooms and set aside.

Melt remaining butter and blend in flour and seasonings. Cook a minute or two, then stir in broth. Cook over low heat, stirring frequently, until smooth and thick. Blend in cream. Add almonds, turkey, sauteed onions, and mushrooms and mix thoroughly. Heat through and stir in sherry. Serve with Chinese noodles, rice, or hot cream puffs. Garnish with parsley. Freezes nicely. Serves 14 to 16.

To freeze: Prepare without adding sherry. Cool. Pour into containers. Freeze. To serve: Heat in double boiler for 1 hour or until thoroughly hot. Add sherry.

HOSPITALITY HOUSE TURKEY CASSEROLE

1 pkg. seasoned cubed Pepperidge
   Farm dressing
1 stick melted butter
1 c. water
2½ c. diced, cooked turkey
½ c. chopped onion
½ c. diced celery

¼ c. chopped green onions and tops
½ c. mayonnaise
¾ tsp. salt
2 eggs
1½ c. milk
1 can cream of chicken soup
1 c. shredded Cheddar cheese

Lightly mix dressing, melted butter, and water. Place ½ mixture in buttered 9x13 inch casserole dish. Mix turkey, onion, celery, onions, mayonnaise, and salt. Spread over dressing mixture and top with remaining dressing mixture. Cover with foil overnight and refrigerate. Remove from refrigerator 1 hour before baking. Spread cream of chicken soup over top. Bake, uncovered, at 325° for 45 minutes. Spread Cheddar cheese over top and bake an additional 10 minutes. *Delicious!*

BROILED TURKEY WITH RASPBERRY SAUCE

Another time serve the sauce with slices from a roast turkey breast portion.

6 boneless turkey breast steaks or
   tenderloins (about 1½ lb.
   total)
1 Tbsp. lemon juice
1 Tbsp. water
2 tsp. soy sauce

1 (10 oz.) pkg. frozen red
   raspberries, thawed
2 Tbsp. dry white wine
1 Tbsp. orange juice
2 tsp. cornstarch
Fresh raspberries (optional)

Rinse the turkey steaks, then pat dry with paper towels. Place on the unheated rack of broiler pan. In a small bowl, combine the lemon juice, water, and soy sauce. Brush turkey steaks with lemon mixture. Broil 5 inches from the heat for 5 minutes. Turn and broil 5 to 6 minutes more or till tender, brushing the steaks occasionally with lemon mixture.

Meanwhile, place the thawed raspberries in a blender container or food processor bowl. Cover and blend or process till smooth. Sieve mixture and discard seeds.

In a small saucepan, combine the wine, orange juice, and cornstarch. Add the sieved raspberries. Cook and stir till thickened and bubbly; cook and stir 2 minutes more. Serve sauce with turkey. Garnish with fresh raspberries if desired. Makes 6 servings.

ORANGE-BASTED TURKEY BREAST

1 c. water
2 Tbsp. frozen orange juice
   concentrate, thawed
1 tsp. instant chicken bouillon
   granules

1 tsp. Dijon-style mustard
¼ tsp. dried thyme, crushed, or
   ground sage
1 (2 to 2½ lb.) turkey breast portion
4 tsp. cornstarch

In a small bowl, combine the water, orange juice concentrate, chicken bouillon granules, mustard, and thyme or sage. Reserve ¼ cup orange juice mixture to baste turkey. Set remaining mixture aside for sauce.

Remove skin and any fat from turkey breast. Place breast on a rack in a shallow roasting pan. Brush some of the ¼ cup orange basting mixture over turkey. Roast, uncovered, in a 325° oven for 1¾ to 2 hours or till thermometer registers 170°, brushing occasionally with orange basting mixture.

In a small saucepan, combine the reserved orange juice mixture and cornstarch. Cook and stir till thickened and bubbly; cook and stir 2 minutes more. Pass sauce with turkey. Serves 8.

SAUTEED TURKEY IN PUFF PASTRY

4 Tbsp. butter
1 Tbsp. flour
1¼ c. chicken or turkey broth
2 Tbsp. sherry
3 c. brown gravy
Salt and pepper

3 c. turkey meat, cut into ½ inch
   cubes
8 puff pastry shells, baked and kept
   warm
Scallions, chopped (for garnish)

1413-96

Melt butter in a heavy saucepan. Saute turkey meat 3 to 5 minutes on each side until done. Cook on low to prevent browning. Remove turkey and set aside. Add flour and cook 3 to 5 minutes to form a roux. Add broth slowly and stir constantly to prevent lumping. Simmer until thickened. Stir in sherry and brown gravy. Season to taste with salt and pepper. Add diced and cooked turkey meat. Heat through. Divide chicken evenly among 8 pastry shells. Garnish with chopped scallions. Serve immediately. Serves 8.

CREPES WITH TURKEY AND SHERRY

Basic Crepes:

1 c. cold milk	**½ tsp. salt**
1 c. cold water	**2 c. all-purpose flour**
4 eggs	**4 Tbsp. butter, melted**

Put ingredients into blender in the preceding order. Whirl 1 minute. With spatula, scrape down sides and blend 1 more minute. Refrigerate at least 2 hours. Heat a 7 inch crepe pan or heavy skillet over medium-high heat until very hot. Pour in a scant ¼ cup of batter, tilting in all directions to spread batter over bottom pan. Pour out any excess and return to heat for 1 minute. Turn crepe when bottom is lightly browned and cook 30 seconds on second side. Slide crepe onto waxed paper and repeat with remaining batter. Crepes may be used immediately, refrigerated overnight, or freeze with waxed paper in between and wrap all in aluminum foil to freeze. Date and keep no longer than 3 months.

Turkey Filling:

¼ c. butter	**4 water chestnuts, diced**
2 c. sliced mushrooms	**2 c. turkey, cooked and finely cut**
6 green onions, finely chopped	**Paprika**
¼ c. chopped pimento	

Melt butter in skillet; add mushrooms. Cook 4 minutes. Add onion. Cook 2 minutes. Add remaining ingredients. Heat.

Wine Sauce:

¼ c. butter	**2 c. milk**
¼ c. flour	**1 tsp. Worcestershire sauce**
¼ c. sherry	**Salt and pepper to taste**

Melt butter in saucepan; stir in flour. Add sherry, milk, and seasonings. Cook until thickened. Add enough Wine Sauce to Turkey Filling to moisten. Place some filling on each crepe; roll and place in shallow baking dish. Pour remaining Wine Sauce over crepes. Bake at 375° for 10 minutes. Place under broiler just enough to lightly brown. Makes 16 crepes.

SKILLET STROGANOFF

To keep the sour cream from curdling, remove the pan from the heat before stirring it in.

½ lb. ground raw turkey breast
½ lb. lean ground pork
1 c. fresh rye bread crumbs
1 Tbsp. dried parsley flakes
½ tsp. dried tarragon
½ tsp. onion powder
2 egg whites
Vegetable cooking spray
2 c. water

1 Tbsp. beef-flavored bouillon
   granules
1 (4 oz.) can mushroom stems and
   pieces, drained
2½ c. uncooked medium egg
   noodles
½ c. lowfat sour cream
½ c. sliced green onions

Combine turkey, pork, and next 5 ingredients (bread crumbs through egg whites) in a bowl and stir well. Shape mixture into 24 (1 inch) meatballs. Coat a large nonstick skillet with cooking spray and place over medium-high heat until hot. Add meatballs and cook 6 minutes, browning on all sides. Drain well. Wipe drippings from skillet with a paper towel.

Return meatballs to skillet. Add water, bouillon granules, and mushrooms; bring to a boil. Stir in noodles; cover, reduce heat, and simmer 10 minutes or until noodles are tender, stirring occasionally. Remove from heat; stir in sour cream. Sprinkle with green onions. Yield: 6 servings (serving size 1 cup).

Notes

Beef, Pork, Lamb, Veal and Wild Game

MEAT ROASTING GUIDE

Cut	Weight Pounds	Approx. Time (Hours) (325° oven)	Internal Temperature
BEEF			
Standing rib roast			
(10 inch) ribs	4	1¾	140° (rare)
(If using shorter cut (8-inch)		2	160° (medium)
ribs, allow 30 min. longer)		2½	170° (well done)
	8	2½	140° (rare)
		3	160° (medium)
		4½	170° (well done)
Rolled ribs	4	2	140° (rare)
		2½	160° (medium)
		3	170° (well done)
	6	3	140° (rare)
		3¼	160° (medium)
		4	170° (well done)
Rolled rump	5	2¼	140° (rare)
(Roast only if high quality.		3	160° (medium)
Otherwise, braise.)		3¼	170° (well done)
Sirloin tip	3	1½	140° (rare)
(Roast only if high quality.		2	160° (medium)
Otherwise, braise.)		2¼	170° (well done)
LAMB			
Leg	6	3	175° (medium)
		3½	180° (well done)
	8	4	175° (medium)
		4½	180° (well done)
VEAL			
Leg (piece)	5	2½ to 3	170° (well done)
Shoulder	6	3½	170° (well done)
Rolled shoulder	3 to 5	3 to 3½	170° (well done)

POULTRY ROASTING GUIDE

Type of Poultry	Ready-To-Cook Weight	Oven Temperature	Approx. Total Roasting Time
TURKEY	6 to 8 lb.	325°	2½ to 3 hr.
	8 to 12 lb.	325°	3 to 3½ hr.
	12 to 16 lb.	325°	3½ to 4 hr.
	16 to 20 lb.	325°	4 to 4½ hr.
	20 to 24 lb.	300°	5 to 6 hr.
CHICKEN	2 to 2½ lb.	400°	1 to 1½ hr.
(Unstuffed)	2½ to 4 lb.	400°	1½ to 2½ hr.
	4 to 8 lb.	325°	3 to 5 hr.
DUCK	3 to 5 lb.	325°	2½ to 3 hr.
(Unstuffed)			

NOTE: Small chickens are roasted at 400° so that they brown well in the short cooking time. They may also be done at 325° but will take longer and will not be as brown. Increase cooking time 15 to 20 minutes for stuffed chicken and duck.

BEEF, PORK, LAMB, VEAL AND WILD GAME

OUR HOUSE OLD ENGLISH DINNER

Use 1 (8 pound) standing 3 rib roast. Bringing meat to room temperature before cooking is unnecessary. Roast may go directly from the refrigerator to the oven.

Preheat oven to 450°. It will take about 15 minutes for most ovens to reach this temperature. For the most predictable results, insert a meat thermometer into the thickest part of the beef, being careful not to let the tip of the thermometer touch any fat or bone.

Place the beef, fat side up, in a large shallow roasting pan. It is unnecessary to use a rack, since the ribs of the roast form a natural rack.

Roast the beef undisturbed in the middle of the oven for 20 minutes. Reduce the heat to 325° and continue to roast, without basting, for about 90 minutes or until the beef is cooked to your taste. A meat thermometer will register 130° to 140° when the beef is rare, 150° to 160° when medium, and 160° to 170° when it is well done. If you are not using a thermometer, start timing the roast after you reduce the heat to 325°. You can estimate approximately 12 minutes per pound for rare beef, 15 minutes per pound for medium, and 20 minutes per pound for well done.

Transfer the beef to a heated platter and let it rest for at least 15 minutes for easier carving. If you plan to accompany the beef with Yorkshire Pudding, increase the oven heat to 400° as soon as the beef is cooked. Transfer the roast from the oven to a heated platter; drape foil loosely over it and set aside in warm place while the pudding bakes. If you have two ovens, time the pudding to finish cooking during the 15 minutes that the roast rests.

To carve, first remove a thin slice of beef from the large end of the roast so that it will stand firmly on this end. Insert a large fork below the top rib and carve slices of beef from the top, separating each slice from the bone as you proceed. Traditionally, roast beef is served with its own juices and with a horseradish sauce. Yorkshire Pudding and Horseradish Sauce follow. Serves 6 to 8.

YORKSHIRE PUDDING

2 eggs	1 c. milk
½ tsp. salt	2 Tbsp. roast beef
1 c. flour	Drippings or lard

To make the batter in a blender, combine the eggs, salt, flour, and milk in the blender jar and blend at high speed for 2 to 3 seconds. Turn off the machine, scrape down the sides of the jar, and blend again for 40 seconds. To make the batter by hand, beat the eggs and salt with a whisk or rotary or electric beater until frothy. Slowly add the flour, beating constantly, then pour in the milk in a thin stream and beat until the mixture is smooth and creamy. Refrigerate for at least 1 hour.

Preheat the oven to 400°. In a 10 x 15 x 2½ inch roasting pan, heat the fat over moderate heat until it splutters. Briefly beat the batter again and pour it into the pan. Bake in the middle of the oven for 15 minutes; reduce the heat to 375° and bake for 15 minutes longer or until the pudding has risen over the top of the pan and is crisp and brown. With a sharp knife, divide the pudding into portions and serve immediately. Serves 6 to 8.

Yorkshire Pudding is always served with roast beef. The same batter is used to make Toad-in-the-Hole.

HORSERADISH SAUCE

¼ c. bottled horseradish, drained
   and squeezed dry in a towel
1 Tbsp. white wine vinegar
1 tsp. sugar

¼ tsp. dry English mustard
½ tsp. salt
½ tsp. white pepper
½ c. chilled heavy cream

In a small bowl, stir the horseradish, vinegar, sugar, mustard, salt, and white pepper together until well blended. Beat the cream with a whisk or a rotary or electric beater until stiff enough to form unwavering peaks on the beater when it is lifted from the bowl. Pour the horseradish mixture over the cream and, with a rubber spatula, fold together lightly but thoroughly. Taste for seasoning. Makes about 1 cup.

Serve the sauce from a sauce boat as an accompaniment to roast beef or to such fish as smoked trout, smoked eel, and grilled salmon.

BEEF WELLINGTON WITH BRANDY SAUCE

3 Tbsp. butter
4 lb. beef tenderloin
Flour
2 c. mushrooms, chopped
2 tsp. chives, chopped

1 dash of cognac
¼ can liver pate
Ground pepper to taste
½ lb. puff pastry dough
2 egg yolks, beaten

Preheat oven to 350°. Melt butter in large, heavy skillet. Dust the meat with flour and brown quickly on all sides. Remove the meat and set aside in a warm place. Saute the mushrooms in the same pan in which beef was browned, adding more butter, if necessary. Add the chives and cognac. Remove from the stove and blend in the liver pate. Cool slightly. Split the meat lengthwise through the center. Spread the mushroom and liver pate mixture on the center of the filet. Sprinkle with pepper. On a floured board, roll the pastry out thinly, and large enough to completely wrap the dough around the meat. Secure the ends by wrapping them under the roll. Set on a greased cooking sheet and brush the pastry entirely with the egg yolks. Bake at 350° for 30 to 40 minutes. Remove from the pan and let stand for about 15 minutes before serving. Serve with Brandy Sauce. Serves 8 to 10.

Brandy Sauce:

6 Tbsp. unsalted butter
¼ c. plus 2 Tbsp. brown sugar
Grated rind of ½ lemon

Squeeze of lemon juice
2 to 3 Tbsp. brandy (or to taste)

Cream butter, then gradually beat in the sugar with the lemon rind and juice. When soft and light, beat in enough brandy, a little at a time, to flavor the butter well. Place in a small bowl and chill before serving. Rum or cognac may be substituted for the brandy.

BOLICHI - STUFFED EYE OF THE ROUND OF BEEF

3 to 4 lb. eye of the round plus piece of suet
1 chorizo sausage, chopped
1 medium slice cured ham, chopped
1 clove garlic, minced
1 medium Spanish onion, chopped
½ green pepper, chopped

Salt and pepper
Paprika
3 Tbsp. bacon drippings
¾ c. hot water
1 bay leaf
4 whole cloves

Ask butcher to cut lengthwise pocket in center of beef, leaving opposite end closed. Mix sausage, ham, garlic, onion, and pepper and stuff roast, packing well but not too tightly. Secure open end with skewers or wire. Salt and pepper all over and sprinkle generously with paprika. Brown well in bacon drippings over medium heat. Turn often to get an even browning because the better the browning, the more delicious the sauce. When browned, add hot water, scraping the pan well. Lay suet on top of meat; add bay leaf and cloves to liquid. Cover and place in 325° oven. Baste occasionally and cook about 3 hours or until the meat is fork tender.

During the last 30 minutes, potato balls may be added. Serve Bolichi cut in round slices and pass gravy separately. Serves 8 to 10. *Beautiful presentation.*

BRANDY MARINATED TOP OF THE ROUND

1 top of the round (2 to 3 inches thick)
1 Tbsp. lemon juice
½ c. soy sauce
½ tsp. Worcestershire sauce
1 dash of liquid red pepper

1 dash of ground ginger
1 tsp. sugar
1 clove garlic
2 Tbsp. brandy or bourbon (or more if desired)

Place meat in plastic bag. Pour in marinade. Marinate 36 hours, turning occasionally to coat meat. Grill over high heat to sear meat, turn heat down, and cook. Cut on diagonal into thin slices to serve.

COLA ROAST

1 tsp. salt
½ tsp. pepper
½ tsp. garlic salt
1 (4 to 5 lb.) bottom round roast
3 Tbsp. vegetable oil

1 (10 oz.) can cola
12 oz. bottle chili sauce
2 Tbsp. Worcestershire sauce
2 Tbsp. hot sauce

Combine salt, pepper, and garlic salt. Rub over surface of roast. Brown roast on all sides in vegetable oil in Dutch oven. Drain off drippings. Combine remaining ingredients. Pour over roast. Cover and bake at 325° for 3 hours or until tender. Serves 8 to 10.

PEPPER STEAK

2 lb. round steak, well trimmed and
  cut in half inch strips
2 cloves garlic (1 whole clove and
  1 minced clove)
2 Tbsp. olive oil
2 large green peppers, cut into
  strips

2 large onions, chopped
1 large can sliced mushrooms
2 tsp. salt
½ tsp. pepper
¾ c. red wine

Brown strips of round steak in skillet with olive oil and 1 whole garlic. Add green pepper and onion. Continue to cook until tender, then add mushrooms, black pepper, and salt, along with the minced garlic. Add the red wine. Cook slowly for 1½ hours. Serve with rice or noodles. Serves 4 to 6.

PEPPERED STEAK WITH JACK DANIEL'S SAUCE

Sauce:

2 Tbsp. minced shallots
1 Tbsp. red wine vinegar
1½ tsp. black pepper, cracked

1 c. chicken broth
2 c. beef broth

Steaks:

2 tenderloin steaks (about 8 oz.
  each)
2 tsp. black pepper, cracked
½ tsp. dried thyme
½ tsp. dried rosemary

½ tsp. dried marjoram
¼ c. olive oil
1 Tbsp. Jack Daniel's or other
  whiskey

For sauce: Bring shallots, vinegar, and 1½ teaspoons pepper to a boil in heavy medium saucepan. Boil, uncovered, until almost no liquid remains in pan. Add beef and chicken broth. Boil until reduced to ½ cup (about 20 minutes).

Place steaks in baking dish. Rub remaining 2 teaspoons pepper, thyme, rosemary, and marjoram onto both sides of steaks. Add oil over meat. Turn to coat other side. Let stand, covered, 1 hour at room temperature. Remove meat from marinade. Heat heavy large skillet over medium high heat. Add steaks and brown on both sides. Reduce heat to medium and cook to desired doneness. Transfer steaks to serving plates. Add sauce to skillet. Bring to a boil. Stir in whiskey. Spoon sauce over steaks. Serves 2.

CHINESE PEPPER STEAK

1 env. dry onion soup mix
1½ c. boiling water
4 Tbsp. vegetable oil
1 clove garlic
1 lb. round steak, cut into pieces or
  strips

Flour
1 Tbsp. soy sauce
2 green peppers, cut into strips
1 Tbsp. cornstarch
3 Tbsp. cold water
Hot cooked rice or noodles

Combine soup mix and boiling water and set aside. Heat oil in large skillet. Saute garlic in oil. Remove garlic and discard. Roll steak strips in flour and brown meat quickly in oil over high heat. Add soup mixture, soy sauce, and peppers. Blend cornstarch in cold water and pour over meat mixture. Cover and cook over low heat until tender. Serve over rice or noodles. Serves 4 to 6.

STRIPPED STEAK

4 Tbsp. butter
1 onion, chopped
1 (4 oz.) can mushrooms
1½ lb. round steak, cut in long bite-
    size strips
Salt and pepper to taste
1 Tbsp. B-V sauce

2 tsp. Worcestershire sauce
2 Tbsp. flour
1 (10 oz.) can beef consomme
1 c. water
1 Tbsp. prepared mustard
2 Tbsp. brown sugar
1 tsp. soy sauce

Melt butter in large skillet. Add chopped onion and mushrooms. Saute for 5 minutes. Add strips of steak and cook over medium heat until meat is browned. Remove from heat. Add consomme, water, and other ingredients. Return to medium heat until it reaches a simmer. Cover and cook on low heat 1½ hours or until tender. Serve over egg noodles, frozen or homemade. Serves 4.

Delicious for family, or top with parsley to decorate for guests.

STRIPPED STEAK 2

4 Tbsp. butter or oleo
1 medium onion, chopped
1 (4 oz.) can mushroom slices,
    drained
1½ lb. round steak, trimmed and cut
    into bite-size pieces
2 Tbsp. flour

1 can golden mushroom soup
1 c. red wine
1 Tbsp. prepared mustard
2 Tbsp. brown sugar
1 to 2 tsp. Worcestershire sauce
Salt and pepper to taste

Melt butter in large skillet. Add onion and mushrooms. Saute for 5 minutes. Add strips of round steak and cook until meat is brown. Blend flour into meat mixture. Remove from heat. Add soup, wine, mustard, brown sugar, Worcestershire sauce, salt, and pepper. Return mixture to heat at simmering point. Cover and simmer on low heat until steak is tender (about 1 hour) or bake in oven 4 hours at 300°. Thicken sauce if desired with small amount of flour paste. Serves 4.

Use 2⅔ pounds of meat to serve 6. Can be made the day ahead and reheated before serving.

MARINATED LONDON BROIL

3 to 4 lb. London broil cut steak
1 c. soy sauce
1 c. tomato juice

1 c. brown sugar
1 c. peanut oil
6 cloves garlic, minced

Combine well last 5 ingredients and pour over the steak. Marinate 24 hours, the last 2 at room temperature. Grill over medium coals approximately 20 minutes for medium rare. Serves 4 to 6.

SIRLOIN TIPS IN WINE SAUCE

2 lb. (1 inch thick) lean sirloin or
    round steak, cut into 4x1 inch
    strips
1½ Tbsp. beef bouillon
2 tsp. basil
10 rosemary leaves
1 (26 oz.) can Campbell's tomato
    soup

2 tsp. oregano
1½ green peppers, sliced into 1 inch
    strips
10 fresh mushrooms, sliced
½ c. cream sherry

Brown beef and drain. Set aside. Add bouillon, oregano, basil, and rosemary to tomato soup in a 2 quart pan. Bring to a boil and add beef. Simmer 45 minutes. Add green peppers to mixture 30 minutes before serving and add mushrooms 10 minutes before serving. Add cream sherry just before serving. Serve over rice. Serves 4.

WESTERN TOP SIRLOIN WITH PALE ALE AND CRACKED PEPPER WILD MUSHROOM SAUCE

2 lb. top sirloin or New York steak
    (1 inch thick)
4 Tbsp. freshly crushed black
    peppercorns
3 large garlic cloves, peeled
⅔ c. pale ale plus additional for
    marinade

4 oz. shiitake and oyster
    mushrooms, quartered
2 Tbsp. butter
1 Tbsp. freshly chopped parsley
3 Tbsp. olive oil
Salt to taste

Rub both sides of the steaks with garlic and press crushed peppercorns into both sides. Sprinkle additional pale ale over steaks, cover and refrigerate for 2 hours. Heat a large skillet until very hot and pour in oil. Sprinkle salt over the oil and add steaks. Sear meat for about 3 to 4 minutes on each side or to desired doneness. Remove steaks and keep warm. Add mushrooms to skillet and cook for a minute. Add pale ale and boil until ⅓ of the liquid is left. Remove from heat and add parsley and butter. Stir the mixture until smooth and pour over steaks. Serves 4.

STEAK BURGUNDY

2 lb. round steak
3 Tbsp. flour
3 Tbsp. margarine
½ onion, chopped
1 Tbsp. parsley, finely chopped
1 medium bay leaf

1 medium garlic clove, crushed
¾ tsp. salt
1 dash of pepper
Fresh mushrooms as desired
¾ c. burgundy wine
¾ c. water (or more if desired)

Cut steak into bite-size cubes. Shake in flour to coat. Melt margarine in skillet. Brown steak pieces on all sides. Remove from heat. Add onion and garlic; saute. Add mushrooms, seasonings, meat, burgundy, and water. Bring to a boil. Reduce heat and simmer 1½ to 2 hours. Serve with rice.

DAY AHEAD BRISKET

1 (4 to 5 lb.) fresh beef brisket
1 pkg. dry onion soup
1 medium onion, sliced and
    separated into rings

2 medium stalks celery, chopped
1 c. bottled chili sauce
½ c. water
1 (12 oz.) can beer

Brown brisket on all sides in small amount of cooking oil. Drain grease and arrange onion rings and celery on top of brisket. Combine chili sauce, onion soup, and water. Pour mixture around meat. Add beer and bake, covered, in preheated 350° oven. Allow 45 minutes cooking time per pound of meat. Baste brisket occasionally with cooking liquid. Remove brisket from oven and allow to cool. Refrigerate overnight. Remove grease that rises to the top. Before serving, slice meat across the grain and reheat to serving temperature in cooking liquid. Serves 8 to 10.

HUNGARIAN BEEF STEW

1 Tbsp. shortening
2 large onions, sliced
3½ lb. round steak, cut into 1 inch
    cubes
½ c. water
1½ Tbsp. sweet paprika

1 clove garlic, minced
1 tsp. salt
2 c. fresh tomatoes, peeled and
    diced
¾ c. green pepper, diced
Sliced chili peppers (optional)

Melt shortening in Dutch oven over medium high heat. Reduce heat to low and cook onion about 35 minutes, stirring frequently, until lightly browned. Remove from heat and add beef, sweet paprika, water, garlic, and salt. Bring back to boiling, then reduce heat to very low. Cover and cook 1½ hours or until meat is tender. *The simple but tricky secret of this dish is to let the meat cook in the steam from its own juices and the juices of the onion.* Just before the stew starts to burn, add a few tablespoons of water. repeating whenever liquid evaporates. When meat is tender, reduce liquid as much as possible without burning. At that point you should have a rich, dark, reddish golden sauce neither too thick or thin, resembling the consistency of a good American stew. The texture must be achieved without thickening. Stir in tomatoes, green pepper, and chili peppers. Simmer 10 minutes. Serve immediately over homemade egg noodles, rice, or dumplings.

FOUR HOUR STEW

2 lb. stew meat
1 (15 oz.) can tomato sauce
1 can beef broth bouillon
¼ c. Minute tapioca
5 carrots

3 medium onions
5 medium potatoes
1 c. celery
1 green pepper
1 bay leaf

Cut vegetables as desired. Mix all ingredients in roaster (not necessary to brown meat). Salt and pepper to taste. Cover and bake at 300° for 4 hours (check after 3 hours).

You can add a large can of crushed tomatoes and a little more tapioca if desired.

BERNIE'S MEAT BALLS WITH TOMATO GRAVY

2 lb. ground chuck
1 lb. freshly ground pork (ground
   pork roast is preferred)
Salt and pepper to taste
1 large white onion, grated

3 eggs, well beaten
¼ c. water
½ c. Italian bread crumbs
½ c. Italian cheese

Mix meat, onion, and seasonings together. Add eggs with water. Mix well, but gently. Add bread crumbs and cheese. Mix and shape into round balls or little footballs, being careful not to pack meat. Meat balls will be tough and heavy if meat packed too tightly. Gently shape the meat with the palms of your hands. Fry until lightly brown, but not completely done; or bake in 300° oven on cookie sheet until lightly brown. Add to Tomato Gravy and cook in the gravy for an hour. Serve with pasta and sprinkle Italian cheese on top of plate.

Tomato Gravy:

2 (6 oz.) cans Italian tomato paste
2 (8 oz.) cans tomato sauce
1 large white onion, finely chopped
¼ c. olive oil
4 cloves garlic, crushed
1 Tbsp. sweet fresh basil, finely
   chopped

¾ c. Italian cheese
1 tsp. sugar
1½ c. water
Salt and pepper to taste

Saute onions in olive oil until tender. Add tomato paste, stirring while frying on low heat, being careful not to burn. Stir often until paste begins to change color, approximately 15 to 20 minutes. Add the tomato sauce, water, garlic, basil, ½ cup cheese, sugar, salt, and pepper. Stir and place lid on pot, turning down to low heat. Cook slowly for at least 2 to 3 hours, stirring occasionally. If gravy gets too thick, add more water. At this point, you can add meatballs, roast, or meat of your choice. Add ¼ cup cheese to gravy, continuing to cook slowly for another hour. Correct seasonings before serving, if necessary. Serve with pasta. Serves 6.

A fresh pork hock, cooked from the beginning with the gravy, adds a delicious taste to the gravy, but remember to use a *fresh pork hock*. This recipe can be doubled or tripled easily and gravy frozen for use later.

CALICO BEEF AND BEANS

½ lb. ground beef
½ lb. bacon, fried crisp and
   crumbled
1 c. onion, chopped
1 (1 lb.) can green beans, drained
1 (1 lb.) can butter beans, drained
1 (1 lb.) can pork and beans
   (undrained)

1 (1 lb.) can kidney beans
   (undrained)
⅓ c. catsup
1 Tbsp. mustard
½ tsp. salt
½ c. brown sugar
2 to 3 Tbsp. vinegar

Brown ground beef, onion, and bacon. Drain. In a large pot, combine all ingredients and bring to a boil. Reduce heat and simmer for 1 hour or bake in oven at 350° for 1 hour. Serves 10.

A crock pot can also be used.

MOIST MEAT LOAF

2 lb. fresh ground beef
2 eggs, slightly beaten
1 c. milk
3 Tbsp. melted butter
1 Tbsp. prepared horseradish
3 Tbsp. catsup

2 Tbsp. minced onion
¼ tsp. pepper
½ tsp. salt
1 c. soft bread crumbs
Bacon strips

Mix meat with the eggs, milk, butter, horseradish, catsup, onion, seasonings, and bread crumbs. Pack in greased loaf pan (8x4 inches). Cover with strips of bacon. Bake at 350° for 1 hour until it is browned.

MEXICALI MEAT LOAVES

1 lb. ground beef
½ c. quick or old-fashioned oats
   (uncooked)
1 egg
1 (8 oz.) can tomato sauce
1 (4 oz.) can chopped green chilies,
   drained

1 Tbsp. plus 1 tsp. instant minced
   onion
1 tsp. chili powder
½ tsp. salt
⅛ tsp. garlic powder
½ c. Cheddar cheese, grated

Combine meat, oats, egg, ¼ cup tomato sauce, 2 tablespoons green chilies, 1 tablespoon onion, chili powder, and salt; mix well. Shape to form four 4x2 inch loaves; place in an 8 inch square baking dish. Bake in preheated 375° oven for 20 to 25 minutes. Combine remaining tomato sauce, green chilies, onion, and garlic powder in small saucepan; heat. To serve, spoon sauce over meat loaves. Sprinkle with cheese. Serves 4.

TAMALE PIE

2 lb. hamburger
2 dried onions, chopped
2 pieces garlic, chopped
2 Tbsp. chili powder
1 large can tomato, sieved
2 Tbsp. salt

2 c. yellow corn meal
1 can black olives
1 can corn (whole)
4 c. hot water
3 cans tomato sauce

Put tomatoes, tomato sauce, salt, and hot water in large pot and heat. Take off heat; stir corn meal in gradually. Coat until thickened. Add more corn meal if not thick enough. Fry meat, onions, celery, and garlic in plenty of oil. Add chili powder; add to corn meal mixture. Add corn and olives. Put in greased pan and bake at 275° until brown on top.

MESA VERDE CASSEROLE

2 lb. ground beef
1 large onion
2 Tbsp. beef bouillon
2 (8 oz.) cans diced chili peppers
   (mild)
1½ cans stewed tomatoes

1 doz. flour tortillas
1 pt. sour cream
1 large can refried beans
1 lb. sharp Cheddar, shredded
1 lb. Mozzarella cheese

1413-96

Brown hamburger and onion well. Add tomatoes and chili pepper. Simmer 1½ hours. (Season with salt and pepper and add bouillon.) Add small amounts of water if needed. Mixture should finish a thick mixture.

Layer in greased 9x13 inch baking dish, starting with a tortilla, then meat mixture, then tortilla, refried beans, sour cream, tortilla, cheese, and etc. (Be sure to put a tortilla between each layer.) Top with cheese; cover and bake at 400° for 30 minutes. Top with lettuce, chopped green onions, tomatoes, and shredded cheese. Salsa or taco sauce is good also.

TASTY TOSTADA PIE

1 (9 inch) unbaked pastry shell
1 lb. lean ground beef
½ c. chopped onion
1 Tbsp. instant beef flavored
    bouillon (or 3 cubes)
1 (16 oz.) can refried beans
1 (4 oz.) can chopped green chilies,
    drained

¼ c. tomato sauce
Sour cream
Shredded Cheddar (or Monterey
    Jack) cheese
Shredded lettuce
Chopped tomatoes

Preheat oven to 425°. Bake pastry shell 8 minutes; remove from oven. Reduce oven temperature to 375°. In a large skillet, brown meat with onion and bouillon, stirring until bouillon is dissolved. Remove from heat, stir in beans, chilies, and tomato sauce. Turn into prepared pastry shell. Bake 20 to 25 minutes or until bubbly around edges. Let stand 10 minutes. Garnish with remaining ingredients. Refrigerate leftovers. Serves 6.

TORTILLA BEEF CASSEROLE

1½ lb. ground beef
1 onion, chopped
1 pkg. dry taco seasoning
1 c. water
Garlic salt to taste
Salt and pepper to taste
1 c. medium-hot red taco sauce

10 corn tortillas
2 (10 oz.) pkg. frozen chopped
    spinach
3 c. shredded Monterey Jack cheese
½ lb. cooked ham, diced
1 c. sour cream

Cook ground beef with onion until meat is crumbly. Add taco seasoning and water. Cover and cook 10 minutes. Add salt, pepper, and garlic salt.

In a 9x13 inch casserole, pour in ½ cup taco sauce. Turn 5 tortillas in it to coat and spread in bottom of dish.

Press water out of spinach. Add half of it to the beef mixture. Spoon mixture over tortillas. Sprinkle with half the cheese. Cover with remaining tortillas. Pour taco sauce over. Sprinkle diced ham on top. Spoon sour cream over and top with remaining spinach and cheese. Cover and bake at 375° for 25 minutes. Uncover and bake 25 minutes longer. Serves 8.

SWEDISH MEATBALLS

1 c. Zwieback crumbs or bread
   crumbs
1 c. medium cream or half & half
8 Tbsp. (1 stick) unsalted butter
1 large onion, minced
1 lb. lean chuck beef
½ lb. lean pork
½ lb. veal
1 medium size potato, boiled and
   mashed

1 tsp. salt
½ tsp. freshly ground black pepper
¼ tsp. nutmeg
2 egg yolks, beaten
1 Tbsp. olive oil
2 c. beef broth
2 Tbsp. flour

1. Soak the crumbs in the cream or half & half.

2. In a large, deep frying pan, over medium heat, melt 3 tablespoons butter and cook the onion 2 minutes, or until soft. Do not brown.

3. Grind the beef, pork, and veal together 3 times. In a large bowl, combine and mix well, but lightly, the meat, crumbs, onion, potato, salt, pepper, nutmeg, and egg yolks. Shape into balls 1 to 1½ inches in diameter.

4. In the frying pan in which the onions cooked, heat 3 tablespoons butter and the oil. In a single layer (if necessary cook a few at a time), brown the balls evenly, shaking the pan as they are cooking. When all are brown, return to the pan; pour in the broth. Cover tightly and simmer 15 minutes until cooked thoroughly.

5. Remove with a slotted spoon and keep warm. Thicken the broth in the pan by stirring in kneaded butter (made with the remaining butter kneaded with the flour), cooking the sauce until it has thickened. Taste for seasonings. Serve the meatballs in the sauce. Serves 6.

MEATBALLS FOR SPAGHETTI

1 lb. ground beef
¼ c. freshly grated Romano cheese
½ c. bread crumbs
¼ tsp. black pepper
½ tsp. salt
1 Tbsp. minced onion

3 eggs
1 Tbsp. minced parsley
¼ c. water
1 recipe your favorite marinara
   sauce

Mix all ingredients, except for sauce, and form into 2 inch meatballs. Fry in the fat until brown on all sides. Add meatballs to a large pot of your favorite marinara sauce and cook over low heat 1½ to 2 hours until sauce has thickened and meatballs are thoroughly cooked. Serve with your favorite pasta. Serves 4.

YUMMY BURGERS

1 lb. ground beef
1 small onion, minced
3 Tbsp. catsup

3 Tbsp. mustard
1 can Campbell's chicken gumbo
   soup

Brown meat and onions. Add remaining ingredients. Simmer until thick. Serve on buns. *Good Sunday night quick meal.*

QUICK PIZZABURGERS

For 4 servings you will need:

1 lb. extra lean ground beef
¾ tsp. salt
¼ tsp. coarsely ground black
   pepper
1 tsp. mixed Italian herbs, or ½ tsp.
   each dried oregano and basil
   leaves
½ c. canned pizza flavored tomato
   sauce

4 oz. (¼ lb.) Mozzarella cheese,
   thinly sliced or shredded
4 green or black olives, sliced
4 thick slices toasted and buttered
   Italian style bread or pita
   bread
Lettuce (optional, for garnish)

1. In a bowl, combine the beef with the salt, pepper, and Italian style herbs until well blended.

2. Divide mixture into 4 portions. Shape each into a flat, round cake.

3. In a heavy skillet or under a preheated broiler, cook the meat patties until browned on both sides, 5 to 6 minutes on each side.

4. Top each with the tomato sauce. Slip under broiler until sauce is hot, then top with the cheese. Broil again until cheese is melted.

5. Garnish with sliced black olives and place on top of toasted, buttered, sliced French or Italian style bread or pita bread. Garnish with lettuce, if used, and serve.

CROWN ROAST OF PORK WITH SAUSAGE APPLE STUFFING

This recipe is an exciting change to the traditional Thanksgiving turkey.

1 large crown pork roast
1 mixture of the Sausage Apple
   Stuffing recipe (recipe
   follows)

To make the crown roast, preheat the oven to 450°F. Place roast, bone tips up on a rack in a shallow roasting pan. Season with a little salt and pepper and place chop holders over bone tips.

Place an empty can (one with no paper or painted label) in the center cavity of the roast. The can will assist in keeping the roast's shape during initial cooking.

Reduce the oven temperature to 350° and roast the meat for 25 to 30 minutes per pound. Remove the can and place the Sausage Apple Stuffing in the center cavity for the last hour. The roast is ready when the internal temperature has reached 170° and the stuffing has been in at least 1 full hour.

Remove to a warm platter and garnish with watercress and crab apples. Serves 6 to 8.

SAUSAGE APPLE STUFFING

The Sausage Apple Stuffing is an old-fashioned stuffing that is soft and extra-smooth with sour cream, Madeira, and an enrichment of chicken livers. Apples and

114

sausage add a little sugar and a little spice to this savory stuffing. Makes stuffing for a 14 pound turkey or a large crown roast. It will serve 10 to 12.

1 (24 oz.) loaf egg bread
¾ stick (6 Tbsp.) butter or margarine
½ lb. chicken livers, cleaned and cut in halves
1 lb. bulk pork sausage
2 c. chopped onions
½ c. finely chopped celery
2 medium apples, peeled, cored, and chopped (about 1½ c.)

3 cloves garlic, crushed
½ c. chopped fresh parsley
1 tsp. dried thyme
¾ c. chopped pecans
2 eggs
½ pt. (1 c.) sour cream
¼ c. Madeira wine
Salt and pepper

Preheat oven to 200°F. Cut crusts off bread and cut bread into ½ inch cubes. You should have 8 cups of bread cubes. Place on baking sheets and toast until cubes are dry, stirring occasionally, about 25 minutes. Remove to a large bowl.

In a large skillet, melt 2 tablespoons butter or margarine. Saute chicken livers until brown on the outside but still pink inside, about 3 to 5 minutes. Do not overcook. Remove livers with a slotted spoon; place on chopping board and chop fine. Add to bowl with bread cubes.

Add sausage to same skillet and cook, stirring, until all pink is gone from the meat. Place in bowl with bread cubes. Melt remaining 4 tablespoons butter or margarine in same skillet. Saute onions, celery, apples, and garlic, stirring often until soft, about 8 minutes. Remove to bowl with bread cubes. Add parsley, thyme, and pecans.

In a small bowl, combine eggs, sour cream, and Madeira. Pour over stuffing and toss lightly but thoroughly. Season to taste. Mixture may be refrigerated covered overnight or it may be stored frozen for 1 month.

Preheat oven to 350°F. Use it to stuff the crown roast (see recipe). Or place in a large shallow casserole. Bake, covered, at 350° for 30 to 45 minutes; uncover and bake 30 minutes longer or until top is crisp.

ROAST PORK WITH APPLES AND ORANGES

1 (12 oz.) pork tenderloin
½ c. orange juice
2 green onions, thinly sliced (¼ c.)
1 clove garlic, minced
1 tsp. sugar
½ tsp. dried thyme, crushed
¼ tsp. salt

1 Tbsp. margarine
1 red cooking apple, cored and cut into thin wedges
2 oranges, peeled and thinly sliced
Orange juice or water
1 tsp. cornstarch
4 oz. pasta, cooked and drained

Place pork in a plastic bag set in a bowl. For marinade, stir together ½ cup orange juice, green onions, garlic, sugar, thyme, and salt. Pour marinade over pork. Seal bag. Marinate in the refrigerator for 4 to 24 hours, turning bag occasionally to coat pork.

Drain pork, reserving marinade. Place pork on a rack in a roasting pan. Roast, uncovered, in a 425° oven for 25 to 30 minutes or till meat thermometer registers 160°. Cover and let stand 5 minutes.

Meanwhile, melt margarine in a medium skillet over medium heat. Add apples. Cook and stir over medium heat for 4 to 5 minutes or till apples are tender. Add oranges; heat through.

For sauce, add orange juice or water to reserved marinade to make ½ cup. Combine with cornstarch in a saucepan. Cook and stir till thickened and bubbly. Cook and stir 2 minutes more.

To serve, slice pork and serve with fruit mixture and pasta. Drizzle sauce over pork and pasta. Makes 4 servings.

Reserve the marinade and thicken it to make a light sauce for the meat and pasta.

ROAST PORK (CUBAN STYLE)

Leg of pork (fresh ham, approx. 6 lb.)
1 whole garlic bulb (about 5 to 6 cloves), minced
2 Tbsp. salt

1 Tbsp. oregano
2 tsp. cumin
½ tsp. black pepper
¾ c. lemon juice
1 lb. onions, sliced

Make slits in the roast. Mince the garlic. Add salt, oregano, cumin, pepper, and lemon juice. Rub the roast well with this marinade. Cover it with onion slices and let rest for at least 12 hours in the refrigerator. Bake with marinade at 325° for approximately 4 hours or until meat thermometer registers 185°. Serves 8 to 10.

PORK ROAST WITH DRIED CHERRIES AND PORT

1 pork roast
⅓ c. shallots, chopped
Thyme
½ c. Port

⅓ c. chicken broth
¼ c. dried cherries
Parsley, chopped

Bake pork roast as you prefer. Just before serving, remove 1 tablespoon grease from baking pan and place in skillet. Add shallots and pinch of thyme. Cook 1 minute. Add Port, chicken broth, and dried cherries. Bring to boil and reduce by half in approximately 5 minutes or less. Season with salt and pepper and garnish with parsley. Serve roast sliced and pass cherry sauce to spoon over. Serves 4.

TOM'S BONELESS PORK ROAST

1 (3 to 5 lb.) boneless pork roast
1 c. orange juice

½ c. honey
¼ c. brandy

Mix orange juice, honey, and brandy together. Inject mixture into meat with flavor injector. Cook on rotisserie according to meat thermometer reading for pork (170°). Inject once or twice during cooking time. May also cook in oven at 325° for 1½ hours to 2½ hours depending on the size of roast. For extra flavor, marinate roast overnight in mixture. Serves 6 to 8.

MARINATED PORK LOIN ROAST

Use 1 (4 to 5 pound) pork loin roast, boned and rolled.

Marinade:

½ c. soy sauce
½ c. sherry
2 cloves garlic, minced

1 Tbsp. dry mustard
1 tsp. ginger
1 tsp. thyme

Sauce:

1 jar black currant jelly
1 tsp. soy sauce

2 Tbsp. sherry

Preheat oven to 325°. Place meat in plastic bag to marinate. Marinate several hours or overnight. Remove meat from bag and place in roasting pan. Roast, uncovered, for 2½ to 3 hours, basting frequently. Combine sauce ingredients and heat for about 2 minutes. Serve with meat. Serves 10.

ROAST PORK TENDERLOIN WITH COGNAC AND CREAM

1¾ to 2¼ lb. pork tenderloin
¼ c. olive oil
Salt and ground pepper to taste
¼ c. butter

3 Tbsp. dried tarragon (or 6 Tbsp. fresh)
⅓ c. cognac
2 c. heavy cream

Coat the tenderloin with the oil and sprinkle with salt and pepper. Place the tenderloin in a roasting pan and cook in a preheated 425° oven for 30 to 35 minutes.

In a small saucepan, melt the butter over moderate heat until it bubbles. Add the tarragon. Add the cognac a third at a time, setting it aflame after each addition and allowing the flames to die out after each flaming. Add the heavy cream, bring the mixture to a boil, simmer it until it is reduced by half, and season with salt and pepper.

Carve tenderloin into medallions and place on a warm serving plate. Spoon sauce over pork. Serve immediately. Serves 4 to 6.

WINE BRAISED PORK LOIN

2 lb. center cut pork loin roast,
    boned, rolled, and tied
2 tsp. salt
½ tsp. ground pepper

1 bay leaf
1 garlic clove, minced
Pinch of ground allspice

Combine all but pork in small bowl. Pat pork dry and rub with salt mixture. Cover and chill 6 to 24 hours.

3 Tbsp. olive oil
2 onions, chopped
4 garlic cloves, chopped
2 red bell peppers, cut lengthwise
    and halved crosswise
1 c. dry white wine

1 c. canned crushed tomatoes with
    added puree
1 c. canned beef broth
2 bay leaves
1 Tbsp. dried marjoram

Preheat oven to 350°. Wipe pork dry. Heat 2 tablespoons oil in heavy Dutch oven over high heat. Add pork; brown on all sides (about 10 minutes). Transfer pork to plate. Reduce heat to medium and add remaining 1 tablespoon oil. Add onions and saute until tender, about 10 minutes. Add garlic and peppers and saute until peppers begin to soften, about 5 minutes. Add wine, tomatoes, broth, bay leaves, and marjoram.

Add pork, fat side up, and drippings on plate. Bring to boil. Cover; bake until tender, 45 minutes.

Transfer pork to platter and let stand 15 minutes. Reduce sauce to 4 cups; season with salt and pepper if necessary. Slice pork. (Can be prepared one day ahead.) Place half of sauce in baking dish. Top with pork slices, then remaining sauce. Cover and chill. Rewarm in covered dish in 350° oven until heated through, about 30 minutes. Serve with sauce.

SESAME-GARLIC GRILLED PORK TENDERLOIN

Use 1½ pounds pork tenderloin.

Marinade:

4 Tbsp. soy sauce	1 Tbsp. dry sherry
2 Tbsp. sesame oil	4 cloves garlic, peeled and minced
2 Tbsp. brown sugar	2 Tbsp. sesame seeds, toasted
½ tsp. honey	3 to 4 scallions, sliced on diagonal

Combine all ingredients for marinade and marinate pork, covered, overnight in refrigerator. Remove pork from marinade, discarding marinade. Grill pork over medium-hot coals, turning occasionally, for 15 to 20 minutes or until a meat thermometer inserted reads 155°. Remove pork from grill and carve into medallions. Serves 4.

PORK CHOPS WITH FRESH PLUM SAUCE

4 boneless center cut pork chops (1 inch thick)	½ bunch green onions
	½ tsp. beef flavored instant bouillon
1 Tbsp. olive or salad oil	1 c. cranberry-raspberry juice
3 medium red plums, cut into wedges	1 Tbsp. brown sugar
	2 tsp. cornstarch

In a 10 inch skillet, over medium high heat, cook pork chops 5 minutes in olive oil. Turn chops and cook another 5 minutes or until chops are done. Sprinkle with salt. Remove to a warm platter and keep warm. While pork is cooking, cut each plum into eighths. In a 2 cup measuring cup, stir together juice, brown sugar, cornstarch, and beef bouillon.

Remove pork chops from pan and add 1 tablespoon oil to drippings. Cook plum wedges and green onions 2 to 3 minutes until lightly browned. Stir mixture in measuring cup and add to skillet. Heat on high until sauce boils and thickens slightly. Reduce heat to low and simmer 1 minute. Pour over pork. Serves 4.

PORK POCKETS

1 lb. ground pork	½ tsp. pepper
2 c. (7 oz.) frozen hash brown potatoes	1 c. Jack cheese, shredded
	Salt to taste
1 large carrot, finely chopped	Pita bread
¼ c. onions, chopped	

Crumble pork and brown in skillet. Add potatoes, carrots, onions, and pepper. Stir and cook until vegetables are done. Add cheese and salt to taste. Fill ½ pita pocket. Lay in pan and brush with butter. Bake at 500° until lightly browned. Serves 6.

MINI-TIKI RIBS

2 lb. pork spareribs, sawed in half
    to make shorter lengths
¼ c. soy sauce
¼ c. honey
⅓ c. lemon juice
2 Tbsp. catsup
2 Tbsp. syrup from canned
    pineapple

1 Tbsp. brown sugar
1 tsp. dry mustard
½ tsp. powdered ginger
½ tsp. cornstarch
1 (20 oz.) can pineapple chunks,
    drained

Cut spareribs apart in twos. Cover with lightly salted water and simmer 1½ hours. Cool about ½ an hour in the broth, then drain. Place ribs, in a single layer, in a baking pan. Combine all remaining ingredients, except cornstarch and pineapple. Pour over ribs and refrigerate overnight. Drain ribs, saving marinade. Bake in a 400° oven 20 minutes.

Meanwhile, combine drained marinade with cornstarch in a small saucepan and heat to boiling, stirring often. After ribs have baked 20 minutes, spoon part of marinade over them. Continue baking 20 minutes longer, basting frequently with marinade. Add drained pineapple and bake 5 to 10 minutes longer, until ribs are nicely glazed. Serves 4 to 6.

SPARERIBS VIA CALIFORNIA

4 racks baby back ribs
1 jar barbecue sauce
2 Tbsp. soy sauce

2 Tbsp. honey
2 Tbsp. dry mustard
4 cloves garlic, crushed

Parboil ribs for 18 minutes and drain. Combine remaining ingredients and cover ribs. Cover with aluminum foil and bake 2 hours at 325°.

FRENCH-CANADIAN PORK MEAT PIE

1 lb. chopped lean pork
1 medium potato, peeled and
    chopped
1 small onion, chopped
½ tsp. salt
½ tsp. savory

¼ tsp. ground celery seeds
¼ tsp. ground cloves
½ c. water
¼ c. dry bread crumbs
Dough for 9 inch double crust pie

Grind pork, potato, and onion together in meat grinder. Combine in heavy saucepan with next 5 ingredients. Bring to boil, then simmer about 20 minutes, uncovered. Stir in crumbs; cool.

Make pie shell. Put pork ingredients in shell. Cover with second round. Crimp edges. Make slits on top. Bake 35 to 40 minutes at 425°. Serve with chutney or catsup.

TELLURIDE GREEN CHILI BURRITOS

1 (3 lb.) Boston butt cut pork roast, diced into ½ inch pieces
1 large onion, chopped
2 cloves garlic
1 tsp. cumin
1 can cream of mushroom soup

4 (7 oz.) large cans diced green chilies
Grated cheese
Shredded lettuce
Diced tomatoes
Sour cream

Brown pork in 1 tablespoon oil. Add onions, green chilies, and garlic. Cook until onions are tender. Add soup, cumin, salt, and pepper to taste. Spoon into flour tortillas and roll up. Top with shredded cheese and sauce and heat in microwave until cheese is melted. Serve with shredded lettuce, grated cheese, diced tomatoes, and sour cream. Sauce may be frozen for future use.

HAM AND BROCCOLI CASSEROLE

1 c. rice
2 c. chicken broth (may be made of bouillon cubes)
6 Tbsp. butter
6 Tbsp. flour
1 Tbsp. grated onion
1 tsp. mustard

1 tsp. Worcestershire sauce
1 tsp. salt
3 c. milk
1 c. Swiss cheese
1 pkg. boiled ham, sliced
1 pkg. frozen broccoli

Cook rice in chicken broth until tender and broth is absorbed. Make a cheese sauce of the butter, flour, seasonings, milk, and cheese. Mix half of this with rice and place in a casserole dish. Roll ham slices around 2 broccoli spears (have been cooked tender), allowing flowerets to show at each end. Arrange rolls with seam side down on the rice and cheese. Pour remaining cheese sauce in a streak down the center of ham rolls. Place under broiler until sauce is flecked with brown or bake.

SAUSAGE BEAN CASSEROLE

2 cans Great Northern white beans (undrained)
1 lb. Italian sausage
1 large onion, chopped
1 (8 oz.) can tomato sauce

8 oz. wine (dry white or red)
½ tsp. basil
1 large clove garlic, minced
Salt and pepper
Dash of cayenne pepper

Fry sausage and drain. Add onions and saute until soft. Add garlic, spices, tomato sauce, and wine. Simmer for a few minutes. To assemble, put 1 can beans in casserole dish and cover with ½ sauce. Repeat with remaining beans and sauce. Bake ½ hour, covered, at 350°. Uncover and bake an additional ½ hour.

BUTTERFLIED LEG OF LAMB
(For barbecuing or roasting)

Use 1 boned and butterflied leg of lamb.

Marinade:

3 to 4 Tbsp. olive oil
2 Tbsp. soy sauce
Juice of ½ lemon plus the grated
   peel if you wish

½ tsp. rosemary
1 or 2 cloves garlic, pureed
   (optional)

Rub the unboned side of the lamb with a tablespoon of olive oil and place, oiled side down, in a baking pan. Rub the rest of the oil and the soy, lemon juice and optional peel, rosemary, and optional garlic into the top side. Cover with plastic wrap and marinate until you are ready to cook the lamb, an hour or more if possible.

To barbecue the lamb: When the coals are just right, place the lamb in an oiled, hinged (double sided) rack and barbecue, turning every 5 minutes or so and brushing with oil, for 45 minutes to an hour, depending on the heat of your coals and the way you like your lamb. If you want it rosy red, it is done when it begins to take on resistance to your finger, in contrast to its soft raw state. A meat thermometer reading would be 125°. Remove the lamb to a carving board and let it set for 8 to 10 minutes, allowing juices to retreat back into the meat before carving.

To carve, start at either of the small ends and, to make attractively largish slices, begin somewhat back from the edge, angling your knife as though carving a flank steak.

To roast in the oven: Roast the lamb and then finish it off under the broiler. To do so, place the marinated lamb flat, boned side up, in a roasting pan in the upper middle of a preheated 375° oven and roast for 20 to 25 minutes or to a meat thermometer reading of 120°. Do not turn the lamb on its other side. Baste with oil and set for 2 to 3 minutes under a preheated broiler to brown lightly. Always let it set for 8 to 10 minutes outside the oven before carving and carve as suggested.

RACK OF LAMB

3¾ to 4 lb. rack of lamb (8 chops)
1 Tbsp. salt
2 Tbsp. fines herbes (½ Tbsp. each
   fresh tarragon, chives,
   shallots, and parsley, all finely
   chopped; if dried, use half the
   amount)

½ c. bread crumbs
1 Tbsp. parsley, finely chopped
2 cloves garlic, peeled and finely
   chopped

Preheat oven to 450°F. Trim fat from ends of chop bones. Rub meat all over with salt. Score fat and rub in fines herbes on all surfaces. Roast with fat side down 25 minutes. The outside curves of the ribs have a thick coat of fat. Cut from the top, pull away this coating, and discard.

Combine bread crumbs with finely chopped parsley and garlic. Sprinkle the outside surfaces of the lamb with the bread crumbs and return to the oven for 5 minutes for rare, 10 minutes for medium, 15 minutes for well done. Serves 4.

SNOW CAPPED LAMB CHOPS

6 (½ inch) shoulder or sirloin chops
1 can condensed consomme
½ tsp. thyme
½ c. celery, chopped
½ c. green onions and tops, sliced
   (save tops)

1 (3 oz.) can broiled, chopped
   mushrooms or fresh
3 Tbsp. flour
1 Tbsp. parsley flakes
1 c. sour cream

Slowly brown chops in small amount of hot oil. Sprinkle with salt and pepper. Add next 4 ingredients. Cover and simmer 30 to 45 minutes or until meat is done. Stack chops to one side. Drain mushrooms and reserve liquid. Stir mushroom liquid into flour, stirring constantly until thick. Add mushrooms and parsley. Top chops with sour cream; cover and heat 3 minutes. Sprinkle with chopped onion tops. Serves 6.

LEG OF LAMB WITH SPINACH AND APRICOTS

Delight the most discriminating of guests with this savory, show-off entree.

½ lb. dried apricots
3 lb. spinach, washed and trimmed
   of stems
1 medium onion, chopped
2 c. fresh bread crumbs
2 eggs, slightly beaten
½ c. butter or margarine, cut into
   cubes and softened
1 Tbsp. grated lemon rind

1 Tbsp. salt
⅛ tsp. mace
Pepper
1 (6 lb.) leg of lamb, boned but not
   butterflied
Vegetable oil
6 garlic cloves, peeled and slivered
½ c. beef broth

Soak apricots in a bowl of cold water for 4 hours. Drain and chop. In a large pot of boiling, salted water, blanch the spinach for 2 minutes. Drain and refresh under cold water. Squeeze excess water from spinach. Chop the spinach and combine with onions and apricots. Grind this mixture coarsely in a food processor. Place in a bowl and add bread crumbs, eggs, butter, lemon rind, salt, mace, and pepper. Mix well.

Sew closed the large opening in the boned leg of lamb. Through the small opening, stuff the leg loosely with about 1½ cups of the apricot-spinach mixture. Put remaining stuffing in a buttered baking dish and cover with foil. Sew up the small opening and brush the lamb with oil. Place slivers of garlic randomly under the skin of the lamb. Place lamb in an oiled roasting pan and bake in a preheated 450° oven 30 to 45 minutes or until the internal meat temperature reaches 140° for medium rare. Bake the remaining stuffing with the roast.

Transfer lamb to a cutting board, cover and let rest for 15 minutes before slicing. Skim fat from the roasting pan and add beef broth to pan drippings. Season with salt and pepper to taste. Cut lamb into ½ inch slices and spoon sauce over each slice. Serves 6 to 8.

FRENCH LAMB CHOPS

Simple to make, yet sophisticated in taste.

6 small loin lamb chops, boned	2 Tbsp. oregano
1 small bottle Dijon mustard	2 Tbsp. rosemary
1 egg, beaten	2 Tbsp. powdered garlic
2 c. bread crumbs	Salt and pepper to taste

1. Preheat oven to 450°.
2. Brush chops on all sides with mustard, then dip in egg.
3. Combine bread crumbs, oregano, rosemary, and garlic. Mix well.
4. Roll chops in bread crumb mixture.
5. Put chops in buttered baking dish and sprinkle with salt and pepper. Bake for 20 minutes. Serves 4 to 6.

LAMB SHANKS

Lamb is available all year long, but somehow spring lamb is better for this traditional meal. A lovely Sunday dinner that smells good all afternoon.

4 lamb shanks (3 lb.)	1 Tbsp. lemon juice
3 to 4 Tbsp. flour	4 carrots, pared and halved
2 Tbsp. oil	4 small onions
1 clove garlic, crushed	2 stalks celery, quartered
2 tsp. salt	2 potatoes, quartered
1 tsp. oregano	1 Tbsp. flour
¼ tsp. pepper	¼ tsp. Kitchen Bouquet
1 c. chicken bouillon	

1. Preheat oven to 350°.
2. Remove fat from shanks; wipe with a damp towel and coat with flour.
3. Slowly heat oil in Dutch oven. Brown shanks well, turning several times.
4. Add garlic, salt, oregano, pepper, bouillon, and lemon juice. Cover and bake for 1½ hours.
5. Turn shanks and add carrots, onions, celery, and potatoes.
6. Cover and bake for 35 to 45 minutes.
7. Remove meat and vegetables to warm platter and cover.
8. Reserve 1½ cups of liquid from Dutch oven. Skim off fat from liquid and put 1 tablespoon in a saucepan.
9. Blend in flour and gradually stir in remaining skimmed liquid. Add Kitchen Bouquet; bring to boil, stirring for 1 minute. Pour over meat and vegetables. Serves 6.

SHISH KEBOB

Use 2 pounds boneless lamb, cut into ½ inch chunks. Beef can be substituted for lamb.

Marinade:

1 c. pineapple juice	2 garlic cloves, minced
¼ c. soy sauce	1 tsp. ground ginger

Mix all marinade ingredients together. Place meat in large bowl. Pour marinade over meat. Cover and refrigerate for 12 to 24 hours.

When ready, skewer meat and cook over hot coals on barbeque to desired doneness. You may add cubes of onion, green pepper, cherry tomatoes, and mushrooms between meat chunks on each skewer. Serve over rice pilaf. Serves 6 to 8.

KIBBEH

This is the Middle Eastern equivalent of hamburger, meat loaf, meatballs, you name it. It's the favorite ground-meat dish everywhere in that part of the world.

½ c. bulgur (cracked wheat)
½ c. hot chicken broth
1½ lb. lean lamb, ground twice
2 small white onions, minced
½ c. tomato sauce
1 tsp. salt
¼ tsp. freshly ground black pepper
½ tsp. ground cumin

¼ tsp. cinnamon
½ c. chopped fresh broadleaf
   parsley
½ c. pignoli, cooked in 2 Tbsp.
   butter until golden and crisp
4 Tbsp. (½ stick) unsalted butter,
   melted

1. In a bowl, mix the bulgur with the broth. Let stand 1 hour. Drain and spoon the bulgur through cheesecloth, squeezing out all liquid.

2. In a bowl, combine the bulgur, lamb, onions, tomato sauce, salt, pepper, cumin, cinnamon, parsley, and pignoli. Knead with your hands until mixture is smooth and blended. Grease 9x9 inch pan and spread meat evenly. Score with a knife into large diamond-shaped design. Pour the melted butter over and cook, uncovered, in a preheated 400° oven 40 minutes or until top is crisp and golden brown.

3. To serve, cut in diamond-shaped wedges. Serve with Potatoes with Ricotta cheese. Serves 6.

SYRIAN CABBAGE ROLLS

1 (3 lb.) head of cabbage
1 c. raw rice
1½ lb. ground lamb
1 to 2 tsp. salt
Ground pepper to taste

Cinnamon to taste
Allspice to taste
1 (8 oz.) can tomato sauce
1 (28 oz.) can tomato puree

Core cabbage and place in a pot of boiling water. While boiling, loosen each leaf with fork when slightly tender. Remove and drain. Wash and drain rice. Mix with lamb, salt, spices, and tomato sauce. Place 1 tablespoon of rice/meat mixture on inner side of each cabbage leaf. Spread in line and roll up. Place evenly in rows, crisscrossing layers in 2 quart baking dish. Cover cabbage rolls with tomato puree and seal top with aluminum foil. Bake at 300° for 1½ to 2 hours. Serve alone or stuffed into warm pita bread halves. Serves 4.

VEAL MARENGO

3 lb. veal stew meat, cut into 2 inch
    pieces
2 to 3 Tbsp. olive oil
1 c. minced yellow onions
1 tsp. salt
¼ tsp. pepper
2 Tbsp. flour
2 c. dry white wine
1 c. chopped canned tomatoes

½ tsp. basil or tarragon
½ tsp. thyme
½ tsp. ground orange peel
2 cloves garlic, mashed
½ lb. fresh mushrooms, quartered
    if large
2 to 3 Tbsp. minced fresh parsley,
    tarragon, or basil

Preheat oven to 325°. Dry veal chunks on paper towel. Brown in hot oil, a few pieces at a time, and place in 4 quart oven casserole. Lower heat to moderate. Using 1 tablespoon oil, brown onions lightly, 5 to 6 minutes. While onions brown, toss meat with 2 tablespoons flour, salt, and pepper.

Add wine to pan with onions. Boil 1 minute, scraping up juices and browned bits on bottom of pan. Pour wine and onions over meat and bring casserole to a simmer on stove top. Stir in tomatoes. Add herbs, orange peel, and garlic. Cover and set in oven 1¼ to 1½ hours until meat is tender.

Add mushrooms to casserole. Baste with sauce. Continue baking 15 more minutes. To serve, place on a platter surrounded by rice or noodles. Decorate with fresh herbs. Serves 6.

VEAL CHOPS - MILAN STYLE

6 veal loin chops (¾ inch thick)
¾ c. dry unflavored bread crumbs
⅓ c. fresh grated Parmesan cheese
2 eggs

Salt to taste
¼ c. butter
Lemon slices

Pound veal chops lightly. Combine bread crumbs and Parmesan cheese in a small bowl. Spread on aluminum foil. Beat eggs and salt in medium bowl. Dip chops in eggs, then coat with bread crumb mixture. Press mixture into chops and let stand 10 to 15 minutes. Melt butter in large skillet. When butter foams, add chops. Cook over medium heat 4 to 5 minutes on each side or until meat has a golden brown crust. Drain on paper towels. Place chops on warm platter. Garnish with lemon slices and serve.

If veal is not available, thick pork chops may be substituted. Cooking time needs to be extended to be certain pork is well cooked. Serves 6.

VEAL PATTIES WITH TOMATOES, ONIONS, AND HERBS

½ c. minced onions
2 Tbsp. butter
2 medium tomatoes, chopped
1 clove garlic, mashed
¼ tsp. salt
½ tsp. basil or thyme
1 c. stale white bread crumbs
½ c. milk

1 lb. ground veal
1 tsp. salt
¼ tsp. pepper
3 Tbsp. minced parsley
1 egg
½ c. flour
⅔ c. beef bouillon
1 to 2 Tbsp. softened butter

Cook onions in small skillet until tender but not brown. Add tomatoes, garlic, salt, and herbs. Boil until tomato juices evaporate.

Soak bread crumbs in milk for 5 minutes. Put in strainer and press out milk. Add crumbs to tomato mixture. Add meat, seasonings, parsley, and egg; mix well.

Form meat into 6 or 12 balls; flatten to ½ inch thick. Dredge in flour. Cook in well oiled skillet about 15 minutes, turning once. Arrange on platter. Pour fat from pan. Add bouillon and reduce to 3 to 4 tablespoons. Off heat, swirl in butter. Pour sauce over patties. Serves 6.

OSSO BUCO

6 Tbsp. butter	1 c. dry white wine
2 c. finely chopped onions	2 Tbsp. chopped fresh basil
¾ c. chopped carrots (no centers)	1 c. water with 1 beef bouillon cube
¾ c. chopped celery	½ tsp. dried thyme
2 large cloves garlic, minced	1 (28 oz.) can crushed tomatoes
6 veal shanks	6 parsley sprigs
½ c. olive oil	2 bay leaves

Melt butter. Add onions, carrots, celery, and garlic and cook over medium heat 10 to 15 minutes; set aside. Season veal shanks with salt and pepper. Dip into flour; brown in hot olive oil. Remove and set aside. Put onion mixture into pan used to brown veal shanks. Add wine, basil, beef bouillon, thyme, tomatoes, parsley, and bay leaves. Cook 15 to 20 minutes.

In deep ovenproof roasting pan, place veal shanks and cover with vegetable and wine mixture. Season. Cover and bake 1 hour and 45 minutes to 2 hours. Sprinkle with fresh parsley and serve. Serves 6.

VEAL PARMIGIANA

1 lb. veal steak or cutlet, very thinly sliced	⅓ c. grated Parmesan cheese
1 tsp. salt	⅓ c. fine dry bread crumbs
⅛ tsp. pepper	¼ c. oil
1 egg	1 (6 oz.) can tomato paste
Water	1 tsp. salt
¼ c. onion	½ tsp. basil
	6 slices Mozzarella or Swiss cheese

Cut veal into 6 or 8 pieces; sprinkle with salt and pepper. In shallow bowl, lightly beat egg with 2 teaspoons water. On sheet of waxed paper, combine Parmesan and bread crumbs. Dip veal in egg, then in Parmesan mixture. In skillet brown veal on both sides, a few pieces at a time, in oil. Remove to large baking dish. To skillet, add onion and cook until tender. Stir in tomato paste, 2 cups water, salt, and basil. Simmer 5 minutes, scraping up any browned bits from bottom of skillet. Pour most of sauce over veal. Top with cheese; pour remaining sauce over. Bake at 350° for 20 to 25 minutes.

VEAL PARMESAN

1 lb. veal cutlets
¼ c. olive oil
1 clove garlic
1 very small onion, chopped
½ c. mushrooms, sliced

½ c. sherry, Marsala, or Madeira
 wine
1 c. Parmesan cheese, grated
Salt and pepper to taste

Preheat oven to 325°. Have meat department flatten meat or pound it until it's ¼ inch thick. Cut into 3 inch pieces. Brown on both sides in oil over high heat and transfer to a baking dish. Keep warm while preparing sauce. Saute garlic, onion, and mushrooms in same oil as veal over low heat until soft. Season with salt and pepper. Remove from heat and stir in wine and cheese. Pour sauce over veal and bake until meat is tender and bubbling hot. Serve very hot with pasta. Serves 4.

VEAL PAPRIKA

6 slices bacon
1 (3⅓ lb.) boneless veal shoulder,
 cut into ½ inch cubes
⅔ c. onions, chopped or sliced
3 cans chicken broth
3 Tbsp. paprika

1½ tsp. salt
3 Tbsp. flour
½ c. cold water
1 c. sour cream
Toasted almonds

Saute bacon, onions, and veal until onions turn golden brown. Add chicken broth, paprika, and salt. Cover and simmer slowly for 1½ hours. Mix flour, cold water, and sour cream and stir into meat mixture. Stir constantly until thickened. Garnish with toasted almonds and serve over thin noodles. Serves 8.

VEAL PICCATA

This recipe remains one of our favorite veal dishes, and one of the gems of the Italian repertoire.

4 veal scallops (each weighing
 about 6 oz.)
Flour (for dredging)
Salt and freshly ground black
 pepper to taste

2 Tbsp. olive oil
3 Tbsp. unsalted butter
⅓ c. dry white wine
⅓ c. chicken broth
Juice of 1 lemon, freshly squeezed

1. Between pieces of wax paper, pound each piece of veal with a meat mallet until wafer-thin. Do not pound so hard, however, that the meat is perforated or shredded; each piece should be intact. Dredge lightly with flour and season with salt and pepper.

2. Heat the oil in a frying pan. Brown the scallops evenly. Transfer to a warm dish and keep warm.

3. Pour any fat from the pan. Add the butter, wine, broth, and lemon juice. Simmer, stirring, over medium-high heat for 5 minutes. Add the scallops, spooning sauce over them, and serve piping hot. Serves 4.

VEAL SCALLOPINI

6 slices veal, thinly sliced
6 Tbsp. flour
4 Tbsp. butter
3 medium onions, thinly sliced
1 clove garlic, minced
2 bouillon cubes

1 c. boiling water
1 tsp. dry mustard
3 tsp. paprika
3 Tbsp. parsley, minced
4 Tbsp. butter
1 c. sour cream

Dust veal with flour. Melt butter in heavy frying pan. Add onions and garlic, cooking until yellow. Add bouillon cubes and boiling water, stirring until cubes dissolve. Add mustard and paprika. Stir mixture well and pour into bowl. Set aside. Melt 4 additional tablespoons butter in frying pan; add floured meat and cook until browned on both sides. Pour onion mixture over the meat. Cover and cook over low heat for 30 minutes. Stir in sour cream and bring to a boil. Remove from heat and serve.

PENNE WITH VEAL AND TOMATO CREAM SAUCE

1 tsp. olive oil
1 lb. ground veal
1 c. chopped green onions
2 (14½ oz.) cans diced peeled
    tomatoes

1 c. whipping cream
½ c. dry white wine
1 Tbsp. tomato paste
12 oz. penne, freshly cooked
Grated Parmesan cheese

Heat oil in heavy large skillet over medium-high heat. Add veal and green onions and saute until cooked through, breaking up veal with back of spoon, about 6 minutes. Add tomatoes with their liquids, cream, wine, and tomato paste. Simmer until sauce thickens, about 12 minutes. Add cooked pasta and toss until heated through and coated with sauce, about 2 minutes. Season to taste with salt and pepper. Serve, passing Parmesan separately. Makes 4 servings.

QUAIL PAPRIKA
(Hunters delight)

6 quail, cleaned
1 tsp. salt
¼ tsp. pepper
3 Tbsp. flour (divided)
½ c. butter

2 (10¾ oz.) cans cream of
    mushroom soup
1 c. water
3 Tbsp. paprika
¾ c. sour cream

Rub the quail inside and out with salt and pepper. Tie the legs close to the body. Sprinkle with 2 tablespoons of the flour. Brown the quail in butter for 6 minutes. Place the birds in a casserole.

In a mixing bowl, combine the soup, water, and paprika and stir until well blended. Pour the sauce over quail. Bake, covered, in a 350° oven for 25 minutes or until tender. Remove the quail to a warm platter. Stir the remaining flour into the pan juices; add the sour cream. Mix and heat but do not allow the sauce to boil. Season to taste. Pour the sauce over the quail. Serves 2 to 3.

ROAST QUAIL VAN SCHAACK
(For 8 quail)

Stuff quail with celery tops. Sprinkle with salt, pepper, and paprika. Place in roasting pan. Sprinkle 8 peppercorns and 1 crumbled bay leaf around quail. Spread quail with ¼ cup (½ stick) softened butter. Birds should be at room temperature before they go into oven. Roast in oven preheated to 400° for 15 minutes. Remove quail from pan. Stir 1 cup burgundy into drippings. Add 2 teaspoons currant jelly, juice of ½ lemon, and 1 cup gravy (made from other meat or fowl stock or drippings). Add quail to sauce. Sprinkle 1 cup fresh seedless grapes around quail. Simmer 10 minutes. Place quail on slices of crisp toast. Cover with sauce.

GOOSE NUT AND FRUIT STUFFING

Makes enough for 12 to 14 pound bird.

2 (8 oz.) pkg. bread stuffings
3 ripe bananas, mashed
1 c. seedless green or red grapes, halved

2 tart apples, cored and diced
2 oranges, sectioned
1 c. walnuts, broken

Prepare bread stuffing as directed on package. Blend in bananas and remaining ingredients. Mix well. Stuff bird. Bake at 325° until bird is done. Excellent for turkey, too!

TRUFFLE-STUFFED QUAIL, CLEOPATRA

12 small quail
½ lb. veal
¾ c. pate de foie gras
¾ chopped chicken liver
2 small truffles

½ c. butter or margarine
¼ c. sherry
3 egg yolks
Salt and pepper to taste
Grape leaves (optional)

Put all the ingredients, except quail, through good grinder, then mix thoroughly. Stuff quail with mixture. Wrap each bird in grape leaves and roast in a preheated 375°F. oven, no longer than 20 minutes.

To prepare the quail over a grill or at an outdoor function, wrap first in grape leaves, then in buttered aluminum foil. Allow an outdoor fire to burn down to ashes, then bake the quail in the hot ashes for 20 minutes. Yield: 6 servings.

Note: Grape leaves may be omitted. Either fresh or canned ones may be used. Purchase them from specialty food shops or the gourmet section of your favorite food store.

CRANBERRY-STUFFED PHEASANT

2 (about 3 lb.) pheasants, dressed
    for roasting
1 lemon, cut in half
Salt
Paprika
1 c. sugar
¾ c. water
1½ c. fresh cranberries

½ c. dry white wine or white-wine
    vinegar, diluted
⅓ c. butter or margarine
1 c. chopped onions
2 small apples, peeled, cored, and
    chopped
6 strips bacon

Wash pheasants and pat dry. Rub inside and out with lemon, salt, and paprika. Combine sugar, water, and cranberries in a saucepan. Simmer until cranberries are tender, about 10 minutes. Drain cranberries and add wine to syrup.

Preheat oven to 350°F. Melt butter or margarine; add onions and saute until golden. Stir in drained cranberries and apples. Use mixture to stuff pheasants. Sew or skewer openings. Truss pheasants and put on a rack in a shallow roasting pan. Put bacon strip over breasts of pheasant. Roast in moderate oven (350°F.) for 1½ hours, or until pheasants are tender. While pheasants are roasting, baste every 15 minutes with cranberry-syrup-wine mixture. Arrange pheasants on heated platter. Skim fat from pan drippings. Serve pheasant and cranberry stuffing with pan drippings and wild rice if desired.

BRAISED PHEASANT WITH MUSHROOMS

2 slices fat salt pork
1 (2½ to 3 lb.) pheasant
1 tsp. salt
¼ tsp. hot sauce
1 onion, studded with cloves
2 stalks celery, ½ bay leaf, and sprig
    of parsley, tied together
½ tsp. thyme leaves

1 (6 oz.) can frozen Florida orange
    juice concentrate, thawed
    and reconstituted
1 lb. mushrooms, sliced
1 carrot, pared
1 c. chilled or canned Florida orange
    and grapefruit sections

Heat salt pork in Dutch oven or large heatproof casserole; brown on all sides. Finish cleaning bird; cut into quarters. Brown bird in Dutch oven. Add salt, hot sauce, onion, celery, bay leaf, parsley, and reconstituted orange juice. Simmer, covered, 40 minutes. Remove onion, celery, bay leaf, and parsley. Add sliced mushrooms, carrot, and thyme. Continue cooking, covered, about 45 minutes longer, or until meat is tender and leg separates from body. During last 10 minutes of cooking, add orange and grapefruit sections. Yield: 4 servings.

CORNISH HENS, HUNTER STYLE

4 Rock Cornish game hens
1 tsp. (about) garlic powder
¼ c. peanut oil
¼ c. butter
½ c. minced celery
½ c. minced carrots
1 medium onion, chopped
2 medium cloves garlic, minced
1 (1 lb. 12 oz.) can tomatoes
1 green pepper, cut in julienne strips
    about 1 inch long

1 (6 or 8 oz.) can sliced mushrooms
¼ c. brandy or sherry
2 c. chicken stock or bouillon
Salt and pepper to taste
¼ tsp. oregano
⅛ tsp. bouquet garni
3 Tbsp. grated Romano cheese
1 c. fresh or frozen uncooked peas
1 Tbsp. monosodium glutamate

Rub hens inside and out with garlic powder; set aside at room temperature for 30 minutes. Heat oil and butter in Dutch oven. Lightly brown hens on all sides. Remove hens from pan. Add celery, carrots, onion, and garlic to drippings. Saute until onion is transparent. Drain off excess grease if necessary.

Drain tomatoes. Reserve liquid. Dice tomatoes and add them with green pepper to onion mixture. Drain mushrooms. Reserve liquid. Add mushrooms and brandy to onion mixture. Simmer about 3 minutes. Add chicken stock, mushroom and tomato liquids, salt, pepper, oregano, and bouquet garni.

Arrange hens, breasts down, in mixture. Bring to boil, reduce heat and simmer, covered, about 30 minutes or until hens are done. Baste exposed surface of hens occasionally during cooking period. Sprinkle hens with cheese. Add peas. Cover and cook just until peas are tender. Just before serving, stir in monosodium glutamate. Serve hens and sauce with buttered noodles or rice. (If sauce is too thin, thicken it with cornstarch or flour.) Makes 4 servings.

MARINATED GRILLED RABBIT

1 (3 lb.) rabbit, cut in serving size
    pieces
Dry sherry or sauterne or other
    white dinner wine
Salt and pepper

½ c. butter or margarine
1 c. chicken broth (canned or
    bouillon cube may be used)
4 (or 5) drops garlic juice
½ tsp. oregano or rosemary

Place pieces of rabbit in deep glass or stainless steel bowl. Cover with wine; marinate overnight or at least 5 hours. Before barbecuing, prepare baste by combining other ingredients with 1 cup of wine used to marinate rabbit. Place rabbit about 8 inches above coals; cook slowly 45 minutes to 1 hour, turning and basting constantly. (Racks that allow you to turn a dozen pieces at a time work best.) When done, brown as desired by moving rabbit closer to coals. Continue basting; do not allow to become dry. Yield: 6 servings.

JUGGED HARE - HASENPFEFFER

2 legs and saddle of hare, cut in 2 pieces
1½ tsp. salt
4 Tbsp. butter or margarine
1 medium size onion
4 cloves
1½ c. Port wine or claret
12 peppercorns

1 herb bouquet (parsley, thyme, bay leaf)
3 c. hot stock or bouillon
2 Tbsp. butter or margarine
1 Tbsp. flour
1 Tbsp. lemon juice
Red currant jelly

Rinse meat; pat dry. Rub with salt. Saute in 3 tablespoons butter or margarine until brown, about 30 minutes. Place in casserole; add onion stuck with cloves, ¾ cup wine, lemon juice, peppercorns, herbs, and stock. Cover and bake in moderate oven (350°F.) 2½ to 3 hours.

About ½ hour before serving, melt remaining tablespoon of butter or margarine. Blend with flour and stir into hot mixture. Add remaining ¾ cup wine and add any needed seasoning. Cover casserole again; cook 30 minutes. Place pieces of hare on hot serving dish; strain gravy over them. Serve with red currant jelly. Yield: 4 servings.

ELK PICCATA

2 lb. elk steak, cut ½ inch thick, trim all fat
2 Tbsp. olive oil
3 Tbsp. butter
¾ lb. fresh mushrooms, sliced
2 cloves garlic, minced

½ c. dry white wine
3 Tbsp. fresh lemon juice
3 oz. brandy
4 Tbsp. minced parsley
Lemon slices

Sprinkle meat with salt and pepper and pound lightly on both sides. Dust lightly with flour. Heat butter and oil and brown meat on both sides. Remove meat from skillet. Add mushrooms and garlic to pan and cook 1 minute. Return meat to pan; add wine and lemon juice. Cover and simmer for 25 minutes or until meat is tender. Warm brandy; pour over meat and flame. Remove meat and keep warm on platter. Spoon sauce over meat. Garnish with parsley and lemon slices. Serves 4.

ROAST SADDLE OF VENISON

1 saddle of venison
1⅓ c. water
2⅔ c. burgundy wine
2 tsp. mustard seeds
2 bay leaves
1 tsp. thyme
2 onions, sliced

½ tsp. pepper
2 garlic cloves, slivered
1 Tbsp. salt
½ c. sour cream
1 c. red currant jelly
1 Tbsp. brandy
Wild rice

Trim all fat off venison. Combine water, wine, mustard seeds, bay leaves, thyme, onions, and pepper. Pour over meat in glass or porcelain dish. Marinate in refrigerator 24 hours, turning occasionally. Insert slivers of garlic in meat and sprinkle with salt. Bake, uncovered, in 350° oven 2 to 4 hours, depending on size, or until tender, basting often with marinade. Remove meat to warm platter. Skim excess fat from meat drippings and stir in sour cream, jelly, and brandy. Cook until mixture thickens. Spoon sauce over meat or serve separately. Serve with wild rice.

MARINATED VENISON ROAST

2 sliced onions
2 crushed cloves garlic
2 sliced lemons and rind
¼ c. wine vinegar

1 (12 oz.) can beer
⅔ c. salad oil
Salt and freshly ground pepper
1 venison roast

Combine all ingredients, except meat; mix well. Add meat. Marinate in refrigerator 2 or 3 days. Turn meat occasionally. Drain meat; roll in flour. Heat a small amount of oil in heavy pan. Brown meat on all sides. Add marinade.

Roast, covered, at 325° about 30 minutes per pound or until done. (When a long-tine fork inserted in the center of the meat can be removed easily, it should be done.) Strain drippings and thicken with small amount of flour or cornstarch mixed with water.

VENISON POT ROAST WITH CRANBERRIES

5 to 6 lb. venison rump, boned,
    rolled, and tied
¼ lb. salt pork or fat bacon, cubed
2 Tbsp. butter or margarine
2 c. fresh cranberries
½ c. chopped celery
1 c. water

1 tsp. salt
¼ tsp. black pepper
1 to 2 tsp. bottled brown bouquet
    sauce
Flour
2 c. chopped onion

Cut slits in the surface of the roast. Press a cube of salt pork into each slit. Heat butter in a Dutch oven and brown meat in it on all sides. Add remaining ingredients, except flour. Cover and bring to a boil. Reduce heat and simmer for 3 to 4 hours, or until meat is tender. Add more water if necessary. Remove meat from pan and keep warm.

Skim excess fat from the surface of the liquid. Press liquid and pulp through a sieve and measure. Make a smooth paste of flour and a little water, using 1 tablespoon flour for every cup of measured liquid. Reheat liquid and stir in flour-water mixture.

Cook over low heat, stirring constantly, until sauce boils and thickens. Slice meat and serve with mashed potatoes or dumplings. Spoon hot gravy over all. Yield: 6 to 8 servings.

BURGUNDY VENISON STEW

1½ lb. venison, cubed
2 Tbsp. flour
½ tsp. salt
½ tsp. pepper
½ tsp. garlic salt
¼ c. oil
¼ c. butter or margarine

2 stalks celery, chopped
1 onion, chopped
2 cloves garlic, chopped
4 sprigs parsley
1½ c. burgundy, claret, or other red
    dinner wine
½ c. water

Coat venison in flour seasoned with salt, pepper, and garlic salt. In a large, heavy skillet, brown meat in oil and butter or margarine. Add celery and onion; brown well. Add garlic and parsley; brown slightly. Pour over wine and water. Simmer, covered, over low heat or in moderately slow oven (325°F.) for 1 to 1½ hours or until meat is tender. Yield: 6 servings.

Ripe-olive and ham-flecked stuffing balls make a gourmet feast with roast venison. While the roast is cooking, bake the balls separately until crusty and handsomely browned.

To insure a tender, juicy roast, marinate the venison overnight in a spicy burgundy mixture. Be careful not to overcook it. Small pieces of beef suet or salt pork inserted throughout the meat help retain moisture and tenderness too.

VENISON STEW WITH DUMPLINGS

3 lb. venison (use neck meat, shoulder meat, or shoulder chops)
2 tsp. monosodium glutamate (divided)
1½ tsp. salt (divided)
1 tsp. paprika
⅛ tsp. pepper
⅓ c. flour
¼ c. bacon drippings or shortening
3½ c. water
¼ tsp. dry mustard
¼ tsp. celery salt

¼ tsp. poultry seasoning
1 medium onion, sliced
Marrow bones (optional)
1 bay leaf
4 parsley sprigs
2 celery stalks (with leaves)
12 small white onions, peeled
6 medium carrots, scraped and halved
3 medium potatoes, pared and halved
2 tsp. Worcestershire sauce

Trim all tallow, cartilage, and sinew from meat; cut meat into 1½ inch pieces. Sprinkle meat with 1½ teaspoons of the monosodium glutamate. Blend together 1 teaspoon of the salt, paprika, and pepper with flour; roll meat in flour mixture. Melt bacon or shortening in a large, deep kettle. Add meat and brown on all sides. Add water, sliced onion, marrow bones, bay leaf, parsley, and celery. Cover; simmer 2 hours, or until meat is tender.

Refrigerate overnight or several hours. Carefully remove all solidified tallow from the stew, blotting around the edges of kettle with paper toweling. Remove marrow bones, bay leaf, parsley, and celery. Add remaining ½ teaspoon monosodium glutamate, and other ingredients; heat to serving temperature. Drop dumplings by spoonfuls (6) on top of pieces of meat or vegetables. Simmer, uncovered, 10 minutes. Cover tightly and cook vegetables until done. Yield: 4 generous servings.

Drop Dumplings:

2 c. sifted, all-purpose flour
3 tsp. baking powder
1 tsp. salt

2 Tbsp. shortening
1 c. milk

Sift together dry ingredients. Cut in shortening to resemble coarse corn meal. Add milk; mix just enough to combine all ingredients.

HIGH-COUNTRY BARBECUED VENISON OR BEEF

5 lb. venison roast or beef rump
    roast
Salt and pepper
½ c. bacon grease or other
    shortening
1 medium clove garlic, minced
3 c. water
1 lb. 2 oz. bottle (2 c.) commercial
    barbecue sauce
1 c. catsup

1 (8 oz.) can tomato sauce
1 tsp. sugar
2 medium onions, coarsely
    chopped
1 c. celery, cut in fairly large pieces
2 green peppers, cut in fairly large
    pieces
3 or 4 drops of liquid red pepper
    (optional)

Season roast with salt and pepper. Brown it on all sides with garlic in bacon grease. (Since fat on meat varies, drain off excess grease, if necessary, leaving about 4 tablespoons in pan.) Add water; bring to boiling point and cook, covered, in oven preheated to 325°F about 3 hours or until done. (Cooking time may vary considerably, depending on toughness of meat.)

Remove roast from pan and cut it into slices about ¼ inch thick. Add remaining ingredients to the drippings, mixing well. Cook, covered, about 1 hour, or until sauce is thickened, in 325° oven. Add meat slices to sauce, and continue to cook about 30 minutes. Serve meat and sauce on split hard rolls if desired.

VENISON STEAK WITH SAUSAGE STUFFING

2 venison round steaks
1 lb. bulk pork sausage
3 green onions, chopped
2 Tbsp. chopped parsley
1 (4 oz.) can mushroom pieces,
    drained

2 Tbsp. uncooked rice
Salt and pepper to taste
1 egg, beaten
½ to 1 c. burgundy wine

Arrange one steak in bottom of greased, oval casserole. Combine sausage, onion, parsley, mushroom pieces, rice, salt, pepper, and egg. Mix well. Spread half of mixture over steak in casserole. Cover with second steak. Spread remaining sauce mixture on top. Carefully pour ½ cup wine around sides of meat. Bake, covered, in oven preheated to 325° for 2 to 3 hours or until meat is tender. If mixture becomes dry, add more wine during latter part of cooking period. Slice so that each serving has four layers. *This is good.*

VENISON SWISS STEAK

2 lb. venison steaks, cut in serving
    pieces
Cooking oil
1 (1⅜ oz.) pkg. dry onion soup mix
2 small bay leaves

2 tsp. packaged spaghetti sauce
    seasoning
Salt and pepper to taste
1 c. burgundy or other red wine
1 (8 oz.) can tomato sauce

Dredge meat in flour. Brown on both sides in small amount of cooking oil. Drain off grease. Combine dry soup mix, spaghetti sauce seasoning, bay leaves, salt, pepper, wine, and tomato sauce. Pour mixture over meat. Bring to boiling point, reduce heat and simmer, covered, about 1 and ½ hours or until meat is tender. If sauce gets too thick during cooking period, add more wine or water.

VENISON MINCEMEAT

4 lb. lean venison
12 cored, chopped fresh winter
    pears
2 lb. raisins
1 lb. currants
1 lb. mixed candied fruits and peels
4 c. brown sugar
Juice of 4 oranges

Juice of 3 lemons
1 Tbsp. celery salt
2 Tbsp. cinnamon
1 Tbsp. nutmeg
1 tsp. cloves
1 Tbsp. allspice
Cider (about 2 qt.)

Boil venison in salted water until very tender. Separate meat from bones and put through food chopper using coarse blade. Combine with remaining ingredients in large kettle, using enough cider to barely cover mixture. Simmer 2 hours to blend flavors. Stir often to prevent sticking. Pack at once into hot pint jars. Adjust lids. Process in pressure canner at 10 pounds pressure for 60 minutes. Or, mincemeat may be frozen. Recommended storage time: 3 months. Yield: 11 pints (or 11 pies).

Note: This is a very rich mincemeat. When making pie, an additional fresh pear may be chopped and stirred into mixture and it may be thinned with fruit juice.

Venison-Mincemeat Pie:

2 pears
Venison Mincemeat

Pastry for double-crust 9 inch pie

To mincemeat, add pears which have been washed, cored, and diced. Pour into pastry-lined pie plate and cover with lattice crust. Bake at 425°F. for 35 to 45 minutes. Serve warm or cold.

136

Breads,
Rolls

MICROWAVE HINTS

1. Place an open box of hardened brown sugar in the microwave oven with 1 cup hot water. Microwave at high for 1½ to 2 minutes for ½ pound or 2 to 3 minutes for 1 pound.
2. Soften hard ice cream by microwaving at 30% power. One pint will take 15 to 30 seconds; one quart, 30 to 45 seconds; and one-half gallon, 45 seconds to one minute.
3. One stick of butter or margarine will soften in 1 minute when microwaved at 20% power.
4. Soften one 8-ounce package of cream cheese by microwaving at 30% power for 2 to 2½ minutes. One 3-ounce package of cream cheese will soften in 1½ to 2 minutes.
5. Thaw frozen orange juice right in the container. Remove the top metal lid. Place the opened container in the microwave and heat on high power 30 seconds for 6 ounces and 45 seconds for 12 ounces.
6. Thaw whipped topping...a 4½ ounce carton will thaw in 1 minute on the defrost setting. Whipped topping should be slightly firm in the center but it will blend well when stirred. Do not overthaw!
7. Soften jello that has set up too hard - perhaps you were to chill it until slightly thickened and forgot it. Heat on a low power setting for a very short time.
8. Dissolve gelatin in the microwave. Measure liquid in a measuring cup, add jello and heat. There will be less stirring to dissolve the gelatin.
9. Heat hot packs in a microwave oven. A wet fingertip towel will take about 25 seconds. It depends on the temperature of the water used to wet the towel.
10. To scald milk, cook 1 cup milk for 2-2½ minutes, stirring once each minute.
11. To make dry bread crumbs, cut 6 slices bread into ½-inch cubes. Microwave in 3-quart casserole 6-7 minutes, or until dry, stirring after 3 minutes. Crush in blender.
12. Refresh stale potato chips, crackers, or other snacks of such type by putting a plateful in the microwave oven for about 30-45 seconds. Let stand for 1 minute to crisp. Cereals can also be crisped.
13. Melt almond bark for candy or dipping pretzels. One pound will take about 2 minutes, stirring twice. If it hardens while dipping candy, microwave for a few seconds longer.
14. Nuts will be easier to shell if you place 2 cups of nuts in a 1-quart casserole with 1 cup of water. Cook for 4 to 5 minutes and the nut meats will slip out whole after cracking the shell.
15. When thawing hamburger meat, the outside will many times begin cooking before the meat is completely thawed. Defrost for 3 minutes, then remove the outside portions that have defrosted. Continue defrosting the hamburger, taking off the defrosted outside portions at short intervals.
16. To drain the fat from hamburger while it is cooking in the microwave oven (one pound cooks in 5 minutes on high), cook it in a plastic colander placed inside a casserole dish.
17. Cubed meat and chopped vegetables will cook more evenly if cut uniformly.
18. When baking large cakes, brownies, or moist bars, place a juice glass in the center of the baking dish to prevent a soggy middle and ensure uniform baking throughout.
19. Since cakes and quick breads rise higher in a microwave oven, fill pans just half full of batter.
20. For stamp collectors: Place a few drops of water on stamp to be removed from envelope. Heat in the microwave for 20 seconds and the stamp will come right off.
21. Using a round dish instead of a square one eliminates overcooked corners in baking cakes.
22. When preparing chicken in a dish, place meaty pieces around the edges and the bony pieces in the center of the dish.
23. Shaping meatloaf into a ring eliminates undercooked center. A glass set in the center of a dish can serve as the mold.
24. Treat fresh meat cuts for 15 to 20 seconds on high in the microwave oven. This cuts down on meat-spoiling types of bacteria.
25. A crusty coating of chopped walnuts surrounding many microwave-cooked cakes and quick breads enhances the looks and eating quality. Sprinkle a layer of medium finely chopped walnuts evenly onto the bottom and sides of a ring pan or Bundt cake pan. Pour in batter and microwave as recipe directs.
26. Do not salt foods on the surface as it causes dehydration (meats and vegetables) and toughens the food. Salt the meat after you remove it from the oven unless the recipe calls for using salt in the mixture.
27. Heat leftover custard and use it as frosting for a cake.
28. Melt marshmallow creme in the microwave oven. Half of a 7-ounce jar will melt in 35-40 seconds on high. Stir to blend.
29. Toast coconut in the microwave. Watch closely because it browns quickly once it begins to brown. Spread ½ cup coconut in a pie plate and cook for 3-4 minutes, stirring every 30 seconds after 2 minutes.
30. Place a cake dish up on another dish or on a roasting rack if you have difficulty getting the bottom of the cake done. This also works for potatoes and other foods that don't quite get done on the bottom.

BREADS, ROLLS

FRENCH BREAD

½ c. warm water
1 tsp. granulated sugar
1½ pkg. dry yeast
3 c. unbleached flour

2 tsp. salt
1 tsp. sugar
1 c. warm water
Corn meal

In half cup warm water, dissolve 1 teaspoon sugar and yeast. Stir until it foams. Place flour, salt, and 1 teaspoon sugar in food processor bowl with steel blade. Turn on processor and mix dry ingredients. With machine still on, add yeast mixture and 1 cup of warm water. Keep the machine on. When a ball forms in about 5 seconds, count to 60 and turn off. Depending on the flour, you may need to add a tablespoon or so of additional flour. Place dough in a greased bowl and allow to rise in a warm place until doubled. Punch down and shape into 2 long loaves. Spray pans with oil and sprinkle with corn meal. Let rise until doubled. Slash top in three diagonal strips. Bake in a 400° oven for 30 minutes. Makes 2 loaves.

BUTTER CRESCENTS

Start the day on a high note with a cup of tea and these melt-in-your-mouth crescents.

Thirty minutes preparation, 1 hour 40 minutes rising and resting, and 15 minutes baking.

½ c. milk
½ c. (1 stick) butter, softened
⅓ c. granulated sugar
½ tsp. salt

1 pkg. active dry yeast
½ c. warm water (105° to 115°F.)
1 large egg, lightly beaten
3½ to 4 c. all-purpose flour

Glaze:

1 large egg, lightly beaten

In a saucepan, heat milk until bubbles appear around edges of pan. Combine butter, sugar, and salt. Add hot milk; stir well. Cool to lukewarm (95° to 100°F.).

In a small bowl, dissolve yeast in warm water. Let stand until foamy, 5 to 10 minutes.

Beat yeast mixture and egg into milk mixture at low speed. Beat in 2 cups of flour at low speed until smooth. Continue beating until thick. Mix in enough remaining flour until dough pulls away from sides of bowl.

On a floured surface, knead dough very gently until smooth and elastic, 2 to 3 minutes. Place in a large greased bowl, turning to coat. Cover loosely with a damp cloth; let rise in a warm place until doubled, 1 hour.

Punch down dough. On a floured surface, divide dough in half. Cover with a damp cloth; let rest for 10 minutes.

Grease 2 baking sheets. Using a floured rolling pin, roll 1 dough half into a 12 inch circle. Cut circle into 6 wedges. Starting at side opposite point, roll up each wedge.

Place, point sides down, on prepared baking sheets. Curve ends to form crescents. Repeat with remaining dough half.

Cover loosely with a damp cloth; let rise in a warm place until almost doubled, 30 minutes.

Preheat oven to 400°F. Brush crescents with glaze. Bake until golden, 15 minutes. Transfer to a wire rack to cool. Makes 1 dozen crescents.

CHERRY BREAD

Cream:

1 c. sugar
¾ c. butter or margarine
3 eggs

1½ tsp. vanilla
½ tsp. almond extract

Sift together:

3 c. flour
1½ tsp. baking soda

½ tsp. salt

Add to creamed mixture alternately with 1½ cups buttermilk.

Stir in:

1½ c. chopped nuts
1 (16 oz.) jar maraschino cherries,
    chopped (save syrup)

Line bottom of loaf pans with wax paper; pour in and bake at 350° for 55 to 60 minutes or until toothpick inserted in center comes out clean. When cool, frost with Cherry Frosting. Makes 2 regular loaves.

Cherry Frosting - Combine:

2 c. powdered sugar

2 Tbsp. melted butter

Add maraschino juice until right spreading consistency and red food coloring if desired.

FOOTHILLS BEER BREAD

3 c. self-rising flour
2 Tbsp. sugar

1 (12 oz.) bottle beer (room
    temperature)

Mix all ingredients until wet. Place in greased bread pan. Bake 1½ hours in 350° oven. Makes 1 loaf.

GOLDEN CHEESE BREAD

1 c. Cheddar cheese, grated
1 c. Monterey Jack cheese, grated
1 c. mayonnaise
1 bunch green onions, chopped

⅛ tsp. garlic powder
Dash of seasoned salt
1 loaf thin French bread

138

Mix everything together in a bowl. Slice bread lengthwise and butter. Put half of cheese mixture on each half of bread. Wrap in foil and bake in 400° oven for 15 to 20 minutes. Slice thin for hors d'oeuvres or serve with chili or stew or etc.

PRESIDENT'S REFRIGERATOR BRAN MUFFINS

1½ c. sugar
½ c. solid shortening
2 eggs
2½ c. unsifted flour
2½ tsp. baking soda
½ tsp. salt

2 c. buttermilk
1 c. boiling water
1 c. 100% Bran ready to eat cereal
¾ c. seedless raisins
2 c. All-Bran ready to eat cereal

Cream sugar and shortening. Add eggs, one at a time, mixing well after each addition. Add flour, soda, salt, and buttermilk, mixing until smooth. Pour boiling water over 100% Bran cereal and let stand until cereal has absorbed water and has cooled slightly. Blend this mixture into batter. Add raisins and All-Bran cereal, mixing thoroughly. Cover and refrigerate. When ready to bake, spoon batter, without stirring, into greased muffin tins. Bake at 400° for 20 minutes.

Note: Batter may be stored in refrigerator for 5 weeks.

WHOLE WHEAT BRAN BREAD

1½ c. wheat bran or wheat germ
2½ c. whole wheat flour
1 tsp. salt
1½ tsp. baking soda

¼ c. dark brown sugar
2 c. buttermilk
½ c. molasses
1 c. raisins (optional)

Combine dry ingredients. Add milk and molasses. Stir just until mixed well. Pour into greased and floured loaf pan. Bake at 350° for 1 hour and 10 minutes.

"QUICKLY" ORANGE BREAD

¾ c. sugar
½ c. chopped pecans
1 Tbsp. grated orange rind
2 (12 oz.) cans refrigerated
    buttermilk biscuits

1 (3 oz.) cream cheese, cut into 20
    pieces
½ c. butter
1 c. sifted powdered sugar
2 Tbsp. orange juice

Combine the sugar, pecans, and orange rind in bowl and set aside. Separate biscuits; gently separate biscuits in halves. Place a cream cheese piece between the 2 halves; pinch sides to seal. Dip in butter and dredge in the reserved sugar mixture. Stand biscuits on edge in a lightly greased 12 cup Bundt pan, spacing evenly.

Drizzle with remaining butter and sprinkle with remaining sugar mixture. Bake at 350° for 45 minutes or until golden brown. Immediately invert onto serving plate. Combine the powdered sugar and orange juice; drizzle over warm bread. Serve immediately. Great with your morning coffee!

TWIN PEAKS STRAWBERRY BREAD

2 (10 oz.) pkg. frozen strawberries
4 eggs
1¼ c. salad oil
3 c. flour
2 c. sugar

3 tsp. cinnamon
1 tsp. baking soda
1 tsp. salt
1 c. chopped nuts

Grease and flour pans. Stir thawed strawberries, eggs, and oil. In large bowl, combine flour, sugar, and rest of ingredients. Mix well. Add strawberry mixture to dry ingredients and stir until blended. Pour into pans and bake. Bake at 350° for 1 hour in two 9x5 inch loaf pans.

VERY LEMON BREAD

⅓ c. butter, melted
1 c. sugar
3 Tbsp. lemon extract
2 eggs
1½ c. flour

1 tsp. salt
1 tsp. baking powder
½ c. milk
1½ Tbsp. grated lemon rind
½ c. pecans, chopped

Sift together flour, salt, and baking powder. Mix butter, sugar, and extract. Beat eggs into batter. Add dry ingredients alternately with milk, beating just enough to blend. Stir in lemon rind and pecans. Pour into a greased loaf pan. Bake at 350° for 1 hour or until toothpick comes out clean. Cool 10 minutes; remove bread from pan and while still warm, drizzle Lemon Glaze over top and into cracks formed while baking. Store, foil wrapped, for 1 day before slicing.

Lemon Glaze:

¼ c. lemon juice

½ c. sugar

Mix until sugar is dissolved.

ZUCCHINI PINEAPPLE BREAD

3 eggs
2 c. sugar
2 tsp. vanilla
2 c. ground zucchini
1 c. oil
3 c. flour
1 tsp. baking powder

1 tsp. baking soda
1 tsp. salt
1 c. or 15½ oz. can crushed
    pineapple, drained
½ c. raisins
1 c. walnuts or pecans, chopped

In large bowl, add eggs, sugar, vanilla, zucchini, and oil. Mix well. Sift together and add flour, baking powder, baking soda, and salt. Add pineapple, raisins, and nuts. Mix and pour into 3 greased and floured loaf pans and bake at 350° for 45 to 50 minutes. If using 2 large pans, bake 1 hour.

BLUEBERRY-ORANGE NUT BREAD

A beautiful bread that's even better with Orange Butter.

3 c. sifted flour
¾ c. sugar
3 tsp. baking powder
¼ tsp. baking soda
1 tsp. salt
3 eggs

½ c. milk
½ c. butter or margarine, melted
1 Tbsp. grated orange peel
⅔ c. orange juice
1 c. fresh or frozen blueberries
½ c. chopped walnuts

Sift together dry ingredients. Beat together eggs, milk, butter, orange peel, and juice. Stir liquid ingredients into dry ingredients just until moistened. Fold in berries and nuts. Pour into a greased 9x5x3 inch loaf pan and bake at 350° for 55 to 65 minutes. Cool slightly; remove from pan, then cool completely on rack. Wrap tightly to store. Slice and serve with Orange Butter if desired. Makes 1 loaf.

Orange Butter (optional):

½ c. butter or margarine, softened
2 Tbsp. frozen orange juice
    concentrate, thawed

1 Tbsp. powdered sugar

For Orange Butter: Beat butter with mixer until fluffy, then gradually beat in orange juice and sugar.

CHOCOLATE CHIP FRUIT BREAD

½ c. butter or margarine
1 c. sugar
2 eggs
2 c. flour
1 tsp. baking soda
¼ tsp. salt

1 c. mashed ripe banana
¼ c. chopped maraschino cherries
⅓ c. semi-sweet chocolate chips
    (miniature chips preferred)
¼ c. chopped nuts
Powdered sugar glaze (optional)

Cream butter and sugar. Add eggs and beat well. Add flour, baking soda, and salt alternately with banana to egg mixture. Mix in cherries, chocolate chips, and nuts. Pour into greased 4½ x 8½ inch loaf pan and bake at 350° about 60 minutes or until done. If desired, while bread is warm, drizzle with powdered sugar glaze. Can be frozen. Makes 1 loaf.

POPPY SEED BREAD

1 c. sugar
2 eggs
1 c. evaporated milk
1 c. cooking oil
2 c. unsifted flour

2 tsp. baking powder
¼ tsp. salt
1 tsp. vanilla
¼ c. poppy seeds

Mix sugar, eggs, evaporated milk, and cooking oil until blended. Sift together flour, baking powder, and salt and add. Add vanilla and poppy seeds. Bake at 375°; for 4 small loaf pans, 40 to 45 minutes, for 2 bread pans, bake 1 hour. *A delicious old favorite!*

ROCKY FORD PUMPKIN BREAD

2⅔ c. sugar
⅔ c. shortening or 11 Tbsp.
   margarine
4 eggs
2 c. canned pumpkin
3⅓ c. flour, sifted
2 tsp. soda
1 tsp. cinnamon

1 tsp. nutmeg
½ tsp. baking powder
¼ tsp. salt
1 c. pecans or walnuts, finely
   chopped
1 c. raisins
½ c. water

Beat sugar and shortening until creamy. Add eggs, one at a time, until well blended. Add pumpkin. In another bowl, mix sifted flour, soda, baking powder, cinnamon, nutmeg, and salt. Alternate adding flour mixture and water into sugar mixture. Mix raisins and nuts with 1 tablespoon flour and add to batter, blending well. Pour into 2 greased loaf pans and bake at 350° for 1 hour. If using foil pans, 3 are needed. *This is another old family recipe!*

APRICOT BREAD

1 c. dried apricots
¾ c. cold water
Juice of ½ lemon
½ c. shortening
1 c. sugar

2 eggs
2 c. flour
½ tsp. salt
¾ tsp. soda

Dice apricots and add to cold water and bring to a boil. Set aside. Add the lemon juice and let cool. Cream shortening and sugar. Add eggs, then apricots. Sift dry ingredients together, combine and mix until blended only. Bake at 350° for 1 hour in loaf pan.

GRAPE-NUT BREAD

3 tsp. shortening, melted
1½ c. Grape-Nuts cereal
1 c. sour milk
1 c. sugar
2 c. flour (unsifted)

1 tsp. baking powder
½ tsp. baking soda
⅛ tsp. salt
1 egg

Grease loaf pan. Soak Grape-Nuts in milk for 10 minutes. Mix in remaining ingredients, except egg. Add egg, well beaten. Pour into loaf pan. Bake at 350° for 1 hour.

Sour milk: Milk mixed with 1 tablespoon vinegar.

DATE-NUT BREAD

1 (10 oz.) pkg. pitted dates
1 c. boiling water
½ c. sugar
1 tsp. baking soda
½ tsp. salt
1 tsp. baking powder

1 large egg, beaten
1 tsp. vanilla
½ to 1 c. walnuts, chopped, or 1 c.
   whole pecans
2 c. unsifted all-purpose flour

Cut dates into coarse pieces with kitchen scissors dipped in water if necessary. Place dates in large mixing bowl. Cover with boiling water. Let stand until dates are soft and mixture is completely cool. Add sugar, baking soda, salt, baking powder, egg, vanilla, and nuts. Add flour, mixing well by hand or with mixer.

Spoon batter into greased and floured loaf pan, 9x5 inches. Bake in preheated 325° oven 55 minutes to 1 hour or until wooden pick inserted in center comes out clean. If whole pecans are used, bread will take slightly longer to bake. Cool slightly in pan, then turn out onto wire rack and cool completely.

Best if refrigerated overnight before slicing. Slice with very sharp knife. Bread freezes nicely. Makes 1 large loaf.

AVOCADO-CINNAMON LOAF

¾ c. shortening, butter, or
   margarine
2 c. minus 2 Tbsp. sugar
3 extra large eggs
2 c. unsifted flour
3 tsp. cinnamon
¾ tsp. salt
¾ tsp. allspice

1½ tsp. soda
¾ c. plus 2 Tbsp. buttermilk
2 tsp. vanilla
1½ c. large, ripe avocados,
   thoroughly mashed
½ c. chopped walnuts
¾ c. raisins
Corn syrup (optional)

Cream together shortening and sugar until light and fluffy. Add eggs, one at a time, beating well after each addition. Sift together flour, cinnamon, salt, allspice, and soda. Add dry ingredients alternately with buttermilk and vanilla to egg mixture. Add avocado, nuts, and raisins. Mix well. Spoon batter into two greased 8½ x 4½ inch pans. Bake in preheated 375° oven 45 minutes or until wood pick in center comes out clean. Cool in pans about 15 minutes. Invert loaves on wire rack. If desired, brush top of loaves with corn syrup and sprinkle with additional chopped nuts, pressing it into cake with fingertips. If topping is used, place loaves under broiler until bubbly. Loaves freeze nicely. Makes 2 loaves.

APRICOT ROLLS

1 lb. creamed cottage cheese
3½ c. flour (about)

1 lb. butter or margarine

Blend ingredients with hands to form a dough. Add more flour if too soft. If cheese is watery, drain. Shape into 1 inch balls and refrigerate overnight. Dough may be kept under refrigeration for a week. May be frozen in balls.

Filling:

2 c. sugar (approx.)

1 lb. dried apricots

Cook apricots until tender in just enough water to cover; drain and puree. Add sugar while still hot. Cool.

Coating:

1½ c. ground almonds or pecans
2 egg whites, slightly beaten with 2
   Tbsp. water

1¼ c. powdered sugar

Mix nuts with sugar. Roll each dough ball into a 3 inch round (make only 10 at a time so dough will remain cold). Place ¼ to ½ teaspoon of apricot mixture in center. Roll up and pinch closed envelope fashion. Dip into egg white and then roll in nut-sugar mixture. Place on a greased baking sheet. Bake at 375° for 12 minutes or until lightly browned. May be sprinkled with powdered sugar. May be frozen and reheated. Yield: About 7 dozen.

COCOANUT CRUNCH BRUNCH CAKE

Cake:

1 pkg. yellow cake mix (reserve ⅓
    c. for topping)
¾ c. water

⅓ c. oil
2 eggs

Heat oven to 350°. Grease and flour a 9x13 inch Pyrex pan. Blend ingredients for 2 minutes. Pour in pan.

Topping:

2 Tbsp. softened margarine
⅓ c. cake mix
¼ c. firmly packed brown sugar

½ tsp. cinnamon
½ c. cocoanut
⅓ c. chopped pecans

Combine all items and sprinkle 1 cup over batter and swirl into cake batter. Sprinkle remaining topping on top. Bake at 350° for 25 to 30 minutes or until light golden brown.

Glaze: Combine ½ cup powdered sugar, ¼ teaspoon vanilla, and 3 to 4 teaspoons milk and drizzle over warm coffee cake. Serves 10 to 12.

CRANBERRY COFFEE CAKE

1½ c. sifted flour
½ c. sugar
2 tsp. baking powder
1 tsp. salt
½ tsp. baking soda
½ c. chopped walnuts
1 ripe banana, mashed (½ c.)

½ c. milk
1 egg, beaten
¼ c. melted shortening
1 (8 oz.) can jellied cranberry sauce
Pecan halves
¼ c. sugar

Sift together dry ingredients. Stir in walnuts. Combine banana, milk, egg, and shortening; add to flour mixture. Stir to blend. Pour into greased 9x9x2 inch baking pan. Cut jellied cranberry sauce into 4 slices, then into quarters. Arrange on top of batter with a pecan half on each wedge. Sprinkle ¼ cup sugar over all. Bake at 400° for 25 to 30 minutes.

BROADWAY BLUEBERRY COFFEE CAKE

1 large egg
½ c. skim milk
½ c. plain nonfat yogurt
3 Tbsp. vegetable oil
1½ c. fresh blueberries, rinsed and patted dry or frozen unsweetened blueberries

2 c. all-purpose flour
½ c. sugar
4 tsp. baking powder
½ tsp. salt

Topping:

3 Tbsp. sugar
2 Tbsp. chopped walnuts

¼ tsp. cinnamon

Preheat oven to 400°. Coat the inside of an 8 inch square baking pan with nonstick cooking spray. In a large mixing bowl, whisk together egg, milk, yogurt, and oil. Set a sieve on top of the bowl and measure flour, sugar, baking powder, and salt into it. Stir the dry ingredients together while sifting into the liquid mixture. Stir the batter just to blend. Do not overbeat. Fold in blueberries. Turn the batter into the prepared pan.

In a small bowl, stir together sugar, walnuts, and cinnamon; sprinkle over the batter. Bake for 20 to 25 minutes or until the top is golden brown and a tester comes out clean. Let cool in the pan for 10 minutes. Cut into squares and serve warm. Serves 9.

GRANDMA'S KENTUCKY SPOON CORN BREAD

1 pt. milk
½ c. corn meal
3 eggs, beaten separately

½ tsp. salt
½ c. butter

Cook milk, corn meal, and salt for 5 minutes. Add butter and yolks of eggs. Cool 25 minutes. Fold in stiffly beaten egg whites. Pour into buttered baking dish. Bake at 400° for 25 minutes. Serve immediately with spoon.

FILLED CRESCENT ROLLS

Use 1 package crescent rolls.

Filling:

½ c. sour cream or 8 oz. cream cheese
¼ tsp. oregano (generous)

¼ tsp. basil (generous)
½ c. chives (generous)
¼ tsp. dill (optional)

Mix filling and set several hours. Keep at room temperature. Separate crescent rolls and spread mixture on just before baking. Bake as per instructions on crescent roll can.

HEALTHY APPLE-WALNUT MUFFINS

Made with no added fat or sugar, these tasty muffins use fruit and buttermilk to keep them moist.

Fifteen minutes preparation, 25 minutes baking.

2 c. all-purpose flour
1 tsp. baking soda
¼ tsp. ground cinnamon
¼ tsp. ground ginger
¼ tsp. ground allspice
¼ tsp. ground nutmeg
¼ rounded tsp. salt
2 large eggs
1 c. plus 2 Tbsp. frozen, thawed
   apple juice concentrate

⅔ c. buttermilk
2 Tbsp. oat bran
2 small Granny Smith apples,
   peeled, cored, and chopped
⅓ c. chopped walnuts (about 1⅓
   oz.)
1 small Granny Smith apple, peeled,
   cored, and cut into 12 thin
   slices (garnish)

Preheat oven to 375°F. Grease 12 standard size muffin pan cups or line with paper liners.

Mix together flour, baking soda, cinnamon, ginger, allspice, nutmeg, and salt. Mix together eggs, apple juice, and buttermilk. Stir flour mixture and oat bran into egg mixture until dry ingredients are just moistened. Do not overmix. Gently stir in chopped apples and nuts.

Spoon batter into prepared pan, filing cups ⅔ full. Garnish each muffin with an apple slice. Bake muffins until lightly golden and tops spring back when pressed, 25 minutes. Transfer pan to a wire rack to cool slightly. Turn muffins out onto rack to cool completely. Makes 12 muffins.

POPPY SEED MUFFINS

2 c. flour
¼ c. poppy seeds
½ tsp. salt
¼ tsp. baking soda
½ c. softened butter

¾ c. sugar
2 eggs
¾ c. sour cream
1½ tsp. vanilla

Combine flour, poppy seed, salt, and baking soda. In mixer cream butter and sugar until light. Beat in eggs, one at a time. Blend in sour cream and vanilla. Beat in dry ingredients. Spoon batter into 12 greased muffin tins. Bake at 375° for 20 minutes. Cool 5 minutes.

MINI LEMON NUTMEG MUFFINS

1 pkg. Pillsbury nut or date quick
   bread mix
1 c. milk
¼ c. oil

1 egg
1 tsp. grated lemon peel
½ tsp. nutmeg

Glaze:

½ c. sugar
1 Tbsp. lemon juice

1 Tbsp. water
¼ tsp. almond extract

Heat oven to 375°. Generously grease bottoms only of 44 mini muffin cups or line with mini paper baking cups. In large bowl, combine all muffin ingredients; stir 50 to 75 strokes until dry particles are moistened. Bake at 375° for 10 to 15 minutes. Combine glaze ingredients. Dip tops of muffins in glaze while muffins are warm.

BEER MUFFINS

3 c. Bisquick
1 Tbsp. sugar
10 oz. beer

1 pkg. onion soup
½ c. Parmesan cheese (shaker can)

Mix all ingredients together. Batter will be lumpy. Grease 12 muffin tins or spray paper muffin cups with baking spray. Bake at 425° until brown, about 15 minutes.

SWEET POTATO BISCUITS

2 c. flour
¾ tsp. salt
1 Tbsp. baking powder
½ c. shortening

⅔ c. milk
¼ c. sugar
1 c. cooked sweet potatoes, mashed

Sift together dry ingredients. Cut in fat until mixture looks like coarse meal, then cut in sweet potatoes. Add milk. Mix quickly with a fork or pastry blender to form a soft dough and until all of the flour is dampened. Turn out on a floured board; knead lightly and roll to about ½ inch thick. Cut with a floured biscuit cutter. Place in an ungreased pan and bake in a hot oven 450°F. for 10 to 12 minutes. Makes 18 medium biscuits.

ORANGE-GLAZE COFFEE CAKE

Light and refreshing, this cake doubles the flavor and fragrance of fresh orange.

Forty five minutes preparation, 2 hours rising, and 25 to 30 minutes baking.

1 pkg. active dry yeast
¼ c. warm water (105° to 115°F.)
½ c. warm milk (105° to 115°F.)
½ c. fresh orange juice
½ c. granulated sugar
½ c. Ricotta cheese

1 Tbsp. grated orange zest
½ tsp. salt
1 large egg, lightly beaten
3½ to 4 c. all-purpose flour
1 large egg, lightly beaten (glaze)

Icing:

1 c. confectioners sugar

1½ to 2 Tbsp. fresh orange juice

In a large bowl, dissolve yeast in warm water. Let stand until foamy, 5 to 10 minutes.

Stir the warm milk, orange juice, sugar, Ricotta cheese, orange zest, salt, and egg into the yeast mixture.

Using heavy-duty electric mixer fitted with the paddle attachment and set on low speed, beat 2 cups flour into the yeast mixture until a wet dough forms. Beat in the remaining flour, ½ cup at a time, until a stiff dough forms.

Turn dough out onto a lightly floured surface and knead until smooth and elastic, 5 to 10 minutes, adding more flour as needed to prevent sticking.

Place the dough in a large greased bowl, turning to coat. Cover loosely with a damp cloth and let rise in a warm place until doubled, about 1½ hours.

Grease a 10 inch springform pan. Punch down the dough. Turn out onto a lightly floured surface and knead for 1 to 2 minutes.

Divide the dough into 3 equal pieces. Roll each piece into a 20 inch long rope. Braid the ropes together.

Coil braided dough in prepared pan; tuck ends under. Cover loosely with a damp cloth and let rise in a warm place until almost doubled, 30 minutes.

Preheat oven to 425°F. Brush the dough with glaze. Bake until the top of the cake is golden brown, 25 to 30 minutes. Turn the cake out onto a wire rack to cool slightly. Makes 12 servings.

To prepare icing, in a small bowl, stir together confectioners sugar and orange juice until smooth. Spread icing over warm cake. Serve warm.

CHERRY STRUDEL

This old-world favorite gets a quick and easy update from ready-made phyllo pastry.

Thirty minutes preparation, 15 to 20 minutes baking.

Filling:

1¼ c. granulated sugar	**⅓ c. water**
½ c. firmly packed light brown sugar	**2 tsp. grated lemon or orange zest**
1½ Tbsp. cornstarch	**½ tsp. vanilla or almond extract**
4 c. pitted, tart, fresh or frozen, thawed cherries	**¼ tsp. ground allspice**
	⅛ tsp. ground cinnamon

Pastry:

8 sheets phyllo pastry (thawed if frozen)	**3 Tbsp. butter, melted**

Topping: Use 1 tablespoon confectioners sugar.

To prepare filling, in a medium saucepan, mix together granulated sugar, brown sugar, and cornstarch. Stir in cherries, water, lemon zest, and vanilla. Cook over medium heat until bubbling and thickened.

Reduce heat to low; add allspice and cinnamon and cook, stirring occasionally, for 15 minutes. Remove pan from heat. Cool completely. Preheat oven to 400°F. Grease a baking sheet.

To prepare pastry, unfold sheets of phyllo so they lie flat. Stack 4 sheets on plastic wrap. Brush top sheet with 1 tablespoon melted butter. Keep remaining sheets covered with plastic wrap and a damp cloth to prevent them drying out.

Spread half filling along a short side of top pastry sheet. Starting with short side and using plastic wrap as a guide, roll up pastry, jellyroll style. Fold ends under.

Place strudel, seam side down, on prepared baking sheet. Brush with ½ tablespoon melted butter. Repeat with remaining phyllo, melted butter, and filling to make second strudel.

Bake until golden, 15 to 20 minutes. Transfer baking sheet to a wire rack to cool for 15 minutes. Transfer strudel to a cutting board to cool completely. Sprinkle with confectioners sugar. Makes 10 servings.

BAKED FRENCH TOAST WITH ALMOND SYRUP

Everyone can be served at the same time.

½ c. butter or margarine, melted
(divided)
7 eggs, beaten
⅔ c. milk

¼ c. brown sugar
1 (16 oz.) loaf French bread, cut into
slices (16 (¾ inch) slices)
Almond Syrup

Divide ¼ cup of the melted butter evenly into two 15x10x1 inch jellyroll pans and spread over entire bottom of pans. Combine the remaining ¼ cup butter, eggs, milk, and brown sugar. Mix well. Dip slices of bread into egg mixture, coating well. Arrange on pans. Allow to set at least 15 minutes. Drizzle any remaining egg mixture over slices that look dry.

Bake in preheated 450° oven about 18 to 20 minutes, turning once after about 10 minutes. Serve with Almond Syrup or maple syrup if desired. Makes 8 servings of 2 slices each.

Almond Syrup:

2 Tbsp. butter or margarine
½ c. sliced or slivered almonds
1½ c. light brown sugar

½ c. water
¼ tsp. almond extract

Melt butter in a small saucepan; add almonds and saute over medium heat until golden (watch carefully so almonds don't burn). Stir in sugar, water, and almond extract and continue stirring until sugar is dissolved. Simmer 2 to 3 minutes. Serve warm. Makes 1½ cups.

CRANBERRY-GLAZED STUFFED FRENCH TOAST

Glaze:

1¼ c. firmly packed brown sugar
½ c. butter or margarine
2 Tbsp. light corn syrup

1 (12 oz.) pkg. cran-fruit cranberry-
raspberry crushed fruit

Egg mixture:

1 c. milk
1 c. light cream
6 eggs

1 tsp. vanilla
¼ tsp. salt

Filling:

2 (3 oz.) pkg. cream cheese,
softened
1 c. chopped walnuts or pecans

1 (16 oz.) loaf French bread (3 to 4
inches wide), cut into 1 inch
slices

Grease a 13x9 inch baking pan. For glaze, combine brown sugar, butter or margarine, and corn syrup in a medium saucepan. Bring to a boil, stirring frequently. Reduce heat and simmer 2 minutes, stirring occasionally. Stir in crushed fruit. Immediately pour into prepared pan. Set aside.

Combine all egg mixture ingredients in a large mixing bowl. Beat using an electric mixer or wire whisk until well blended. Set aside.

Combine filling ingredients in a small bowl. Spread 1 side of each slice with about 1 tablespoon filling. Place each slice vertically on top of glaze, top crust down, forming 2 rows. Pour egg mixture evenly over bread. Cover and refrigerate 8 to 10 hours.

Preheat oven to 350°. Bake, covered, for about 1 hour and 10 minutes or until set. Let stand 5 minutes; invert onto a serving platter or jellyroll pan. Makes 10 servings.

CHEESE-STUFFED FRENCH TOAST WITH STRAWBERRY SAUCE

12 (1 oz.) diagonally cut slices French bread
¼ c. sifted powdered sugar
1 (8 oz.) tub reduced-fat cream cheese
2½ c. 1% lowfat milk
⅓ c. sugar

½ tsp. vanilla extract
4 egg whites
2 eggs
Vegetable cooking spray
Strawberry Sauce
Candied Lemon Rind

Cut a horizontal slit through bottom crust of each slice of bread to form a pocket. Combine powdered sugar and cream cheese; stir well. Spread mixture evenly into pockets of bread. Place 6 bread slices in each of two large, shallow baking dishes; set aside.

Combine milk, sugar, vanilla extract, egg whites, and eggs in a bowl; beat well with a wire whisk. Pour milk mixture evenly over bread slices. Cover and chill 1 hour or until liquid is absorbed.

Coat a large nonstick skillet with cooking spray and place over medium heat until hot. Arrange half of bread slices in skillet, and cook 3 minutes. Turn bread over and cook 3 minutes or until browned; remove from skillet. Repeat procedure with the remaining bread slices.

Serve with Strawberry Sauce and garnish with Candied Lemon Rind. Yield: 6 servings (serving size 2 slices toast and ½ cup sauce).

Calories 517 (19% from fat); Protein 17.8 g; Fat 10.9 g (sat 5.4 g, mono 3.9 g, poly 1.2 g); Carb 89.5 g; Fiber 4 g; Chol 101 mg; Iron 2.2 mg; Sodium 653; Calc 242 mg.

Strawberry Sauce:

4 c. sliced strawberries
⅓ c. honey

3 Tbsp. fresh lemon juice

Combine all ingredients in a bowl; stir well. Cover and let stand 1 hour. Yield: 3 cups (serving size ½ cup).

Candied Lemon Rind:

1 large lemon
¼ c. sugar (divided)

1 Tbsp. water

Using a vegetable peeler, carefully remove rind from lemon. Cut rind into ⅛ inch thick strips; set aside.

Combine 2 tablespoons sugar and water in a 2 cup glass measure. Microwave at HIGH 1 minute; stir in rind strips. Microwave at HIGH 2 minutes, stirring every 30 seconds. Add remaining 2 tablespoons sugar and toss well. Spread rind in a single layer on wax paper; let stand at room temperature until dry. Store in an airtight container. Yield: ¼ cup.

GOLDEN BEER PANCAKES

3 c. sifted flour
3 tsp. baking powder
¾ tsp. salt
1 Tbsp. sugar

2 eggs, separated
1 c. beer
1½ c. milk
⅓ c. melted butter or oil

Sift together flour, baking powder, salt, and sugar. Beat egg yolks with fork. Stir in beer, milk, and butter and add to the dry ingredients. Beat until smooth. Beat egg whites until stiff. Fold into the batter.

Heat griddle, grease lightly and drop spoonfuls of batter onto griddle. Bake until batter rises and entire surface is dotted with holes. Turn and bake the second side. Serve hot with maple syrup. Makes about 24 pancakes.

ZUCCHINI PANCAKES

3 c. coarsely grated zucchini
1 egg, lightly beaten
Pinch of nutmeg
Salt and freshly ground pepper

½ c. all-purpose flour
1 tsp. baking powder
Oil
Parmesan cheese (garnish)

Combine zucchini and egg and mix well. Add nutmeg, salt, and pepper to taste. Sift flour and baking powder over mixture and blend thoroughly. Place large skillet over medium-high heat or heat griddle. Oil lightly. Use ¼ cup batter for each pancake and cook until lightly golden, turning once. Transfer to platter and sprinkle with Parmesan. Makes 4 servings.

CHEESE CROISSANT "al" ORANGE

2 Tbsp. butter
2 Tbsp. sugar
1½ tsp. cornstarch
½ c. orange juice
1 c. Ricotta cheese (8 oz.)

1 (8 oz.) orange flavored yogurt (1 c.)
1 (11 oz.) can mandarin oranges, drained
4 croissants

Melt butter. Add sugar and cornstarch to orange juice. Add to butter. Cook until thick, stirring constantly. Cool. Stir together cheese and yogurt. Fold in orange sections. Split croissants. Divide cheese among croissants and spoon sauce over each. Makes four large servings. Use small croissants for 8 servings. *Great breakfast!*

Notes

Desserts

Common Baking Dishes and Pans

Spring Form Pan

Layer Cake or Pie Pan

Ring Mold

Baking or Square Pan

Loaf Pan

Brioche Pan

Angel Cake Pan

Bundt Tube

Equivalent Dishes

4-CUP BAKING DISH
= 9″ pie plate
= 8″ x $1^1 4$″ layer cake pan
= $7^3 8$″ x $3^5 8$″ x $2^1 4$″ loaf pan

6-CUP BAKING DISH
= 8″ or 9″ x $1^1 2$″ layer cake pan
= 10″ pie pan
= $8^1 2$″ x $3^5 8$″ x $2^5 8$″ loaf pan

8-CUP BAKING DISH
= 8″ x 8″ x 2″ square pan
= 11″ x 7″ x $1^1 2$″ baking pan
= 9″ x 5″ x 3″ loaf pan

10-CUP BAKING DISH
= 9″ x 9″ x 2″ square pan
= $11^3 4$″ x $7^1 2$″ x $1^3 4$″ baking pan
= 15″ x 10″ x 1″ flat jelly roll pan

12-CUP BAKING DISH OR MORE
= $13^1 2$″ x $8^1 2$″ x 2″ glass baking dish
= 13″ x 9″ x 2″ metal baking pan
= 14″ x $10^1 2$″ x $2^1 2$″ roasting pan

Total Volume of Pans

TUBE PANS

$7^1 2$″ x 3″ Bundt tube	6 cups
9″ x $3^1 2$″ fancy or Bundt tube	9 cups
9″ x $3^1 2$″ angel cake pan	12 cups
10″ x $3^3 4$″ Bundt tube	12 cups
9″ x $3^1 2$″ fancy tube mold	12 cups
10″ x 4″ fancy tube mold	16 cups
10″ x 4″ angel cake pan	18 cups

SPRING FORM PANS

8″ x 3″ pan	12 cups
9″ x 3″ pan	16 cups

RING MOLDS

$8^1 2$″ x $2^1 4$″ mold	$4^1 2$ cups
$9^1 4$″ x $2^3 4$″ mold	8 cups

BRIOCHE PAN

$9^1 2$″ x $3^1 4$″ pan	8 cups

DESSERTS

KAHLUA TIRAMISU FOR TWO

12 small packaged ladyfingers
2 egg yolks
½ c. powdered sugar
4 oz. softened cream cheese, beaten
    until fluffy
⅓ c. whipping cream, whipped

½ tsp. instant espresso powder
1 Tbsp. water
¼ c. Kahlua
1 oz. semi-sweet chocolate,
    chopped finely
2 tsp. unsweetened cocoa powder

Place ladyfingers on baking sheet; toast at 325°F. for 10 minutes. Whisk yolks with powdered sugar until smooth and thick. Whisk in cream cheese. Fold in whipped cream. Dissolve espresso in water and Kahlua. Combine chopped chocolate and cocoa. Place 2 tablespoons cheese mixture in bottom of each (2 liter) 12 ounce wine glasses. Top each with 3 ladyfingers; sprinkle with 3 to 4 teaspoons Kahlua mixture. Top with ⅓ cup cheese mixture and sprinkle with ¼ chocolate mixture. Arrange 3 ladyfingers over chocolate; sprinkle more Kahlua and top each with half of remaining cheese mixture. Sprinkle with remaining chocolate. Chill, covered, several hours or overnight. Serves 2.

STRAWBERRY TIRAMISU

¾ lb. Mascarpone cheese (1½ c. at
    room temperature)*
3 Tbsp. confectioners sugar
3 Tbsp. orange flavored liqueur
1½ c. heavy cream

1 pt. strawberries, rinsed and hulled
¼ c. granulated sugar
¼ c. orange juice
24 sponge ladyfingers

In medium bowl, whisk Mascarpone cheese, confectioners sugar, and 1 tablespoon of the orange liqueur until well blended.

In large chilled bowl with electric mixer at medium speed, beat heavy cream until soft peaks form; gently fold whipped cream into Mascarpone mixture until blended. In blender or food processor, blend together remaining liqueur, the strawberries, granulated sugar, and orange juice to a smooth puree. Pour strawberries mixture into shallow bowl.

Dip 12 ladyfingers in strawberry mixture to coat; arrange in a 9 inch square glass dish, side by side, in 2 rows of six, rows touching. Spread ½ cup of the strawberry mixture evenly over rows. Spread half of the cream mixture on top. Repeat with remaining ladyfingers; arrange over cream layer. Spread with remaining strawberry mixture. Spread with remaining cream, smoothing top with spatula. Cover and refrigerate at least 8 hours or overnight.

To serve, cut into 9 squares. Place on dessert plates and dust each with cocoa powder and top with a sliced fanned strawberry.

* If Mascarpone cheese is unavailable, puree in blender or food processor 2 tablespoons of the heavy cream with 1¼ cups Ricotta cheese, 3 tablespoons softened cream cheese, and 1 teaspoon fresh lemon juice until smooth.

Guaranteed rave reviews from guests.

TRIPLE-CHOCOLATE CHEESECAKE

This tastes like a creamy frozen fudge pop.

¼ c. sugar
1 Tbsp. stick margarine
1 Tbsp. egg white
1⅓ c. chocolate graham cracker
  crumbs (about 16 crackers)
Vegetable cooking spray
3 Tbsp. dark rum
3 (1 oz.) sq. semi-sweet chocolate
¼ c. chocolate syrup
1 (8 oz.) block nonfat cream cheese,
  softened

1 (8 oz.) block Neufchatel cheese,
  softened
1 c. sugar
2 Tbsp. unsweetened cocoa
1 tsp. vanilla extract
¼ tsp. salt
2 eggs
½ c. lowfat sour cream
1 Tbsp. sugar
2 tsp. unsweetened cocoa
Chocolate curls (optional)

Preheat oven to 350°. Place first 3 ingredients in a bowl; beat at medium speed of a mixer until blended. Add crumbs; stir well. Firmly press mixture into bottom and 1 inch up sides of an 8 inch springform pan coated with cooking spray. Bake at 350° for 10 minutes; let cool on a wire rack.

Combine rum and chocolate squares in the top of a double boiler. Cook over simmering water 2 minutes or until chocolate melts, stirring frequently. Remove from heat; add chocolate syrup, stirring until smooth.

Preheat oven to 300°. Place cheeses in a large bowl; beat at medium speed of a mixer until smooth. Add 1 cup sugar, 2 tablespoons cocoa, vanilla, and salt; beat until smooth. Add rum mixture; beat at low speed until well blended. Add eggs, 1 at a time, beating well after each addition.

Pour cheese mixture into prepared pan; bake at 300° for 40 minutes or until almost set. Combine sour cream, 1 tablespoon sugar, and 2 teaspoons cocoa; stir well. Turn oven off and spread sour cream mixture over cheesecake. Let cheesecake stand for 45 minutes in oven with door closed. Remove cheesecake from oven and let cool to room temperature. Cover and chill at least 8 hours. Garnish with chocolate curls if desired. Yield: 12 servings (serving size 1 wedge).

17TH STREET CHEESECAKE

⅔ c. all-purpose flour
2 Tbsp. sugar
2 Tbsp. chilled stick margarine, cut
  into small pieces
1 Tbsp. ice water
Vegetable cooking spray
3 (8 oz.) blocks nonfat cream
  cheese, softened
2 (8 oz.) blocks Neufchatel cheese,
  softened

1¾ c. sugar
3 Tbsp. all-purpose flour
1 Tbsp. vanilla extract
1½ tsp. grated orange rind
1 tsp. grated lemon rind
¼ tsp. salt
5 eggs
Lemon zest (optional)
Orange slices (optional)
Lemon slices (optional)

Preheat oven to 400°. Place ⅔ cup flour and 2 tablespoons sugar in a food processor and pulse 2 times or until combined. Add chilled margarine; pulse 6 times or until mixture resembles coarse meal. With processor on, slowly pour ice water through food chute, processing just until blended (do not allow dough to form a ball).

Firmly press mixture into bottom of a 9 inch springform pan coated with cooking spray. Bake at 400° for 10 minutes; let cool on a wire rack.

Preheat oven to 525° or to highest oven setting. Combine cheeses in a large bowl; beat at high speed of a mixer until smooth. Add 1¾ cups sugar and next 5 ingredients (sugar through salt); beat well. Add eggs, 1 at a time, beating well after each addition.

Pour cheese mixture into prepared pan; bake at 525° for 7 minutes. Reduce oven temperature to 200° and bake 45 minutes or until almost set. Remove cheesecake from oven and let cool to room temperature. Cover and chill at least 8 hours. Garnish with lemon zest, orange slices, and lemon slices if desired. Yield: 16 servings (serving size 1 wedge).

WHITE CHOCOLATE RASPBERRY CHEESECAKE SANTACAFE

For the crust:

2 c. graham cracker crumbs
1 c. slivered blanched almonds

¼ c. clarified butter in its liquid
   (unchilled) form

For the filling:

8 oz. fine quality white chocolate
   (preferably Callebaut)
4 (8 oz.) pkg. cream cheese,
   softened
½ c. plus 2 Tbsp. sugar

4 large whole eggs
2 large egg yolks
2 Tbsp. all-purpose flour
1 tsp. vanilla

You will also need 2 pints raspberries.

Make the crust: In food processor, blend together the graham cracker crumbs and the almonds until the almonds are ground fine; add the butter and combine the mixture well. Press the mixture onto the bottom and ⅔ of the way up the side of a 10 inch springform pan.

Make the filling: In a metal bowl set over a pan of barely simmering water, melt the chocolate, stirring until it is smooth, and remove the bowl from the heat. In a large bowl with an electric mixer, beat the cream cheese until it is light and fluffy. Add the sugar and beat in the whole eggs and the egg yolks, 1 at a time, beating well after each addition. Beat in the flour and the vanilla and add the melted chocolate in a slow stream, beating until the filling is combined well.

Scatter the raspberries over the bottom of the crust; pour the filling over them and bake the cheesecake in the middle of a preheated 250°F. oven for 1 hour or until the top is firm to the touch. Let the cheesecake cool in the pan on a rack; chill it, covered loosely overnight and remove the side of the pan. For a whole one, bake a little longer.

Rasberry Sauce:

2 (10 oz.) pkg. frozen raspberries in
   syrup, thawed

¼ c. sugar
3 Tbsp. Grand Marnier liqueur

Use syrup from only one package of raspberries, draining the other. Combine all ingredients in food processor or blender; strain puree to remove seeds. Chill until ready to use. Drizzle over plate, place cheesecake on top.

This sauce freezes beautifully and looks elegant with the cheesecake.

FROZEN CHOCOLATE MOUSSE TORTE

1 (7 oz.) pkg. almond paste
1 Tbsp. cocoa
5 eggs
6 oz. semi-sweet chocolate
2 tsp. instant coffee
1 Tbsp. brandy or water

2 Tbsp. sugar
½ c. whipping cream
Semi-sweet chocolate bar for
    garnish (at room temperature;
    optional)

In the bowl of a food processor or the small bowl of an electric mixer, break almond paste into small pieces. Add cocoa and 2 of the eggs. Whirl or beat until mixture is smooth. Pour into a greased and flour-dusted 10 inch cheesecake pan with either a removable bottom or spring-release sides. Bake in a 375° oven for 15 minutes or until cake springs back when lightly touched. Cool on a wire rack.

Separate two of the remaining eggs; set aside whites. In the top of a double boiler, stir chocolate over hot, not boiling, water until melted. In a large mixing bowl, beat the egg yolks with remaining whole egg. Beat in coffee, brandy, and melted chocolate.

Beat egg whites until foamy; gradually add sugar and beat until moist, stiff peaks form. Fold into chocolate mixture. Whip the cream and fold into chocolate mixture. Spread evenly over cooled cake and freeze until firm, at least 3 hours.

To serve, remove sides of pan and thaw torte about 10 minutes. Garnish with chocolate curls, if desired. Makes 12 to 16 servings.

A little bit of this rich chocolate mousse torte goes a long way. Served frozen, it's an elegant finale to any meal.

ALMOND ROCA TORTE

Meringue:

6 egg whites (room temperature)
2 tsp. vanilla
½ tsp. cream of tartar

⅛ tsp. salt
2 c. sugar

Filling:

7 oz. almond roca, crushed
⅛ tsp. salt

2 c. whipping cream, whipped
¼ c. sugar

Add the cream of tartar to the egg whites and beat until soft peaks form. Add vanilla and salt. Gradually add the sugar, beating until very stiff. Line two 9 inch cake pans with plain ungreased brown paper. Grease sides of pans. Spread the meringue evenly in the pans. Bake in a very slow oven, 275°, for 1 hour the night before serving. Turn off oven and let dry, with the door closed, overnight. Remove carefully from pans.

Filling: Whip the cream until stiff. Add the sugar, salt, and crushed almond roca. Spread ½ of the mixture between the layers of meringue. Frost the sides and top with the remainder. Chill 4 hours or longer. Serves 12.

Make a day ahead and serve each slice with a bright red strawberry!

FRENCH CHERRY CLAFOUTI

Nonstick spray coating
3 eggs
⅓ c. sugar
Several drops of almond extract
1¼ c. skim milk
⅓ c. all-purpose flour

2 c. pitted, dark sweet cherries, or
1 (16½ oz.) can pitted, dark
sweet cherries, well drained
Sifted powdered sugar (optional)
Finely shredded orange peel
(optional)

Generously spray a 2 quart square baking dish or a 10 inch quiche dish with nonstick coating. Beat together eggs, sugar, and almond extract in medium bowl with wire whisk till combined. Blend in milk. Gradually add flour, beating with whisk till smooth. Pour batter into prepared dish. Sprinkle cherries atop batter.

Bake in a 350° oven for 25 to 30 minutes or till a knife inserted near the center comes out clean. If desired, sprinkle with sifted powdered sugar and shredded orange peel. Makes 8 servings.

Clafouti is a traditional French, custard-like dessert, but its summer-ripe flavor and rich texture make it pleasing for breakfast, too.

PEACH UPSIDE PUDDING

2 qt. peaches
⅓ c. peach juice
½ tsp. cinnamon
2 Tbsp. melted butter

2 eggs
¾ c. sugar
2 c. bread crumbs

Line a buttered dish with peaches. Pour juice over the peaches. Beat eggs until light; add sugar and beat thoroughly. Add cinnamon, bread crumbs, and melted butter. Pour mixture over peaches. Bake in 400° oven for 25 minutes or until the bread crumbs are brown and crusty. Serve in dessert dishes or compote. Serves 6.

AMARETTO BREAD PUDDING

1 loaf French bread
1 qt. half & half or milk
2 Tbsp. butter
3 eggs

1½ c. sugar
2 Tbsp. almond extract
¾ c. golden raisins
¾ c. sliced almonds

Break up bread and cover with half & half. Cover and let stand 1 hour. Preheat oven to 325°. Grease 9x13x2 inch dish with the butter. Beat eggs, sugar, and almond extract. Stir into bread mixture. Gently fold in raisins and almonds. Spread evenly in dish. Place on middle rack and bake 50 minutes. Remove and cool.

Amaretto Sauce:

8 Tbsp. unsalted butter
1 c. powdered sugar

1 egg, beaten
4 Tbsp. Amaretto liqueur

Using double boiler, stir together butter and sugar until very hot. Remove from heat. Whisk the egg well into butter and sugar mixture. Add liqueur. To serve, cut pudding into 12 to 15 pieces. Spoon sauce over and serve immediately.

The bread pudding freezes well. The sauce will keep in the refrigerator for several weeks.

PUMPKIN DESSERT

3 eggs
1 (16 oz.) can pumpkin

1 c. sugar
1 can evaporated milk

Combine these ingredients and pour into 9x13 inch baking dish. Sprinkle with spice cake mix and drizzle 1 brick of melted butter over top. Sprinkle ½ cup nuts over top. Bake at 350° for 45 to 60 minutes.

A quick and easy dessert to make.

BLACK FOREST DESSERT

1 cube butter or margarine
1 c. flour

1 c. pecans, chopped

For the crust, mix together butter, flour, and pecans. Pat all ingredients in a glass 9x13 inch dish. Bake at 350° for 30 minutes. Cool.

8 oz. cream cheese
1 c. powdered sugar

1 c. Dream Whip, whipped
½ tsp. vanilla

Fold together preceding 4 ingredients and spread on cooled shell.

3 oz. butterscotch instant pudding
3 oz. vanilla instant pudding

2½ c. milk

Whip together butterscotch pudding and vanilla pudding with milk and spread over cheese. Whip Dream Whip and pour over pudding. Sprinkle 1 cup chopped pecans. Refrigerate overnight or let set at least 4 hours.

This dessert is always well received!

MARDI GRAS TORTE

1 egg
¾ c. sugar
½ c. flour
1 tsp. baking powder
⅛ tsp. salt
½ c. coarsely chopped walnuts or
    pecans

1½ c. small cubed *red* apples (*not
    peeled*)
1 tsp. brandy flavoring
Whipped cream
Nutmeg

Grease 9 inch pie pan. Beat 1 egg white until stiff; add yolk and beat until stiff. Add ¾ cup sugar, a little at a time, beating after each addition. Sift together ½ cup flour, 1 teaspoon baking powder, and ⅛ teaspoon salt. Fold flour mixture into egg mixture, adding a little flour mixture at a time, making about 4 additions in all.

Fold in ½ cup coarsely chopped walnuts or pecans, 1½ cups of small cubed *red* apples, and 1 teaspoon brandy flavoring. Bake at 350° for 45 to 55 minutes or until golden brown.

Serve warm or cold with whipped cream and sprinkle generously with freshly grated nutmeg. Recipe serves 6, or may be doubled exactly and baked in two pans to serve 12.

DEATH BY CHOCOLATE

1 (18 oz.) box fudge brownie mix
¼ to ½ c. coffee liquor
3 (3.5 oz.) pkg. instant chocolate
   mousse

8 chocolate covered toffee candy
   bars (Heath bars)
1 (12 oz.) container frozen whipped
   topping, thawed

Preheat oven according to brownie package directions. Bake brownies according to directions and let cool. Prick holes in the tops of brownies with a fork and pour the coffee liquor over brownies; set aside. Prepare chocolate mousse according to package directions. Break candy bars into small pieces in food processor or by gently tapping the wrapped bars with a hammer. Break up half the brownies into small pieces and place in the bottom or a large glass bowl of trifle dish. Cover with half the mousse, then half the candy, and then half the whipped topping. Repeat layers with the remaining ingredients.

Note: Instead of the coffee liquor, you may substitute a mixture of 1 teaspoon sugar and 4 tablespoons black coffee, or just leave out the coffee flavoring entirely.

ALMOND LEMON PIE

6 Tbsp. slivered or chopped
   almonds
1 (3 oz.) pkg. lemon gelatin
⅛ tsp. salt
1 c. boiling water

1 c. mashed banana
2 Tbsp. lemon juice
1 c. dairy sour cream
Baked, cooled 9 inch pastry or
   graham cracker pie shell

Spread out almonds in shallow pan and toast in 350° oven about 10 minutes. Dissolve gelatin and salt in boiling water and chill until it begins to thicken. Mash banana and mix at once with lemon juice and ¾ cup sour cream. Fold with 2 tablespoons almonds into slightly thickened gelatin and turn into pie shell. Chill until firm, about 2 hours. Dollop remaining sour cream on top and sprinkle with the remaining toasted almonds. Serves 6 to 8.

BAUR'S FAMOUS MIJA PIE

1 c. sugar
¼ tsp. salt
¼ c. milk
4 Tbsp. cornstarch
2 egg yolks
1½ c. milk, scalded
4½ tsp. cocoa

2 oz. German's sweet chocolate,
   grated
¼ c. milk
½ tsp. vanilla
1 tsp. butter
4 oz. ground Mija candy or almond
   toffee, Heath bars

Combine sugar, cornstarch, and salt. Add ¼ cup milk, mixing well. Blend in egg yolks.

Scald 1½ cups milk over hot water in top of double boiler. Add corn starch mixture to scalded milk, stirring constantly. Beat well with wire whip or rotary beater until smooth. Cook mixture over hot water, stirring frequently, until clear and thickened.

Meanwhile, dissolve cocoa in ¼ cup milk. Add cocoa and grated chocolate to cornstarch mixture. Continue to cook, stirring until chocolate is melted and mixture is thickened.

Remove mixture from heat. Add butter and vanilla, stirring until butter is melted. Refrigerate mixture until it is thoroughly chilled. Turn it into baked pie shell. Sprinkle ground Mija over top. Chill.

Baur's was a famous restaurant on Curtis Street in Denver. They originated the ice cream soda.

LAYERED LEMON PIE

Crust:

20 chocolate wafers   **¼ c. melted butter**

A prepared chocolate crust could be used.

Filling:

¼ c. butter   **⅛ tsp. salt**
⅓ c. lemon juice   **3 slightly beaten eggs**
¾ c. sugar   **1 pt. vanilla ice cream**

Crust: Crumble chocolate wafers. Mix with melted butter and pat into 9 inch pie pan. Bake 8 minutes at 350°.

Filling: Melt butter; stir in lemon juice, sugar, and salt. Stir to dissolve. Pour half into 3 slightly beaten eggs. Return eggs to rest of butter mixture and cook over medium heat until thick. Chill. Divide ice cream in half. Put half into crust. The ice cream can be placed in the microwave to soften, then spread around and return to freeze to harden. Pour half of the lemon mixture over the ice cream. Freeze. Repeat layers. Freeze.

Garnish with cookie crumbs or chocolate curls. Let stand 10 minutes at room temperature to serve. Serves 8.

Interesting combination - *good!*

LEMON CHESS PIE

½ c. butter   **¾ c. lemon juice**
2 c. sugar   **Grated rind of 3 lemons**
1 Tbsp. flour   **1 unbaked pie shell**
5 eggs

Cream butter and sugar. Add flour, then well beaten eggs. Add lemon juice and rind. Mix well and pour into uncooked pie shell. Bake at 325° until light brown, about 45 minutes.

LEMON CHIFFON PIE

1 baked pie shell   **1 Tbsp. grated lemon rind or zest**
½ c. sugar   **4 egg yolks**
1 env. unflavored gelatin   **4 egg whites**
⅔ c. water   **½ tsp. cream of tartar**
½ c. fresh lemon juice   **½ c. sugar**

Combine sugar, gelatin, water, lemon juice, lemon rind, and eggs, cooking over medium heat and bring to a boil. Stir in lemon rind. Cool.

160

Combine egg whites, cream of tartar, and sugar and beat until stiff and peaks form. Fold into cooled mixture, mixing well. Pile into baked pie shell. Chill.

MIRACLE PIE

1 c. sugar
¼ c. butter
4 eggs
½ c. flour
2 c. milk

1 c. coconut
¼ tsp. salt
½ tsp. baking powder
1 tsp. vanilla

Put all ingredients into blender. Blend thoroughly. Pour into a 10 inch pie plate that has been greased and floured. Bake at 350° for 60 minutes. A crust will form on bottom, pie filling in center, and coconut topping above.

PUMPKIN ICE CREAM PIE

1 qt. vanilla ice cream, softened
¾ can canned pumpkin (15 oz.)
¼ c. honey
½ tsp. cinnamon
¼ tsp. ground ginger
¼ tsp. salt

⅛ tsp. nutmeg
⅛ tsp. ground cloves
1 baked 9 inch pie shell, cooled
⅓ c. chopped pecans
Whipped cream
Pecan halves

Combine first 8 ingredients in mixing bowl and blend well. Pour into pie shell. Sprinkle with chopped nuts. Freeze until serving time. Garnish with whipped cream and pecan halves just before serving. This pie is so simple to make you will serve often.

I REMEMBER "MAMA'S STRAWBERRY PIE"

1 baked 9 inch pie crust
2 egg yolks
¾ c. granulated sugar
¼ tsp. salt
2½ Tbsp. cornstarch

2 c. scalded milk
1 qt. washed, hulled strawberries
Sweetened whipped cream
1 tsp. rum flavoring

Prepare and bake a 9 inch pie crust using either your favorite pastry recipe or any popular mix of your choice. Cool slightly. Prepare a custard as follows.

Beat 2 egg yolks. Beat in gradually granulated sugar, salt, and cornstarch. Pour over the preceding 2 cups scalded milk. Cook and stir the custard over very low heat. Stir constantly until it thickens. Have ready one quart of washed, hulled strawberries. Arrange them in the baked pie shell. Pour the hot custard over the berries. Chill thoroughly. When ready to serve, garnish with mounds of sweetened whipped cream. Add a teaspoon rum flavoring and additional whole berries if desired.

FROZEN CHOCOLATE PIE WITH PECAN CRUST

6 (1 oz.) sq. semi-sweet chocolate
½ tsp. instant coffee granules
2 eggs, beaten
3 Tbsp. Kahlua
¼ c. powdered sugar
¾ c. whipping cream

1 tsp. vanilla extract
Pecan Crust
¾ c. whipping cream
1 Tbsp. Kahlua
Grated chocolate

Place chocolate squares and coffee granules in top of a double boiler; bring water to a boil. Reduce heat to low; cook until chocolate melts. Gradually stir about ¼ of melted chocolate into eggs, mixing well. Add to remaining chocolate in double boiler. Gradually stir in Kahlua and powdered sugar. Cook, stirring constantly, until mixture reaches 165°. Cool to room temperature. Beat ¾ cup whipping cream until soft peaks form; fold into chocolate mixture. Stir in vanilla. Spoon into Pecan Crust. Cover and freeze. Transfer pie from freezer to refrigerator 1 hour before serving.

Beat ¾ cup whipping cream in a medium mixing bowl until foamy. Gradually add 1 tablespoon Kahlua, beating until stiff peaks form. Pipe or dollop whipped cream around edge of pie. Sprinkle with grated chocolate. Yield: One 9 inch pie.

Pecan Crust:

2 c. coarsely chopped pecans
⅓ c. firmly packed brown sugar

3 Tbsp. butter, melted
2 tsp. Kahlua

Combine all ingredients, mixing well. Firmly press mixture evenly over bottom and up the sides of a 9 inch pie plate. Bake at 350° for 10 to 12 minutes. Press sides of crust with back of spoon. Cool. Yield: 1 (9 inch) pie shell.

DESSERT PIZZA PIE

Crust:

1¼ c. all-purpose white flour
2 tsp. baking powder
¼ tsp. salt
½ c. nonfat *or* lowfat cottage cheese
⅓ c. sugar
3 Tbsp. vegetable oil (preferably
    canola oil)

2 Tbsp. lowfat milk
1½ tsp. pure vanilla extract
1 Tbsp. (approx.) corn meal (for
    preparing pan)

Toppings:

½ c. Raspberry Marinara Sauce
1 c. diced pineapple
1 kiwi fruit, peeled and diced
¼ c. dried strawberries or dried
    cranberries

2½ tsp. sugar
1 (2 oz.) block white chocolate

To make crust: In a small bowl, whisk flour, baking powder, and salt. In a food processor, puree cottage cheese. Add sugar, oil, milk, and vanilla and process until smooth. Add the dry ingredients and pulse 4 to 5 times just until the dough clumps together. Turn out onto a lightly floured work surface and press the dough into a ball. Knead several times, but do not overwork. Dust with flour, wrap in plastic wrap, and refrigerate for at least 15 minutes while you prepare toppings.

To assemble and bake pizza: Set oven rack at lowest position; preheat oven to 400°F. Spray a 12 inch pizza pan or large baking sheet with nonstick cooking spray. Sprinkle with corn meal, shaking off excess.

On a lightly floured work surface, roll the dough flat into a 12 inch disk about ¼ inch thick. Roll the dough back over a rolling pin and transfer to the prepared pizza pan or baking sheet. Finish the edges by turning them under. To glaze the border, brush it very lightly with a little milk and sprinkle with ½ teaspoon of the sugar.

Spread the crust with Raspberry Marinara Sauce and scatter pineapple, kiwi, and dried strawberries or cranberries on top. Sprinkle with 2 teaspoons sugar. Bake until the crust is golden and crisp, about 20 minutes.

While the pizza is baking, gently warm white chocolate in the microwave at 30% power until sightly softened, but not melted, 20 to 40 seconds, then grate the softened chocolate on a vegetable grater. (If chocolate breaks into fine shreds, rather than large ones, continue to microwave, checking every 10 seconds.)

Remove from the oven and immediately sprinkle the grated white chocolate over top; let stand until melted. Cut the pizza into wedges and serve hot or at room temperature. Makes one 12 inch pie for 8 servings.

Raspberry Marinara Sauce:

1 (12 oz.) pkg. unsweetened frozen raspberries, thawed (3 c.)
¼ c. sugar

2 tsp. fresh lemon juice
1 tsp. balsamic vinegar

In a food processor, puree raspberries, sugar, lemon juice, and balsamic vinegar until smooth. Strain through a fine sieve into a bowl. (The sauce can be stored, covered, in the refrigerator for up to 4 days or frozen for longer storage.) Makes about 1½ cups.

Note: This recipe makes enough sauce for both ravioli and pizza. It is also a good all-purpose dessert topping.

NO-CRUST CRANBERRY NUT PIE

This is a delicious holiday pie that's a snap to make. It's perfect for the cook who doesn't like to make pie crusts.

For 1 pie:

Fresh cranberries (1 pkg. makes 2 pies)
½ c. pecans
1 c. sugar

½ c. flour
⅜ c. melted butter or margarine
1 egg

Line bottom of well greased 8 inch pie with fresh cranberries and sprinkle with the pecans and ½ cup sugar. Beat egg well. Gradually add remaining sugar until thoroughly mixed. Add flour and shortening, beating well. Pour batter over cranberries. Bake at 325° for 45 minutes until crust is golden brown. Delicious with whipped cream, vanilla ice cream, or vanilla frozen yogurt.

PEARL STREET ORANGE ICEBOX CAKE

1 sponge or angel food bar or pound
    cake
1 orange
1 lemon

¾ c. sugar
2 whole eggs
½ pt. whipped cream

    Split cake to make 4 layers. Mix together the filling of sugar and the juice of the lemon and the orange and a little rind of each. Beat slightly 2 whole eggs and add to preceding mixture. Cook in double boiler until thickened. Cool. Add ½ pint whipped cream. Spread on all layers and cover sides and top. Chill. Slice. Serves 8 to 10. Best if made the day before serving.

1922 CHRISTMAS CAKE OR SPICE CAKE

2 c. brown sugar
2 c. raisins
2 c. boiling water
¾ c. shortening
½ to 1 tsp. cinnamon
½ to 1 tsp. cloves

½ to 1 tsp. nutmeg
¼ tsp. salt
2 tsp. baking soda
3½ c. sifted flour
1 c. chopped nuts (optional)

    Mix together brown sugar, raisins, boiling water, shortening, cinnamon, cloves, nutmeg, and salt. Boil this mixture for 5 minutes. Dissolve 2 level teaspoons of baking soda in a little water and add to boiled mixture. Let cool. When nearly cold, add 3⅓ cups sifted flour. You may add 1 cup nuts if desired. Bake in 2 loaf pans, greased and floured, 1 hour at 350°.

    This can be baked in 4 small loaves at 350° for 45 minutes.

HERSHEY CHOCOLATE SYRUP CAKE

1 c. margarine
½ tsp. salt
4 eggs
1 c. sugar

1 c. flour
1 tsp. vanilla
1 c. chopped nuts
1 (16 oz.) can Hershey's syrup

    Cream margarine and sugar thoroughly. Add eggs, one at a time. Add syrup, flour mixture, vanilla, and nuts. Bake at 350° for 35 to 45 minutes in a 9x12 inch baking dish.

    Icing:

1 c. sugar
¼ c. milk
2 tsp. vanilla

¼ c. cocoa
¼ butter

    Bring to a boil until thickens. Cool and beat until creamy. Add powdered sugar until desired consistency.

CHOCOLATE TURTLE CAKE

1 box German chocolate cake mix
¾ c. margarine, melted
1 c. evaporated milk

1 (14 oz.) pkg. caramels
1 c. pecans or walnuts, chopped
1 c. chocolate chips

164

Mix cake as directed on box. Add melted margarine and ⅔ cup milk. Pour half of batter into greased and floured 13x9 inch pan. Bake 10 to 15 minutes at 350°. While cake bakes, melt caramels with remaining milk. Remove cake from oven and pour caramel mixture over cake. Sprinkle with nuts and chocolate chips. Add remaining half of batter. Return cake to oven and bake 20 minutes. Serve with ice cream or whipped cream.

ORANGE-TIPPED WALNUT BISCOTTI

2 c. unsifted all-purpose flour
2 tsp. baking powder
¾ tsp. ground cinnamon
¼ tsp. ground nutmeg
⅛ tsp. ground allspice
½ stick (¼ c.) butter (at room
  temperature)

⅔ c. sugar
1 tsp. grated orange rind
1 large whole egg
2 large egg whites
1 tsp. vanilla
½ c. coarsely chopped walnuts
Orange Icing (recipe follows)

Stir together flour, baking powder, cinnamon, nutmeg, and allspice. In large bowl of mixer, beat butter, sugar, and orange rind until well blended. Beat in whole egg, then egg whites. Beat in vanilla. Gradually add flour mixture, beating until blended. Stir in walnuts. Divide dough in half. On lightly floured board, shape each portion into a long loaf about 2 inches in diameter. (Dough will be sticky.) Place loaves about 3 inches apart on oiled baking sheet. Flatten each loaf to thickness of about ½ inch. Bake on center shelf in preheated 350° oven until firm to touch, about 15 minutes.

Remove baking sheet from oven. Cut hot loaves crosswise into ½ inch thick slices. Turn slices cut sides down and spread out slightly on baking sheet. Return to oven and bake until biscotti look dry and are lightly brown, about 10 minutes. Transfer biscotti to racks to cool. Spread Orange Icing over about 1 inch of one end of each cookie. Let stand until icing is firm, about 15 minutes. This recipe, containing a small amount of butter, makes biscotti with crisp cookie-like texture. Biscotti can be stored in airtight container for at least a month. Makes about 4 dozen.

Orange Icing: Mix 1 cup sifted powdered sugar and 1 teaspoon grated orange rind. Stir in 1 to 2 tablespoon orange juice or just enough for good spreading consistency.

SPICED BISCOTTI

2¼ c. unsifted all-purpose flour
1 tsp. baking powder
½ tsp. baking soda
¼ tsp. salt
¼ tsp. black pepper
½ tsp. ground cloves
½ tsp. ground cinnamon

½ tsp. ground ginger
1 c. sugar
2 large eggs plus 2 yolks
½ tsp. vanilla
½ c. hazelnut liqueur or other liquid
  of choice

Sift flour, baking powder, soda, salt, pepper, cloves, cinnamon, and ginger into small bowl. Whisk sugar, whole eggs, and yolks to a light lemon color in large bowl. Stir in vanilla and liqueur. Sift dry ingredients over egg mixture, then fold in until dough is just combined. Preheat oven to 350° with oven rack placed in center position. Divide dough in half. Turn each portion onto oiled baking sheet covered with parchment paper. Using floured hands, quickly stretch each portion of dough into a rough log about 13 inches long and 2 inches in diameter. Place logs about 3 inches apart on baking sheet.

Pat each log to smooth it. Bake, turning baking sheet once, until loaves are golden and just beginning to crack on top, about 35 minutes.

Cool loaves 10 minutes. Lower oven temperature to 325°. Cut each loaf diagonally into ½ inch slices with serrated knife. Lay slices about ½ inch apart on baking sheet, cut sides up. Return to oven. Bake 8 minutes. Turn each over. Bake about 7 minutes longer or until crisp and golden brown. Transfer to wire racks to cool completely.

This recipe, containing no shortening, makes the traditional hard biscotti that should be quickly dunked in coffee, tea, or wine just long enough to soften them. Biscotti can be stored in an airtight container for at least a month. Makes about 3 dozen.

Variations: Omit hazelnut liqueur. Soak ¾ cup currants, chopped raisins or dates in ¼ cup brandy or Marsala at least 1 hour. Add to sugar-egg mixture.

LEMON ICE

Juice of 7 lemons   **4 c. sugar**
1 Tbsp. zest of lemon

Let set overnight. Add 1 pint of half & half. Put in ice cream freezer. When serving, pour a little sauterne wine over for an unusual effect.

This unusual dessert has been enjoyed by our family for many years.

MARGARITA SORBET

1½ c. water   **½ c. fresh orange juice**
¾ c. sugar   **2 Tbsp. fresh lime juice**
1 pt. strawberries, rinsed and hulled   **2 Tbsp. tequila**

Strawberry Sauce:

½ pt. strawberries, rinsed and   **1 Tbsp. sugar**
hulled

Garnish:

Shaved fresh coconut   **Mint sprigs**

In small saucepan over high heat, bring water and sugar to boil; reduce heat. Simmer 3 minutes until sugar is dissolved. Refrigerate until syrup is cold.

In blender or food processor, puree strawberries. Add cold syrup, juices, and tequila; blend.

In electric ice cream maker, freeze mixture according to manufacturer's directions. (Or pour mixture into chilled metal pan; freeze until solid. With metal spoon, break up into large chunks; transfer to food processor. Blend until slushy and smooth. For smoothest consistency, refreeze in metal pan and process again until slushy and smooth.) Freeze until ready to serve.

Sauce: In blender or food processor, puree strawberries and sugar; strain through fine-mesh sieve. Discard seeds.

To serve: Place 3 small scoops of sorbet into each of 8 dessert bowls. Drizzle with Strawberry Sauce. Garnish with coconut and mint sprigs.

FRESH FRUIT SORBETS

For dessert, serve 1 scoop each of two or three intensely flavored fruit sorbets in footed dishes.

⅔ c. boiling water
⅔ c. sugar
2 c. fruit puree (peach, apricot,
    raspberry, pear, or
    strawberry; need about 4 c.
    fresh fruit)

Pour boiling water over sugar in small bowl. Stir till sugar is dissolved. Cover and chill.

Sieve fruit puree if necessary. Combine puree and sugar syrup. Freeze in ice cream freezer according to manufacturer's directions. (Or transfer to a shallow pan. Cover and freeze till firm. Break into small chunks. Transfer to a chilled bowl. Beat with an electric mixer till smooth but not melted. Return to pan, cover, and freeze till firm. Let stand 5 to 10 minutes before scooping.) Makes 6 to 8 servings.

STRAWBERRY-BANANA FREEZE

2 (6 oz.) containers fat-free
    strawberry yogurt
2 Tbsp. skim milk

2 medium ripe bananas
Red food coloring (optional)

Line an 8x8x2 inch baking pan or 2 quart square baking dish with plastic wrap. Spoon yogurt into the pan. Cover and freeze about 3 hours or till completely frozen.

Remove yogurt from pan; peel away plastic wrap. Cut or break frozen yogurt into chunks. Peel bananas; cut into large chunks. Add to blender container or food processor bowl along with skim milk. Add a drop of a red food coloring, if desired. Process till pureed. Add yogurt pieces, a few at a time, processing till smooth, stopping blender and pushing pieces down as needed. Transfer to bowl. Cover and freeze about 30 minutes or till soft-serve consistency. Serve in dessert dishes. Makes 4 servings.

PEANUT BUTTER CHOCOLATE ICE CREAM

2 eggs
⅓ c. sugar
1 c. crunchy peanut butter
½ c. light corn syrup

2 c. heavy cream
1 c. milk
2 tsp. vanilla
¾ c. semi-sweet chocolate chips

Beat eggs until frothy. Gradually beat in sugar. Add peanut butter and corn syrup. Stir in cream, vanilla, and milk. Add mixture to ice cream maker. When ice cream is completed, stir in chocolate chips.

This is so creamy you won't be able to resist!

CHOCOLATE MOUSSE

1 (6 oz.) pkg. semi-sweet chocolate
    chips
2 eggs

3 Tbsp. strong hot coffee
1½ Tbsp. brandy
¾ c. scalded milk

Combine in blender eggs and chocolate chips at high speed for 1 to 2 minutes. Add hot coffee, brandy, and scalded milk last. Makes 6 servings.

Very nice when served in demitasse cups.

GERMAN CHOCOLATE CARAMEL SQUARES

1 (14 oz.) bag caramels	¾ c. butter, melted
1 (5 oz.) can evaporated milk	1 c. chopped walnuts
1 pkg. German chocolate cake mix	1 (6 oz.) pkg. chocolate chips

Combine caramels and ⅓ cup evaporated milk and melt together in microwave at 50% power. In separate bowl, combine cake mix (dry), ⅓ cup evaporated milk, and melted butter. Add chopped nuts. Spoon half of this cake mixture into 9x13 inch greased pan and bake 6 minutes at 350°. Remove from oven and sprinkle with chocolate chips. Pour caramel mixture over. Drop remaining cake mixture over by using 2 teaspoons and dropping batter over pan until nearly covered. Bake an additional 20 minutes at 350°. Cool completely before cutting into 1 inch squares. These cookies freeze well. They travel well and are tremendously popular! *Enjoy!!!!*

KAHLUA CHOCOLATE BARS

12 oz. praline, crushed	10 oz. semi-sweet chocolate,
¼ c. peanut oil	chopped
14 oz. milk chocolate, crushed	1¼ c. whipping cream
6 oz. Gaufrette cookies (about 20),	2 tsp. Kahlua
crushed	Cocoa powder

Combine praline and oil. Set aside. Melt milk chocolate; combine with crushed cookies and praline. Place 22 x 4 x 1¼ inch bottomless mold on wax paper-lined baking sheet. Spread mixture evenly over bottom. Chill. Melt semi-sweet chocolate. Cool slightly. Whip cream with Kahlua. Fold into melted semi-sweet chocolate. Spread over chocolate layer. Chill to set. Run knife around edge of mold; remove. Dust with cocoa power. Cut into 36 bars. Serves 12.

Note: Gaufrette cookies and the mold are available at specialty stores.

KAHLUA TOFFEE BARS

Cookie Base (recipe follows)	1 tsp. baking powder
2 large eggs	½ tsp. salt
¼ c. Kahlua	1 c. flaked coconut
1 c. brown sugar, packed	1 c. filberts or pecans, chopped
¼ c. sifted all-purpose flour	

Prepare Cookie Base. Spread over bottom of greased and floured (or parchment lined) 13 x 9 x 2 pan. Bake at 350°F. for 10 to 12 minutes. Beat eggs in small bowl. Beat in Kahlua and brown sugar until fluffy. Resift flour with baking powder and salt. Stir into creamed mixture. Fold in coconut and nuts. Pour over partially baked crust and return to oven. Bake 20 minutes longer or just until top is set. Remove from oven and cool on wire rack. Cut into bars, about 1½ x 2½ inches. Makes 2 dozen bars.

Cookie Base: Cream together ¼ cup each butter and shortening and ½ cup firmly packed brown sugar. Stir in 1 cup sifted all-purpose flour, mixing well.

Variation: To make frosted bars, beat 1½ cups sifted powdered sugar, 3 tablespoons softened butter, and 1 tablespoon Kahlua together until smooth. Press through small rosette tube, if desired.

NANCY REAGAN'S VIENNA BARS

½ c. butter
¾ c. sugar
⅛ tsp. salt
1 large egg yolk
1¼ c. all-purpose flour

½ c. red raspberry preserves
2 large egg whites
4 oz. finely chopped or ground
   almonds

Mix butter, flour, salt, egg yolk, and ¼ cup of sugar. Pat into the bottom of a greased 9 inch square Pyrex pan. Bake 15 to 20 minutes at 350° until lightly browned. Spread with preserves. Beat 2 egg whites until stiff. Fold in remaining sugar and nuts. Spread over preserves. Bake about 25 minutes at 350°. Cut bars in 1½ x 3 inches while still warm.

LEMON BARS

Lime juice adds extra tartness.

1 c. butter
¼ tsp. salt
½ c. powdered sugar
2 c. flour
4 eggs, slightly beaten
Grated rind of 1 lemon

5 Tbsp. lemon juice
1 Tbsp. lime juice
2 c. sugar
¼ c. flour
Powdered sugar

Blend butter, salt, powdered sugar, and 2 cups of flour together well and press into greased 9x13 inch baking pan. Bake at 350° for 15 to 20 minutes, or until golden.

Mix remaining ingredients together; pour over baked layer and bake in 325° oven for 20 to 25 minutes or until firm. Dust with powdered sugar. Cut when cool. Store in refrigerator. Makes 5 dozen.

LOWFAT LEMON BARS

1 pkg. 1 step angel food cake mix
   (Duncan Hines)

21 oz. can lemon pie filling
   (Wilderness)

Mix the ingredients together. Pat into a greased jellyroll pan and bake in a preheated 350° oven for 30 minutes. You can sprinkle with chopped nuts before baking. Cool and cut into 24 bars.

Fat: 6 grams. Cholesterol: 0.

These bars are good for dieters and baked quickly. *Yummy.*

NUTTY CARAMEL BARS

3 sticks (1½ c.) butter
½ c. granulated sugar
1 extra large egg
1 tsp. vanilla
2 c. unsifted all-purpose flour

¼ c. honey
¾ c. firmly packed light brown sugar
¼ c. whipping cream
1 (10 or 12 oz.) can lightly salted
    mixed whole nuts

In large bowl of mixer or in food processor, beat 2 sticks butter with granulated sugar until light and fluffy. Beat in egg and vanilla. Stir in flour until well mixed. Spread dough evenly in greased 9x13 inch baking pan. Dough will be soft.

Use metal spatula dipped in cold water to spread dough if necessary. Bake on center shelf of preheated 350° oven for 15 minutes or just until edges are brown and center looks dry. Remove to wire rack while preparing topping. Maintain oven temperature.

In medium, heavy, deep saucepan, over medium heat, melt remaining 1 stick butter with honey. Stir in brown sugar and bring to a rolling boil. Boil without stirring, exactly 2 minutes. Remove from heat. Stir in cream and nuts. Immediately spoon caramel mixture evenly over crust. Bake on center shelf of oven about 10 minutes or until caramel bubbles merrily around edges. Cool completely on wire rack. With very sharp knife, cut into 2x2 inch bars. Store tightly covered in container at room temperature. Makes 24 bars.

BOW MAR BANANA BARS

1 c. flour
¾ c. sugar
1 egg
½ tsp. baking powder
½ tsp. salt
¼ tsp. soda

4 Tbsp. chopped nuts
¼ tsp. cloves
¼ tsp. allspice
¼ c. butter
⅓ c. banana, mashed
¾ tsp. cinnamon

Cream butter and bananas. Add sugar and egg. Add ¼ cup milk alternately with dry ingredients. Add nuts and spread in a greased 9x13 inch baking dish. Bake at 350° for 22 to 25 minutes. While warm spread with following frosting.

Frosting:

2 Tbsp. butter
1 Tbsp. hot water

2 tsp. lemon juice
1 c. powdered sugar

ZUCCHINI BARS

¾ c. butter or margarine
½ c. sugar
½ c. brown sugar
2 eggs
1 tsp. vanilla
1¾ c. flour
½ tsp. salt

1½ tsp. baking powder
¾ c. coconut
¾ c. dates, diced
¾ c. raisins
¼ to ½ c. nuts, chopped (optional)
2 c. zucchini, shredded

Frosting:

1 Tbsp. butter or margarine, melted
2 Tbsp. milk
¼ tsp. cinnamon

1 tsp. vanilla
1 c. powdered sugar
1 c. broken nuts (optional)

Beat butter, sugar, brown sugar, eggs, and vanilla until smooth and creamy. Add flour, salt, and baking powder. Stir in coconut, dates, raisins, nuts, and zucchini. Place in a greased 10x15 inch pan. Bake in a preheated 350° oven for 35 to 40 minutes. Cool slightly before frosting.

Frosting: Combine first 5 ingredients. Frost cooled cookies. Sprinkle with nuts if desired. Yield: 36 bar cookies.

CHOCOLATE MARSHMALLOW SLICE

Cream:

1 c. powdered sugar
1 whole egg

1 Tbsp. soft margarine or butter

Add:

3 sq. melted chocolate
1 pkg. multi-colored miniature
  marshmallows

Mix well. Divide into 2 parts. Roll out in long rolls; roll in coconut or nutmeats, or leave plain. Chill, then slice.

Very colorful on your holiday cookie plate.

ROYAL GORGE CHOCOLATE REVEL BARS

1 c. margarine or butter
2½ c. all-purpose flour or 1½ c. all-
  purpose flour and 1 c. whole
  wheat flour
2 c. packed brown sugar
2 eggs
4 tsp. vanilla

1 tsp. baking soda
3 c. quick-cooking rolled oats
1½ c. semi-sweet chocolate pieces
1 (14 oz.) can or 1¼ c. sweetened
  condensed milk
2 Tbsp. margarine or butter
½ c. chopped nuts

In a large mixer bowl, beat the 1 cup margarine or butter at medium speed for 30 seconds. Add about half the flour, all of the brown sugar, eggs, 2 teaspoons vanilla, and baking soda. Beat on low speed until thoroughly combined. Beat in remaining flour. Stir in oats.

In medium saucepan, cook chocolate pieces, sweetened condensed milk, and 2 tablespoons margarine or butter over low heat, stirring frequently. Stir in remaining vanilla and nuts.

Pat ⅔ of the oat mixture, about 3½ cups, into a 15x10 inch baking pan. Spread chocolate mixture over and dot with remaining oat mixture. Bake at 350° for 25 minutes or until top is lightly golden. Cut into bars. Makes 60 bars. *Freezes and ships well.*

GUILT-FREE BROWNIES

Nonstick spray coating
1¼ c. all-purpose flour
1 c. sugar
¾ c. unsweetened cocoa powder
1 tsp. baking powder
¾ c. refrigerated or frozen egg
    product, thawed
½ c. fat-free dairy sour cream or
    plain yogurt

½ c. applesauce
¼ c. cooking oil
1 tsp. vanilla
½ c. reduced-fat semi-sweet
    chocolate flavor baking
    pieces or ¼ c. chopped walnuts
Sifted powdered sugar (optional)

Spray a 13x9x2 inch baking pan with nonstick coating; set pan aside.

Combine flour, sugar, cocoa, and baking powder in a large mixing bowl. Make a well in center of ingredients. Combine egg product, sour cream or yogurt, applesauce, oil, and vanilla. Stir into dry ingredients just till moistened. Fold in baking pieces or nuts. Spread in prepared pan.

Bake in a 350° oven about 25 minutes or till a wooden toothpick inserted in center comes out clean. Cool in the pan on wire cooling rack. Sprinkle with sifted powdered sugar if desired. Makes 32 servings.

TEXAS BROWNIES

2 c. all-purpose flour
2 c. granulated sugar
½ c. or 1 cube butter or margarine
½ c. shortening
1 c. strong brewed coffee or water

½ c. dark, unsweetened cocoa
½ c. buttermilk
2 eggs
1 tsp. baking soda
1 tsp. vanilla

Frosting:

½ c. or 1 cube butter or margarine
4 Tbsp. dark cocoa
¼ c. milk

3½ c. unsifted powdered sugar
1 tsp. vanilla

In a large mixing bowl, combine the flour and the sugar. In heavy saucepan, combine butter, shortening, coffee or water, and cocoa. Stir and heat to boiling. Pour boiling mixture over the flour and sugar in the bowl. Add the buttermilk, eggs, baking soda, and vanilla. Mix well, using a wooden spoon or high speed on electric mixer. Pour into a well buttered 17½ x 11 inch jellyroll pan. Bake at 400° for 20 minutes or until brownies test done in the center. While brownies bake, prepare the frosting.

In a saucepan, combine the butter, cocoa, and milk. Heat to boiling, stirring. Mix in the powdered sugar and vanilla until frosting is smooth. Pour warm frosting over brownies as soon as you take them out of the oven. Cool. Cut in 48 bars.

Tip: If you don't have buttermilk on hand, substitute 2 teaspoons vinegar or lemon juice. Mix into ½ cup milk. Or use powdered buttermilk. Mix according to package directions.

These tender brownies are quick to prepare, using ingredients that are handy in the kitchen. This recipe makes a large pan. Great for potluck.

MONACO BROWNIES WITH CARAMEL

16 oz. caramels
2⅓ c. evaporated milk
¾ c. melted margarine

1 devils food cake mix
1½ c. chopped walnuts
12 oz. chocolate chips

Combine caramels and ⅓ cup milk and cook over low heat, stirring constantly until caramels are melted. Set aside. Grease and flour 9x13 inch pan. Combine margarine, cake mix, and ⅓ cup milk in large bowl and mix. Press half the dough in pan, reserving other half for topping. Bake at 350° for 6 minutes. Take out of oven and sprinkle chocolate chips and then spread caramel mixture evenly over chips. Crumble reserved dough mix over caramels evenly. Return to oven and bake 15 to 18 minutes. Cool. Refrigerate 30 minutes to set caramel. Cut into squares.

CHOCOLATE MACAROON SQUARES

½ c. butter, cut up
¾ c. sugar
1¼ c. flour
4 large egg whites

1½ tsp. vanilla
3 c. shredded dry coconut
1 c. pecans, finely chopped
1½ c. semi-sweet chocolate chips

In a food processor or with fingers, whirl or rub butter, ¼ cup sugar, and 1 cup flour until dough begins to hold together. Press evenly in bottom of a 9 inch square pan. Bake crust in a 350° oven 10 to 15 minutes or until golden brown.

In a large bowl, beat egg whites until frothy. Add vanilla and remaining ½ cup sugar and ¼ cup flour; mix until smooth. Stir in coconut. Sprinkle chocolate and nuts evenly over pastry. Spoon coconut mixture over chocolate and nuts. Spread evenly with spatula. Continue baking until macaroon topping is golden and slightly wet looking, about 25 minutes. Cool in pan on a rack. Using a very sharp knife, cut into 36 (1½ inch) squares.

QUICK TURTLE COOKIES

2 c. flour
1 cube butter plus ⅔ c.
1½ c. brown sugar

1 c. pecan halves
1 c. milk chocolate chips

Mix together flour, 1 stick butter, and 1 cup brown sugar. Pat into 13x9 inch pan. Stir to boiling ⅔ cup butter and ½ cup brown sugar; boil 1 minute. Layer 1 cup pecan halves over crust and pour caramel over all. Bake 20 minutes at 350°. Remove from oven and sprinkle with 1 cup milk chocolate chips. Let melt 2 to 3 minutes and swirl. Cut into bars when cool.

HIGH COUNTRY NO ROLL SUGAR COOKIES

1 c. sugar minus 3 Tbsp.
1 c. butter or margarine
1 extra large egg
1 tsp. vanilla

2 c. flour
½ tsp. salt
½ tsp. soda
½ tsp. cream of tartar

Cream sugar, butter, and egg until fluffy. Mix remaining ingredients with sugar mixture. Mix well with spoon, then with hands. Dough will be stiff. Pinch off dough size of a walnut and roll. Place balls on ungreased pan about 2 inches apart. Dip bottom of glass in sugar and press each ball until it forms a circle. Sprinkle additional sugar on cookies. Bake at 400° about 10 minutes or until golden brown. Remove from pan while still hot.

PECAN SANDWICH COOKIES

½ c. butter
1 c. flour

⅔ c. ground pecans
⅓ c. sugar

Filling and frosting: Melt 1 cup chocolate chips and add ½ cup sour cream; stir.

Sift flour and sugar. Add to creamed butter. Mix with ground pecans. (If stiff, mix with hands.) Roll dough on floured pastry sheet to ¼ inch or less. Cut 2 inch rounds. Place on cookie sheet and bake at 375° for 7 to 10 minutes. Watch closely as these cookies burn easily. Cool. Prepare filling. Place thin layer of filling on flat (bottom) of cookie; attach additional flat of cookie to filling (two bottoms together). Top cookie with frosting and a pecan half. Makes 18 cookies.

Spectacular for the holidays! Extremely rich!!!!

IRISH PUFFS

3 c. crushed vanilla wafers
¾ c. confectioners sugar
3 Tbsp. light corn syrup
1½ tsp. cocoa powder (not a mix)

1 c. chopped pecans
½ c. Bailey's Irish cream
Confectioners sugar

Combine vanilla wafers, pecans, ¾ cup sugar, Bailey's, corn syrup, and cocoa powder in a medium bowl with a wooden spoon until mixture is well blended. Shape into 1 inch balls, rolling between palms of hand. Spread confectioners sugar on wax paper and roll balls in sugar to coat well. Allow to dry on wire rack 1 hour. Store in metal tin, between wax paper with a tight fitting lid. *A no bake cookie.*

RED ROCKS MACADAMIA NUT-CHIP COOKIES

1 c. butter
½ c. sugar
1½ c. flour

1 c. white chocolate chips
1 c. macadamia nuts

Mix and chill. Drop by heaping teaspoon on cookie sheet. Bake at 350° for 20 minutes.

C U BUFFALO CHIPS

2 c. margarine
2 c. sugar
2 c. corn flakes
2 c. oatmeal
2 tsp. soda
1 large pkg. chocolate chips

2 c. brown sugar, packed
4 eggs, beaten
2 tsp. vanilla
4 c. flour
2 tsp. baking powder
1 c. chopped nuts

Cream margarine and sugar. Stir in eggs. Sift flour, soda, and baking powder. Add to creamed mixture and mix thoroughly. Add chocolate chips and nuts. Drop by an *ice cream scoop* on ungreased cookie sheet. Bake at 350° for 20 minutes. Cookies have an even better flavor if frozen before eating.

MONTVIEW APRICOT SQUARES

1 c. butter or margarine
1 c. sugar
1 egg yolk
2 c. flour

¾ c. finely chopped pecans
1 (10 oz.) jar apricot jam or
  preserves

Preheat oven to 350°. Cream butter and sugar in large bowl. Add yolk and mix well. Add flour. Add nuts and blend well. Dough will be soft. Divide dough in half. Spread ½ evenly on bottom of 9x13 inch pan. Cover with jam and spread carefully to edges. Cover with remaining dough by spoonfuls over jam. Bake until golden brown, about 40 to 45 minutes. Let cool slightly and cut into squares. Makes 40.

When spreading dough in pan and adding jam and nuts, use small spoonfuls as it's easier to spread.

VERSATILE CREAM CHEESE COOKIES

1 c. shortening
1 (3 oz.) pkg. cream cheese
1 c. sugar
1 tsp. baking powder
1 egg

½ tsp. vanilla
2½ c. flour
1 tsp. orange or lemon rind
  (optional)
1 Tbsp. orange or lemon juice

Cream shortening. Gradually work in cheese and sugar until well blended. Beat in remaining ingredients. Drop by teaspoon on cookie sheet or use a cookie press. (Use food coloring if desired). Dough may be chilled until firm and rolled and cut with cookie cutters. Bake in a preheated 375° oven for 10 minutes. Yield: 3 to 5 dozen cookies.

GINGER CRINKLES
(Cookies)

⅔ c. oil

1 c. sugar

Mix the oil and sugar together.

1 egg

¼ c. molasses

Add to the oil and sugar mixture.

2 c. flour
2 tsp. baking soda
½ tsp. salt

1 tsp. ginger
1 tsp. cinnamon

Sift together and add to preceding. Roll into small balls and roll in granulated sugar. Place on greased baking sheet. Bake at 325° for 8 to 10 minutes. Remove from pan and cool. Store cookies in airtight can.

PUMPKIN COOKIES

Cookie Dough:

1 c. (2 sticks) butter
1 c. light brown sugar, firmly packed
1 egg
1 c. canned pumpkin
2 c. all-purpose flour
1½ c. golden raisins

2 tsp. grated orange peel
1 tsp. baking powder
1 tsp. pumpkin pie spice
½ tsp. baking soda
½ tsp. salt

Preheat oven to 350°. Cream butter in large mixing bowl; gradually add sugar and mix until blended. Beat in egg and pumpkin until blended. Mix ¼ cup flour with raisins and orange peel. Combine remaining flour, baking powder, pumpkin spice, soda, and salt. Gradually add to creamed mixture, beating just until blended. Stir in raisin mixture. Drop by rounded teaspoons onto buttered cookie sheets. Bake 12 to 15 minutes. Remove from wire racks to cool.

Frosting:

3 Tbsp. butter, softened
3½ c. confectioners sugar

¼ c. orange juice

Beat butter, 2 cups of sugar, and orange juice together until smooth. Add remaining sugar, beating until frosting is smooth.

For Halloween, decorate as pumpkin faces with candy corn, jelly beans, and etc.

WINTER PARK CARROT BARS

Use 4 eggs, beaten well.

Add:

2 c. sugar
2 tsp. soda

2 tsp. cinnamon

Add:

1 c. oil
1 tsp. salt

3 small jars baby carrot food
2 c. flour (last)

Bake in 12x18 inch pan for 25 minutes at 350°.

Frost with Cream Cheese Frosting:

1 (8 oz.) pkg. cream cheese
2 tsp. vanilla

½ stick butter
1 lb. powdered sugar

Warm cheese and butter at room temperature. Cream together thoroughly and add vanilla. Gradually beat in the sugar and spread. *Great for ski trips.*

176

ROCKY MOUNTAIN ZUCCHINI COOKIES

1 c. margarine or shortening
2 eggs
1 c. white sugar
1 tsp. salt
1 c. brown sugar
1 c. zucchini, grated and drained

1 Tbsp. cinnamon
4 c. flour
1 c. nuts or coconut
½ tsp. soda, dissolved in 1 Tbsp. warm water
1 tsp. vanilla

Mix shortening, sugar, eggs, and salt; cream well. Add zucchini. Add cinnamon, flour, soda, vanilla, and nuts. Mix well and drop by teaspoon on cookie sheet (lightly greased). Bake 12 to 14 minutes at 350°.

POPPY SEED COOKIES

1 c. sugar
Peel of 1 orange
1 egg yolk
1 c. (2 sticks) unsalted butter, cut into 8 pieces

½ tsp. salt
½ tsp. freshly grated nutmeg
1 c. unbleached all-purpose flour
1 c. cake flour
¼ c. poppy seed

Mince orange peel finely and combine with sugar, mincing together. Add egg yolk and mix 1 minute. Add butter, salt, and nutmeg. Mix until light and fluffy, about 1 minute. Add remaining ingredients and mix thoroughly but do not overmix.

Divide dough into 4 equal portions. Arrange each on sheet of plastic wrap. Using plastic as aide, shape dough into 2x4 inch cylinders. Seal and refrigerate until firm, 1 hour. (Can be prepared ahead to this point and frozen.)

Position rack in center of oven and preheat to 350°F. Cut dough into ¼ inch slices. Arrange on baking sheet, spacing 1½ inches apart. Bake until edges are lightly browned, about 8 minutes. Transfer to wire rack and let cool. Store in airtight container. Makes about 5 dozen. *A fresh taste!*

CAPPUCCINO THINS

4 oz. sweet cooking chocolate, cut into 1 inch pieces
½ c. plus 2 Tbsp. sugar
½ c. firmly packed light brown sugar
1 egg yolk
1 Tbsp. freeze-dried instant coffee powder

1 tsp. cinnamon
1 Tbsp. unsweetened cocoa
¾ tsp. salt
1 c. (2 sticks) unsalted butter, cut into 8 pieces
1 c. cake flour
1 c. unbleached all-purpose flour

Chop chocolate until it resembles coarse meal. Transfer to small bowl and set aside. Combine sugars, egg yolk, coffee and cocoa powders, cinnamon, and salt in work bowl and mix about a minute. Add butter and mix 1 minute. Add flours and chocolate and mix just until flour is incorporated into dough. Do not overmix.

Divide dough into 4 equal portions and arrange each on a sheet of plastic wrap. Using as aide, shape dough into 1x4 inch cylinders. Seal and refrigerate until firm (1 hour). Can be prepared ahead to this point and frozen.

Position rack in center of oven and preheat to 350°F. Cut dough into ¼ inch slices. Arrange on baking sheet, spacing 1½ inches apart. Bake until set, about 8 minutes, and transfer cookies to wire rack. Let cool completely and store in airtight container. Makes about 5 dozen. *Wonderful with coffee!*

NO COOK ORANGE BALLS

1 (12 to 16 oz.) pkg. vanilla wafers
    or wafer crumbs
¼ to ½ c. chopped nuts (any kind)

¼ c. melted butter or margarine
1 c. undiluted frozen orange juice
1 c. powdered sugar

Crush wafers and mix with other ingredients. Make balls and roll in powdered sugar. Use more sugar if needed.

Miscellaneous

TEMPERATURE TESTS
FOR CANDY MAKING

There are two different methods of determining when candy has been cooked to the proper consistency. One is by using a candy thermometer in order to record degrees, the other is by using the cold water test. The chart below will prove useful in helping to follow candy recipes:

TYPE OF CANDY	DEGREES	COLD WATER
Fondant, Fudge	234 - 238°	Soft Ball
Divinity, Caramels	245 - 248°	Firm Ball
Taffy	265 - 270°	Hard Ball
Butterscotch	275 - 280°	Light Crack
Peanut Brittle	285 - 290°	Hard Crack
Caramelized Sugar	310 - 321°	Caramelized

In using the cold water test, use a fresh cupful of cold water for each test. When testing, remove the candy from the fire and pour about ½ teaspoon of candy into the cold water. Pick the candy up in the fingers and roll into a ball if possible.

In the SOFT BALL TEST the candy will roll into a soft ball which quickly loses its shape when removed from the water.

In the FIRM BALL TEST the candy will roll into a firm, but not hard ball. It will flatten out a few minutes after being removed from the water.

In the HARD BALL TEST the candy will roll into a hard ball which has lost almost all plasticity and will roll around on a plate on removal from the water.

In the LIGHT CRACK TEST the candy will form brittle threads which will soften on removal from the water.

In the HARD CRACK TEST the candy will form brittle threads in the water which will remain brittle after being removed from the water.

In CARAMELIZING the sugar first melts then becomes a golden brown. It will form a hard brittle ball in cold water.

MISCELLANEOUS

WATERMELON PICO DE GALLO

Cube into a ¼ inch dice:

½ c. jicima
1½ c. watermelon
¼ c. honeydew
¼ c. cantaloupe
¼ c. red onion

1 jalapeno, chopped
2 Tbsp. lime juice
½ c. cilantro, chopped
½ tsp. salt

Mix ingredients together in bowl. Chill before serving. Refreshing as a dip with blue corn meal tortillas.

WATSON'S SALSA

2 c. medium salsa
1 can black beans, drained
1½ c. corn (3 ears fresh corn)
2 red peppers

2 medium tomatoes, seeded and
   chopped fine
1 bunch green onions, chopped
1 to 2 bunches cilantro, chopped

Roast skins of red peppers until black; skin, seed, and slice. Put into bowl; add remaining ingredients. Will last 2 to 3 weeks in refrigerator. Also good served on chicken. *Very good.*

ORANGE-BASIL SALSA

¼ c. snipped fresh basil or snipped
   fresh mint
¼ c. finely copped red onion
1 tsp. finely shredded orange peel

2 oranges, peeled, sectioned, and
   chopped (1 c.)
Dash of salt

Stir together all ingredients. Cover and refrigerate till ready to serve. Serve chilled or at room temperature. Makes about ¾ cup.

PARSLEY PARMESAN MARINADE

¾ c. canola or safflower oil
⅓ c. balsamic vinegar
2 shallots, minced
3 Tbsp. minced fresh parsley

2 Tbsp. freshly grated Parmesan
   cheese
Salt and freshly ground pepper

In a bowl, whisk together oil, vinegar, shallots, parsley, and cheese. Add salt and pepper to taste. Makes about 1⅓ cups.

ROSEMARY WALNUT MARINADE

3 Tbsp. balsamic vinegar
3 Tbsp. seasoned rice wine vinegar
2 Tbsp. fresh rosemary
1 tsp. Dijon mustard

½ c. olive oil
½ c. canola or safflower oil
½ c. walnut pieces
Salt and freshly ground pepper

In a food processor, put vinegars, rosemary, mustard, and oils, and process with a steel blade for about 40 seconds, stopping once to scrape down the sides. Through the feed tube, add the walnut pieces and process until they are finely ground, not pureed. Add salt and pepper to taste. Makes 1½ cups.

GINGER CILANTRO MARINADE

½ c. canola or safflower oil
3 Tbsp. seasoned rice wine vinegar
2 Tbsp. plain white wine vinegar (no herbs)
3 Tbsp. minced fresh cilantro

1 Tbsp. grated fresh ginger
1 Tbsp. "lite" soy sauce
2 tsp. toasted sesame oil
2 large cloves garlic, pressed

In a bowl, whisk together oil, vinegars, cilantro, ginger, soy sauce, sesame oil, and garlic until well mixed. If using this on blanched or sauteed vegetables, toss them with the dressing when they are hot. Makes about 1 cup.

BARBECUE SAUCE

1 c. catsup
½ c. brown sugar
¼ c. vinegar

1 Tbsp. Worcestershire sauce
¼ c. water

Mix and simmer for 15 minutes.

PESTO

2 c. fresh basil leaves, packed
3 cloves garlic
¼ c. pine nuts
1 tsp. salt

¾ c. extra virgin olive oil
½ c. freshly grated Parmesan cheese
¼ c. freshly grated Romano cheese

In a food processor or blender, combine the basil, garlic, pine nuts, and salt. Process until smooth. With the processor running, add oil through the feed tube and process until well blended. Pour the basil mixture into a bowl and mix in the cheeses.

MASTE KHIAR

4 cucumbers
¼ c. fresh mint, chopped

3 (8 oz.) containers plain yogurt
Salt and freshly ground pepper

Peel cucumbers and cut into small cubes. Add mint and 2 containers of yogurt. Salt and pepper to taste. Mix and chill for 2 hours. Drain excess water and add remaining yogurt. Stir mixture; chill briefly and serve. Serves 6 to 8. Use as a salad, side dish, or appetizer.

TEXAS CORN DIP

¼ c. butter or margarine
½ c. whipping cream (unwhipped)
1 c. American cheese, grated
¼ tsp. paprika

½ tsp. salt
¼ tsp. pepper
6 ears corn, cooked and drained

Melt butter in chafing dish over hot water. Add cream, cheese, paprika, salt, and pepper. Cook over low heat, stirring, until cheese is melted and mixture is well blended and hot. Keep mixture warm to keep it from becoming too thick. Roll hot, cooked corn in sauce, turning until it is completely coated. If sauce becomes too thick, thin it by adding a small amount of milk. Recipe may be doubled. Sauce takes the place of butter on corn. It also is delicious served over cooked cauliflower, broccoli, and other vegetables of your choice. Makes about 1 cup.

CHILI RING

2 Tbsp. gelatin
½ c. cold water
1 c. chili sauce
1 c. mayonnaise

1 c. cottage cheese
1 c. whipping cream
1 can shrimp (optional)

Dissolve gelatin in water. Heat chili sauce, mayonnaise, and cottage cheese and combine with gelatin and cream. Pour into bowl or mold to chill and set. Serve with chicken or potato salad. *Easy and good.*

STUFFING SUPREME

2 cans bean sprouts
2 cans mushrooms
4 tsp. beef bouillon
2 onions, chopped
2 green peppers, chopped

3 c. celery, chopped
2 cloves garlic, minced or pressed
1 (8 oz.) can tomato sauce
2 tsp. salt
1 tsp. pepper

Drain liquid from sprouts and mushrooms; combine with other ingredients. Stuff turkey or cook in casserole at 350° for 30 to 40 minutes. This is good hot, cold, or uncooked! *Very good.*

MUSTARD MOUSSE

1 env. unflavored gelatin
¼ c. lemon juice
4 eggs
¾ c. sugar
3 Tbsp. Dijon mustard

½ tsp. salt
½ c. cider vinegar (or white)
1 c. whipping cream, whipped
½ c. water
2 Tbsp. parsley, chopped (optional)

In a small bowl, pour the lemon juice over gelatin and let stand 5 minutes. In a double boiler, mix eggs, sugar, mustard, salt, vinegar, and water. Beat with wire whip until blended. Add gelatin and stir constantly over hot water until thick. Don't boil. Cool by putting cold water in bottom of boiler and let stand and set while whipping cream. Fold into egg mixture. Pour into an oiled mold holding about 4 cups. Refrigerate until set, several hours or overnight. May be kept up to 3 days.

Sweet and tart; brings out the flavor of pork, beef, or ham.

CRANBERRY-APPLE RELISH

1 c. sugar
¼ tsp. cinnamon
¼ tsp. cloves
¼ tsp. allspice
½ c. apple juice

4 c. fresh cranberries
2 medium Red Delicious apples,
    peeled, cored, and chopped
½ c. walnuts, chopped

    Mix sugar, spices, and apple juice in a deep 2 quart microwave-safe casserole. Stir in cranberries and apples. Cover loosely with waxed paper. Microwave on HIGH for 8 to 10 minutes, stirring twice, until cranberries pop. Uncover; microwave 2 to 3 minutes more, until slightly thickened. Stir in walnuts. Let cool before serving. Makes 4½ cups.

PEACH CHUTNEY

1 (1 lb.) can peach slices in natural
    juices, drained
¾ c. cider vinegar
½ c. brown sugar
½ small onion, minced

1 apple, peeled, cored, and coarsely
    chopped
1 tsp. pickling spices
Juice of ½ lemon

    Chop peaches coarsely. Combine with remaining ingredients in large saucepan; simmer 20 minutes or until thickened slightly. Cool and cover until serving. Serve cold or at room temperature. Makes 2 cups.

ANOTHER CRANBERRY CHUTNEY

4 c. fresh cranberries
¼ c. walnuts
½ tsp. cinnamon
½ c. white raisins
1 green apple, peeled, cored, and
    chopped

1 Tbsp. vinegar
2 c. sugar
½ tsp. ginger
½ c. orange concentrate

    Simmer all ingredients, except walnuts, in saucepan until cranberries pop. Remove from heat and add nuts. Pour into sterile jars. Recipe can be doubled.

A.L.D. CRANBERRY CHUTNEY

1 pkg. cranberries
1 large apple, peeled, cored, and
    chopped
½ c. raisins
½ c. orange juice concentrate
2 Tbsp. orange rind, grated
Red food coloring

1 Tbsp. cider vinegar
2 tsp. cinnamon
3 c. sugar
1 tsp. ginger
1 tsp. cloves
½ c. walnuts, chopped

    Mix all ingredients, except walnuts, together in saucepan. Heat to boiling, decrease heat and cook until cranberries pop. Stir frequently. Remove from heat; cool. Add walnuts.

BAKED PINEAPPLE

½ c. butter, softened
¾ c. sugar
Dash of salt
3 eggs

1 (15 oz.) can chunk pineapple,
   drained
5 slices white bread, cubed

Cream butter and sugar together. Add eggs, beating well. Stir in remaining ingredients. Bake, uncovered, at 325° for 40 to 50 minutes. *Great served with ham!*

PALSADIS FRESH PEACH SAUCE

2 fresh peaches, peeled and sliced
1 (8 oz.) ctn. nonfat dairy sour cream
½ c. firmly packed brown sugar

2 tsp. Dijon mustard
1 Tbsp. bourbon
¼ tsp. salt

Combine all ingredients in a saucepan and place over low heat, stirring gently until heated through. Drizzle over chicken breasts to taste.

WESTCLIFF BOURBON PEACHES

From "An Appetite for Passion Cookbook" by Laura Esquivel and John Willoughby, Miramax Books.

1 c. sugar
1½ c. water
1 c. cider vinegar
8 small, ripe peaches, peeled,
   quartered, and pitted

10 whole cloves
½ c. bourbon whiskey
4 sprigs fresh mint

Combine the sugar, water, and vinegar in a saucepan and bring to a boil. Add the peaches and cloves, simmer for 5 minutes, and remove from the heat. Allow to cool to room temperature, then pour into a quart jar. Add the bourbon and mint; cover tightly and refrigerate for at least 1 week. Will keep for up to 6 weeks covered and refrigerated. Suggested as an accompaniment to grilled venison steaks.

CRANBERRY-CITRUS SAUCE

1 small orange (unpeeled), sliced
2⅓ c. orange juice
2 c. sugar
2 Tbsp. plus 2 tsp. fresh lemon juice

2 (12 oz.) bags cranberries
3 Tbsp. plus 1 tsp. Triple Sec or
   other orange liqueur
   (optional)

Finely grind orange in processor. Combine orange juice, sugar, and lemon juice in heavy large saucepan. Bring to boil, stirring until sugar dissolves. Reduce heat and simmer 5 minutes. Add ground orange and cranberries and cook until berries begin to pop, stirring occasionally, about 8 minutes. Remove from heat. Stir in Triple Sec. Cool completely. (Can be prepared up to 4 days ahead.) Cover and refrigerate. Serve cold or at room temperature. Makes 5 cups.

CAPER, SHALLOT, AND PARSLEY SAUCE

½ c. white wine tarragon vinegar
2 tsp. fresh lemon juice
2 Tbsp. water
½ tsp. sugar
2 Tbsp. olive oil

¼ c. shallot, finely chopped
3 Tbsp. fresh parsley leaves, minced
2 Tbsp. capers, chopped
Salt and pepper to taste

In a small bowl, combine well all the ingredients. Makes 1 cup.

JALAPENA JELLY

1 c. canned jalapena peppers with seeds
1 medium bell pepper
1¼ c. vinegar (divided)

6 c. sugar
8 oz. Certo
4 to 5 drops of green food coloring

Put both peppers and ¼ cup vinegar together in blender and blend. Place sugar in saucepan; add blender mixture. Add 1 cup vinegar. Cook over low heat. Boil slowly for 15 minutes, skimming off foam. Add Certo and food coloring. Return to boiling, stirring constantly. Boil 1 minute. Cool slightly and pour into containers. Serve on crackers with cream cheese.

SWEET RED AND GREEN PEPPER JAM

12 red and green peppers
1 Tbsp. salt

2 c. vinegar
2 c. sugar

Grind peppers; add salt and let stand overnight. Drain well. Add vinegar and sugar. Stir over medium heat until mixture boils. Lower heat and simmer until thick as jam. Seal in hot jars.

KIWI AND PEAR PRESERVES

4 kiwi (about 1¼ c.)
1 large ripe pear
4 c. sugar
2 tsp. lime or lemon juice

½ (6 oz.) liquid pectin
½ tsp. lime or lemon peel, finely shredded

Peel and coarsely chop the kiwi. Peel, core, and coarsely chop pear. In a large bowl, mash both fruits with a fork. Stir in sugar. Let stand 10 minutes. Combine the pectin, peel, and juice. Add to fruit mixture. Stir for 3 minutes. Ladle at once into clean hot jars, leaving a ½ inch head space. Seal and label. Let stand overnight. Store in refrigerator. Makes 5 cups.

PLUM CONSERVE

3 lb. plums, pitted and chopped*
1 lb. seeded raisins
3 oranges with rind, seeded and chopped

2 lemons (juice only)
3 lb. sugar
1 lb. walnuts, chopped

Combine all ingredients in large saucepan. Cook over medium heat, stirring occasionally, until fruit is thick and clear. Distribute into sterilized glasses and seal, or put into freezable glasses and store in freezer or refrigerator.

* Blue plums, greengage or plums from ornamental trees.

SPICED PEACH JAM

4 c. peaches, chopped	½ to 1 tsp. cloves
1 box Sure-Jell	½ to 1 tsp. cinnamon
5½ c. sugar	½ to 1 tsp. allspice

Follow Sure-Jell direction for jam.

SWEET DILL PICKLES

2 qt. dill pickles	1 Tbsp. black pepper
2½ c. cider vinegar	4 c. sugar
2 Tbsp. whole allspice	1 c. brown sugar

Make syrup and boil 5 minutes. Drain pickles and cut into chunks. Add pickles to syrup and bring to boil. Let stand in syrup 24 hours.

REFRIGERATOR ONION RING PICKLES

1½ lb. small crisp onions	½ c. water
18 whole cloves	1 c. sugar
18 black peppercorns	2 tsp. salt
3 tsp. mustard seed	1½ tsp. turmeric
1½ tsp. celery seed	½ tsp. cinnamon
2 c. white or apple cider vinegar	

Peel onions and slice ¼ inch thick; separate the slices into rings. Divide into three one pint canning jars. To each jar, add 6 whole cloves, 6 peppercorns, 1 teaspoon mustard seed, and ½ teaspoon celery seed. Combine vinegar, water, sugar, salt, turmeric, and cinnamon in a steel or enamel saucepan; heat to boiling, then simmer 2 minutes. Pour mixture into the jars. Let them cool, then cover each jar with double plastic wrap and apply a cap. No need to seal jars. Let the pickles mellow for one month in the refrigerator before serving. Always store in the refrigerator.

Excellent condiment with most meals; unique!

FRUIT-FLAVOR VINEGARS

Heat 2 cups white wine vinegar and 1 cup fresh or frozen tart red cherries, blueberries, or raspberries in a small stainless steel or enamel saucepan to boiling. Reduce heat; boil gently, uncovered, for 3 minutes. Remove from heat and cover loosely with cheesecloth; cool. Uncover and pour mixture into a clean 1 pint jar. Cover jar tightly with a nonmetal lid. Let stand in a cool, dark place for 2 weeks.

Line a colander with several layers of 100% cotton cheesecloth. Pour vinegar mixture through colander into a bowl. Discard fruit. Transfer vinegar to a clean 1½ pint jar or bottle. Cover tightly with a nonmetal lid; store in a cool, dark place up to 6 months.

HERB VINEGAR

Wash ½ cup tightly packed fresh tarragon, thyme, mint, rosemary, or basil leaves; pat dry. Combine herbs and 2 cups white wine vinegar in a small stainless steel or enamel saucepan. Bring almost to boiling. Remove from heat; cover loosely with cheesecloth. Cool. Uncover and pour mixture into a clean 1 pint jar. Cover jar tightly with a nonmetal lid. Let stand in a cool, dark place for 2 weeks.

Line a colander with several layers of 100% cotton cheesecloth. Pour vinegar mixture through colander into a bowl. Discard herbs. Transfer vinegar to a clean 1 pint jar or bottle. Cover tightly with a nonmetal lid; store in a cool, dark place up to 6 months.

PECAN PRALINE SAUCE

1 Tbsp. butter
½ c. buttermilk
1 c. sugar

¾ c. pecans, chopped
½ tsp. baking soda
Vanilla ice cream

In a heavy saucepan or the top of a double boiler, melt butter over low heat. Add the remaining ingredients. Stir over low heat until slightly thickened. Serve warm over vanilla ice cream, pound cake, in small meringues.

PEACH FROZEN YOGURT

5 medium peaches, peeled and
    pitted, or 5 c. frozen sliced
    peaches, thawed
1 (8 oz.) ctn. vanilla lowfat yogurt

2 Tbsp. honey
1 tsp. vanilla
⅛ tsp. ground nutmeg

Place fruit in a blender container or food processor. Cover and blend or process till smooth. Add yogurt, honey, vanilla, and nutmeg; cover and blend or process till combined. Transfer to a 9x9x2 inch pan. Cover and freeze 2 to 3 hours or till almost firm.

Break frozen mixture into small chunks. Transfer to a chilled bowl. Beat with an electric mixer till smooth but not melted. Return to pan. Cover and freeze till firm. Let stand at room temperature for 10 minutes before scooping. Makes 8 (½ cup) servings.

CREAM CARAMELS

1 large can condensed milk
⅔ c. light corn syrup
1½ c. sugar
1 tsp. vanilla

8 Tbsp. butter
4 Tbsp. flour
4 Tbsp. corn starch
Nuts (optional)

Put sugar, corn syrup, and 1 cup condensed milk into saucepan and stir constantly until it boils. Slowly add the rest of the condensed milk. Do not let boiling stop. Cook until a soft ball forms in cold water. Cream the butter, flour, and corn starch together; add to cooked mixture and cook until a firm ball forms in cold water. Nuts may be added here. Turn into buttered pan. Let stand overnight. Cut into squares when cool.

186

OLD-FASHIONED BASIC FUDGE

2 c. sugar
¾ c. milk
2 Tbsp. butter, cut into small pieces

4 Tbsp. cocoa
2 Tbsp. light corn syrup
2 tsp. vanilla

Oil an 8x8 inch pan. Combine the sugar, cocoa, milk, and corn syrup in 3 quart heavy pot, stirring to blend all ingredients. Over low heat and stirring slowly, bring to a boil. Continue to stir a few minutes, then let boil to the soft ball stage or 234° on candy thermometer. Remove from heat; add butter without stirring and set on a cooling surface. Do not stir until syrup is lukewarm or 110°, then add vanilla and stir without stopping until mixture loses its gloss and thickens. Quickly pour into the oiled pan and mark into squares. When firm, cut into pieces and store in airtight container.

PEANUT BUTTER GRANOLA

2 Tbsp. oil
⅓ c. chunky peanut butter
½ c. brown sugar
2½ c. old-fashioned oats

¾ c. raisins
1 c. coconut
½ c. wheat germ
¾ c. nuts

Stir corn oil into peanut butter, then add sugar. Add oats and nuts; stir well. Spread on 2 baking sheets; bake at 300° for 15 to 20 minutes, stirring occasionally. Add raisins, coconut, and wheat germ. Serves 6 to 8.

CANDIED FRUIT SLICES

Very colorful on Christmas cookie tray.

1 c. butter
1 c. sifted powdered sugar
1 egg
1 tsp. vanilla

2¼ c. sifted flour
1 c. pecan halves or large pieces
1 c. green candied cherries, halved
1 c. red candied cherries (whole)

Cream butter; gradually add powdered sugar, then cream together well. Blend in egg and vanilla. Stir in flour and mix well. Stir in pecans and cherries. Divide dough in half and shape each into a 1½ inch diameter roll. Wrap each in waxed paper and chill well, at least 3 hours. Cut into ⅛ inch slices and place on ungreased baking sheets. Bake at 325° for 13 to 15 minutes or until delicately brown on edges. Cool on racks. Makes 6 dozen.

LEMON CURD
(Good)

5 egg yolks
½ c. sugar
2 large lemons (juice and finely
    grated rind)

¼ c. sweet butter

In a heavy saucepan or double boiler, mix yolks and sugar. Stir well. Add juice and rind of lemons. Cook over low heat until thick. Stir constantly. Add butter a little bit at a time. Pour into a clean jar and refrigerate.

Use as a spread on muffins and biscuits. Great with English tea.

Notes

Celebrity and Restaurant Recipes

HEART HEALTHY TIPS
Substitutions, Modifications and Equivalents

Instead of	Use	Instead of	Use
1 c. butter 498 mg cholesterol	7/8 c. polyunsaturated oil-0 mg cholesterol 1 c. tub margarine- 0 mg cholesterol 2 stks margarine- 0 mg cholesterol	1 c. whole milk yogurt, plain- 250 calories	1 c. part skim milk yogurt, plain- 125-145 calories
		1 c. sour cream- 416 calories	1 c. blended low-fat cottage cheese- 208 calories
1 c. heavy cream- 832 calories, 296 mg cholesterol	1 c. evap. skim milk- 176 calories 8 mg cholesterol	1 oz. baking chocolate 8.4 gm sat. fat	3 Tbsp. cocoa powder- 1.7 gm sat. fat PLUS
1 md whole egg- 274 mg cholesterol	1/4 c. egg sub- 0 mg cholesterol*		1 Tbsp. polyunsaturated oil - 1.1 gm sat. fat TOTAL: 2.8 gm sat. fat

*Some egg substitutes do contain cholesterol. Check label to be sure.

To Reduce Cholesterol or Saturated Fats:

1. Select lean cuts of meat.
2. Serve moderate portions.
3. Replace animal fats with appropriate substitutes.

Examples

Instead of	Use
Butter, lard, bacon or bacon fat, and chicken fat	Polyunsaturated margarine or oil
Sour cream	Low-fat yogurt
Whole milk	Skim milk
Whole milk cheeses	Low-fat cheeses
Whole eggs	Egg whites or egg substitutes

To Reduce Calories or Fats:

1. Brown meat by broiling or cooking in non-stick pans with little or no oil.
2. Chill soups, stews, sauces, and broths. Lift off congealed fat (saves 100 calories per Tbsp. of fat removed).
3. Trim fat from meat. Also remove skin from poultry.
4. Use water-packed canned products (canned fish, canned fruits).
5. In recipes for baked products, the sugar can often be reduced 1/4 to 1/3 without harming the final product. Cinnamon and vanilla also give the impression of sweetness.
6. Use fresh fruit whenever possible. If canned fruit must be used, select water-packed varieties, fruit in own juice, or drain heavy syrup from canned fruit.
7. For sauces and dressings, use low-calorie bases (vinegar, mustard, tomato juice, fat-free bouillon) instead of high calorie ones (creams, fats, oils, mayonnaise).

Equivalents for Sugar Substitutes

Brand Name	Amount	Substitution for Sugar
Adolph's Powder	1 tsp.	= 1/4 c.
	4 tsp.	= 1 c.
Equal Powder	1 pkt.	= 2 tsp.
Sweet N'Low Powder	1 pkt.	= 2 tsp.
	1 tsp.	= 1/4 c.
	4 tsp.	= 1 c.
Sweet N'Low Brown	4 tsp.	= 1 c. brown sugar
Sugar Twin Powder	1 tsp.	= 1 tsp.
Sugar Twin Brown Powder	1 tsp.	= 1 tsp. brown sugar
Sweet-10 Liquid	10 drops	= 1 tsp.
	2 Tbsp.	= 1 c.

CELEBRITY AND RESTAURANT RECIPES

SWEDISH GRAVLAX

½ fresh salmon
1 tsp. pepper
1 tsp. salt

1 tsp. dill
1 tsp. sugar

Combine salt, pepper, dill, and sugar. Grind in grinder. Put ⅛ inch mixture on top of salmon. Wrap salmon in Saran Wrap to marinate. Refrigerate 30 hours, then take all marinade off salmon. Slice salmon very thin. Make the following sauce.

Sauce:

½ c. Dijon mustard
1 tsp. dill
1 tsp. sugar

¼ c. lemon juice
Salt and pepper

Serve with toast points and thinly sliced lemon.

Adde Brewster Restaurant

ASSIGNMENTS RESTAURANT CEDAR PLANK SALMON WITH BLACKBERRY SAUCE

4 (8 oz.) salmon filets
1 tsp. kosher salt
½ tsp. white pepper

Cedar plank
½ c. olive oil

For Sauce:

2 pt. fresh blackberries
1 shallot
1 c. white wine
2½ c. stock (this could be fish or
   chicken)

2 Tbsp. honey
1 sprig fresh tarragon

Sauce: In a pan, reduce berries, shallot, and wine by one third of its volume. Add stock, honey, and tarragon and reduce by one third of its volume again. Blend mixture; strain (to get the seeds out) and adjust seasoning with salt and white pepper.

To cook salmon, season filets with salt and pepper and let stand for 20 minutes. Preheat oven to 500° and place oiled cedar plank in the oven by itself for 20 minutes. Lay salmon filets on plank and place in oven for 8 to 10 minutes. Sauce the plate and lay the salmon on top of your sauce. I recommend to serve the salmon with fresh steamed asparagus, marinated Roma tomatoes, and couscous.

I use cedar planks to erect backyard fences. I cut them a little bit smaller than my oven, then wash the plank in my dishwasher to sanitize. I use olive oil to "season" the plank.

Assignments Restaurant, Chef Stephen Kleinman, CEC

BUCKHORN EXCHANGE LAVENDER PEPPER DUCK BREAST WITH RASPBERRY-RED ZINFANDEL SAUCE

Raspberry-Red Zinfandel Sauce:

3 c. cold water
24 oz. of raspberries
1 Tbsp. chicken base
1 c. sugar
1 c. Zinfandel

½ c. dark rum
2 to 3 Tbsp. corn starch
½ c. cold water
2 Tbsp. creme de cassis

1. Combine raspberries and water in a heavy saucepan and bring to boil. Reduce heat; simmer for 5 minutes. Add chicken base and sugar. Stir until sugar dissolves and continue to simmer.
2. Add Zinfandel and rum and continue to simmer until reduced by ¼.
3. Combine cornstarch with ½ cup cold water and add to sauce.
4. Bring sauce back to a boil, simmer for 5 minutes and remove from heat.
5. Stir in creme de cassis.
6. Force sauce through double mesh strainer.

Lavender Pepper Rub:

2 Tbsp. Tellicherry black
   peppercorns
2 Tbsp. sea salt

2 Tbsp. fennel seeds
2 Tbsp. lavender
1 Tbsp. white pepper

Combine all ingredients in a blender and process until all seeds are reduced to a coarse grind.

1. Skin duck breasts and rub with lavender mixture 1 hour prior to cooking.
2. Grill duck breasts over hot fire until medium rare. Allow to stand for 5 minutes and slice.
3. Serve each breast with 2 ounces of sauce.

Buckhorn Exchange, George Carlberg, Executive Chef

BREAD PUDDING

1 loaf bread, diced
½ tsp. allspice
½ tsp. nutmeg
2 tsp. cinnamon

½ c. raisins
Zest of 1 orange
10 oranges, juiced (or frozen
   concentrate)

Toss bread and spices until bread is coated. Reduce orange juice until it is a syrup. A little sugar may be added. Make Royale Sauce.

Royale Sauce:

10 egg yolks
2 whole eggs
2 c. half & half cream
2 c. heavy cream

1 vanilla bean, split and inside
   scraped out
½ c. sugar

In 6 ounce ovenproof dishes, put a small amount of zest, a small amount of orange juice reduction, 7 or more raisins. Add bread until cup is ¾ full and fill with Royale. Let set and add more Royale until cup is almost full. Bake at 300° for 45 minutes in a water bath. Yield: 10 cups.

Castle Pines Country Club, David Lazarus, Chef

SILVER DOLLAR-SIZE CINNAMON ROLL
(Famous for over 30 years)

1 cake yeast	2 eggs
½ c. warm water	4 oz. margarine
2 c. milk	4 heaping tsp. sugar
6 c. flour	1 heaping tsp. salt

Dissolve yeast in warm water. Scald milk and add sugar, salt, and margarine. Cool to lukewarm.

Add 3 cups flour to this mixture and beat by hand until smooth. Into this mixture, beat the unbeaten eggs and yeast. Stir in remaining 3 cups flour and let rise till double in bulk. Makes 4 dozen cinnamon rolls. Roll the dough into a thin long narrow strip.

Spread with melted margarine and sprinkle with a few currants, sugar, and cinnamon, then roll lengthwise. Cut into 1 inch pieces. Let rise. Bake at 400° until done. Spread powdered-sugar icing while hot. Makes 4 dozen.

Historic El Rancho Colorado Restaurant and Mountain Lodge

GAZPACHO

8 cucumbers	1 red pepper
½ lb. tomatoes	1 jalapeno
1 onion	1 c. red wine vinegar
2 stalks celery	1 c. olive oil
1 carrot	Tabasco
3 cloves garlic	Salt and pepper
1 green pepper	

Peel and seed cucumbers. Dice all other vegetables. Add all ingredients to food processor and blend. Should still have a light chunkiness. Garnish with croutons sauteed in olive oil.

Legends-Beaver Creek Resort

JICAMA AND POTATO CRUSTED SALMON, WITH
TOMATO VINAIGRETTE

6 to 8 oz. salmon filets	1 clove garlic
1 jicama, julienne	1 tomato, smoked (if possible)
1 potato, julienne	¼ c. sherry vinegar
1 shallot	¼ c. olive or canola oil
1 to 2½ Tbsp. tomato paste	Salt and pepper

Peel jicama and potato. Julienne into ⅛ x ⅛ x 2½ inches. Use lemon juice to retard rust color if needed. Arrange over salmon filet and cook in Teflon pan with a little oil and salt and pepper until crust is lightly golden brown. Place in oven 6 to 8 minutes.

Vinaigrette: Place shallot and garlic in food processor. Add tomato and puree. Add vinegar and then slowly pour in oil. Add tomato paste and check seasoning. Pool under cooked salmon and serve with a rice pilaf and vegetables. Add a lemon garni.

Legends-Beaver Creek Resort, Michael Hanrahan, Chef

BANANA BREAD WITH NUTMEG BUTTER

3 bananas
½ c. buttermilk

1 tsp. vanilla

Combine and mash together.

2 c. cake flour
1 tsp. baking powder

1 tsp. baking soda
A pinch of salt

Sift all together.

6 oz. unsalted butter

1½ c. sugar

Cream together. Add 2 large eggs to creamed butter and sugar, one at a time. Add ⅓ cup chopped walnuts.

To mix batter:

1. Add to the creamed butter, sugar, and eggs the dry ingredients and banana mixture alternately, starting and ending with dry ingredients. Finish with chopped walnuts.

2. Bake in a buttered and floured loaf pan in 325° oven for approximately 25 to 30 minutes.

Nutmeg Butter:

½ lb. butter
1½ Tbsp. nutmeg

2 Tbsp. brown sugar

1. Let butter set at room temperature till soft.
2. Mix in the rest of the ingredients and chill.

Normandy Restaurant Francais

PAN-SEARED GINGER AND SESAME CRUSTED SEA BASS

Use 4 (6 to 7 ounce) sea bass filets.

Fried Spinach:

½ lb. fresh spinach leaves
2 to 3 inches frying oil in 5 to 6 qt.
  deep pan *or* deep-fryer is
  available

Stem spinach and fry for 2 to 3 minutes, less if needed.

Cilantro Lime Vinaigrette:

1 c. lime juice
½ qt. rice wine vinegar
2 c. olive oil
Pinch of ground cloves

½ tsp. nutmeg
1/16 tsp. cinnamon
2 tsp. cilantro, chopped
1 c. honey

Combine all ingredients thoroughly. Garnish with diced red and green bell pepper.

Sesame Seed Crust:

½ c. black sesame seeds
½ c. white sesame seeds

1 tsp. ginger (ground)
1 tsp. fresh ginger, finely diced

Mix together thoroughly. Encrust bass by rolling in the seeds and patting while rolling.

Grapefruit Compote:

5 grapefruit segments
½ c. sugar
½ qt. red wine vinegar

1 c. Port wine
2 tsp. orange zest

Mix sugar, Port wine, and vinegar together and reduce for ½ hour. Let cool. Add segments to reduction along with zest.

Cooking: Pan-fry sea bass filets in olive oil using a large skillet. Cook for 5 to 7 minutes or until filets are flaking. (Cooking time will depend on the thickness of the fillet.)

Presentation: Place pool of vinaigrette on plate. Form a nest of crisp spinach on the vinaigrette. Place sea bass in the spinach nest and Grapefruit Compote on the side. Yield: 4 servings.

Palace Arms Restaurant, The Brown Palace Hotel

GRILLED BEEF TENDERLOIN

Five spices, lemon grass, and oyster sauce.

Marinade:

1 Tbsp. five spices
1 Tbsp. soy sauce
1 tsp. minced green onion
2 Tbsp. oyster sauce
½ c. pineapple juice
Black pepper

1 tsp. chili paste
½ c. honey
1 tsp. minced lemon grass
½ tsp. minced garlic
1 tsp. curry powder

Additional ingredients:

1½ to 2 lb. beef tenderloin (in one
piece; you can also cut the
beef in 3 oz. pieces)

1 lb. mixed greens

Marinate the meat in marinade 1 hour before cooking. Preheat a grill or BBQ on high temperature. Grill the meat 7 minutes each side for medium rare. Slice into thin slices and serve on a mixed green salad sprinkled with Tamarind Dressing.

You can serve this dish with saute vegetables and potato or rice.

If it is for individual serving, sear the beef pieces on high heat in a saute pan, 3 minutes each side.

Tamarind Dressing:

½ juice from tamarind soaked in
water
1 tsp. chili paste
1 Tbsp. sugar
1 tsp. minced garlic

½ c. fish sauce
1 Tbsp. lime juice
1 tsp. minced lemon grass
½ c. water

Mix all ingredients in jar. Shake well.

Papillion Restaurant

VENISON MEDALLIONS WITH LINGONBERRY SAUCE

4 (4 to 6 oz.) venison medallions
Flour
1 tsp. salt

1 tsp. cracked black pepper
4 Tbsp. olive oil

Season medallions with salt and pepper. Dredge in flour lightly. Saute venison until desired temperature.

Lingonberry Sauce:

1 Tbsp. butter
½ c. lingonberry preserves (may substitute cranberry sauce)
2 Tbsp. fresh lemon juice
2 Tbsp. fresh orange juice

¼ c. cider vinegar
1 Tbsp. cornstarch
1 tsp. salt
3 whole cloves

Melt butter and add jelly, lemon juice, and orange juice. After jelly has melted, add vinegar, corn starch, salt, and cloves. Cook until thickened.

Pinos Restaurant, Jeff Willoughly

ASIAGO CHEESE DIP

1 gal. mayonnaise
2 lb. sour cream
1.5 lb. Asiago cheese, grated

¾ lb. sun-dried tomatoes
1.5 qt. green onions
1.5 qt. mushrooms

Rehydrate the sun-dried tomatoes in hot water. Rinse and chop scallions. Rinse and slice mushrooms. Combine all the ingredients together. Serve it warm and spread it over your favorite bread. *So yummy!!*

Rock Bottom Brewery

TAKU GLACIER LODGE GRILLED SALMON

⅓ c. butter
⅔ c. brown sugar
2 Tbsp. lemon juice

1 Tbsp. dry white wine
8 (10 to 12 oz.) salmon filets

In a medium saucepan, melt butter over medium heat. Stir in brown sugar until dissolved. Add lemon juice and wine. Stir and heat through, about 5 minutes.

Place filets in a well greased grill basket. Grill on an uncovered grill directly over medium coals for 4 to 6 minutes per ½ inch thickness or until fish flakes when tested with a fork. Turn often, basting with each turn. *Enjoy!*

Taku Glacier Lodge, Juneau, AK

TAKU GLACIER LODGE GINGER COOKIES

2 cubes butter	1¼ tsp. soda
1¾ c. granulated sugar	2½ tsp. cinnamon
¾ c. brown sugar	2 Tbsp. powdered ginger
1 egg	1 Tbsp. cloves
⅓ c. molasses	1 Tbsp. nutmeg
2¾ c. unbleached white flour	½ salt

Preheat oven to 350°, with oven racks evenly spaced. Cream butter and sugar together until fluffy. Beat in egg and molasses. Sift together flour, soda, spices, and salt. Using a small ice cream scoop, form golf ball size dough and dip into raw sugar. Place on ungreased cookie sheet with sugar side up. Bake 12 to 15 minutes for soft cookies. Cookies will crack on top. Take longer for crispier cooked. Excellent served warm. *Yum!*

These specialties are served at the Taku Glacier Lodge in the wilderness near Juneau, Alaska. Served buffet style, salmon is served with beans, cole slaw, and spiced apples with cookies for dessert. Guaranteed to please your guests.

Taku Glacier Lodge, Juneau, AK

LEMON CHICKEN FOR TWO

1 oz. olive oil	4 oz. chicken stock
1 (6 oz.) chicken breast, sliced thinly	1 tsp. fresh rosemary, chopped
Juice of 1 lemon	4 oz. black pepper fettuccine
Salt and pepper to taste	

Combine olive oil and chicken breast. Cook, stirring occasionally, for 6 minutes, until chicken is cooked thoroughly. Add lemon juice, salt and pepper, chicken stock, and rosemary. Reduce to desired consistency and serve on black pepper fettuccine.

Fettuccine available at restaurant, Alfafa's, Wild Oats, Safeway, and Nieman-Marcus.

The Villa Palmer Lake, Linda Van Scoten McColl, Proprietor

PEASANTS PASTA

8 oz. herbed margarine	4 tsp. pureed garlic
12 oz. artichoke hearts	6 oz. chopped tomato
8 oz. sliced fresh mushrooms	10 oz. fresh Parmesan/Romano
24 oz. fresh cooked pasta	cheese, grated
6 oz. sliced black olives	

In a large skillet over medium heat, melt garlic and margarine. Add artichoke hearts and fresh mushrooms. Saute lightly. Add black olives and tomato. Add fresh cooked pasta and 7 ounces of the grated Parmesan/Romano mix and toss. Turn immediately into serving dish and sprinkle with remaining cheese mixture. Serves 4.

This recipe is especially good served with a crisp green salad and fresh hot garlic bread.

York St. Cafe and Bar

SWEDISH MEATBALLS

1 lb. hamburger
1 large diced onion

2 Tbsp. flour
Salt and pepper

Mix with fork and fingers; roll into balls, a little larger than golf balls. Brown over slow heat, turning often. Add 1 can (pound) tomatoes (strain pulp of tomatoes through a strainer). Simmer at least 1 full hour. Serve over mashed potatoes.

Hank Brown, United States Senator

PUMPKIN PECAN MINI MUFFINS

½ c. sliced, unblanched almonds
1⅔ c. all-purpose flour
1 c. sugar
1 Tbsp. pumpkin pie spice
1 tsp. baking soda
¼ tsp. baking powder

¼ tsp. salt
2 large eggs
1 c. plain pumpkin
1 stick butter, melted
1 c. chopped pecans

Preheat oven to 350°. Put almonds on a cookie sheet and bake about 5 minutes until just lightly browned. Slide almonds off the cookie sheet so they cool quickly. Thoroughly mix flour, sugar, pie spice, baking soda, baking powder, and salt in a large bowl.

In another bowl, whisk together eggs, pumpkin, butter, pecans, and almonds until well blended. Fold into dry ingredients until they are just moistened. Scoop batter into greased muffin cups and bake for 20 to 25 minutes. Makes 48 mini muffins (or 12 regular muffins).

Bea Romer, First Lady of Colorado

DAN SCHAEFER'S FAVORITE CHILI

5 (28 oz.) cans peeled tomatoes
6 (1 lb.) cans kidney beans
3 lb. extra lean ground beef
1 diced onion
2 diced green peppers
2 Tbsp. chili powder
1 Tbsp. fines herbes

½ Tbsp. cilantro
1 tsp. crushed red pepper flakes
   (more if higher heat level
   desired)
⅛ to ¼ tsp. nutmeg
Salt to taste

Brown ground beef until thoroughly cooked and drain. In a Dutch oven, crush tomatoes and add remaining ingredients. Bring to a boil and simmer, covered, for 20 minutes.

Congressman Dan Schaefer

BAKED ROCKY MOUNTAIN RAINBOW TROUT

6 (1 to 1½ lb.) fresh rainbow trout
6 small yellow onions, quartered
6 lemons, cut into wedges

12 strips smoked bacon (uncooked)
1 Tbsp. butter salt

Rub the cavity of each fish with butter salt. Stuff each fish with onion quarters and lemon wedges. On a section of foil, place a piece of uncooked bacon. Place fish on the bacon and top with a second piece of bacon and wrap tightly in the foil. Bake for 20 to 30 minutes at 350°. The fish can also be cooked on the grill over hot coals for 5 to 7 minutes a side. Serves 6.

Dan Schaefer, Congress of the United States, House of Representatives

GRILLED VEAL OR PORK CHOPS WITH CAPONATA AND RISSOTO FRITTERS

2 Tbsp. crushed garlic
½ tsp. crushed fresh rosemary
½ tsp. freshly ground black pepper
½ tsp. salt

4 (8 oz.) veal or pork chops
Caponata - see recipe below
Rissoto fritters - see recipe below

In a small bowl, blend the garlic, rosemary, pepper and salt into a paste. Rub into chops and let sit at room temperature for two hours.

Prepare a charcoal or gas grill for cooking. Place the chops on the hottest part of the grill and sear quickly on both sides to seal in the juices. Move to a cooler spot on the grill and cook turning once for about 5-7 minutes for medium. Place a chop on each of four warm serving plates. Garnish with caponata and rissoto fritters. Serves 4.

240 Union Restaurant

RISSOTO HERB FRITTERS

¼ c. butter
¼ c. finely chopped yellow onion
½ c. aborio rice
3 c. chicken stock or canned broth
¼ c. freshly grated Parmesan

2 Tbsp. fresh basil, chopped
2 Tbsp. fresh chives, chopped
2 Tbsp. Italian parsley
Salt and pepper
2 c. oil for frying

Bring the chicken stock to a steady simmer in a saucepan. Heat the butter in a heavy saucepan over moderate heat. Add the onion and saute for 1-2 minutes until transparent. Add the rice to the onions, stir 1 minute making sure all grains are well coated. Add simmering stock ½ cup at a time stirring frequently. Wait until each addition is almost completely absorbed before adding the next half cup. After approximately 20 minutes rice should be tender. The rice should not be al dente for the fritters. It should be slightly over-cooked.

Stir in herbs and cheese, salt and pepper to taste and remove rissoto from pan into casserole dish. Cover and refrigerate at least two hours or overnight. Scoop out rissoto with 2 ounce scoop trying not to break the structure of the rissoto. Fry in 360° oil for approximately three minutes, until crisp. Serve with grilled meats or poultry. Makes 12 fritters.

240 Union Restaurant

1413-96

197

CAPONATA

½ c. extra virgin olive oil
4 Italian plum tomatoes, peeled, seeded and chopped
½ yellow onion, minced
1 Tbsp. garlic, minced
Pinch dried basil
Pinch dried oregano
1 large eggplant, peeled and chopped
1 ea. red and yellow pepper, roasted, peeled and chopped
1 c. Kalamata olives
1 c. toasted pine nuts
⅓ c. red wine vinegar
⅓ c. sugar
Salt and freshly ground black pepper

Heat ¼ cup olive oil in a heavy saucepan over high heat, add the tomatoes, onion, garlic and herbs. Lower the heat and saute for 15 to 20 minutes. Remove from heat and set aside.

Sprinkle the eggplant with 4 tablespoons salt, toss, and let sit at room temperature for 20 minutes. Fold the olives and roasted peppers into the tomato mixture.

Thoroughly rinse salt from eggplant with cold water. Pat dry. Heat the remaining ¼ cup olive oil in a clean skillet over high heat. Add the eggplant and saute two minutes, or until tender. Add pine nuts to eggplant and remove from heat. Let cool.

Combine the eggplant mixture with the tomato mixture. In a small saucepan combine vinegar, sugar and ⅓ cup water. Cook for 3 minutes or until sugar is dissolved. Remove from heat and set aside to cool. Stir the vinegar-sugar mixture into the caponata a bit at a time until the desired consistency is reached. The caponata should be thick like a relish. Adjust the seasoning with salt and pepper. Cover and refrigerate until ready to use. The caponata can be made ahead 3-4 days in advance. Allow to return to room temperature before serving.

240 Union Restaurant

Notes

Notes

INDEX OF RECIPES

VEGETABLES

EGG, CHEESE AND PASTA

FISH AND CHICKEN

BEEF, PORK, LAMB, VEAL AND WILD GAME

MISCELLANEOUS

CELEBRITY AND RESTAURANT RECIPES

KITCHEN HINTS

If you've over-salted soup or vegetables, add cut raw potatoes and discard once they have cooked and absorbed the salt.

A teaspoon each of cider vinegar and sugar added to salty soup or vegetables will also remedy the situation.

If you've over-sweetened a dish, add salt.

A teaspoon of cider vinegar will take care of too-sweet vegetable or main dishes.

Pale gravy may be browned by adding a bit of instant coffee straight from the jar . . . no bitter taste, either.

If you will brown the flour well before adding to the liquid when making gravy, you will avoid pale or lumpy gravy.

A different way of browning flour is to put it in a custard cup placed beside meat in the oven. Once the meat is done, the flour will be nice and brown.

Thin gravy can be thickened by adding a mixture of flour or cornstarch and water, which has been mixed to a smooth paste, added gradually, stirring constantly, while bringing to a boil.

Lumpless gravy can be your triumph if you add a pinch of salt to the flour before mixing it with water.

A small amount of baking soda added to gravy will eliminate excess grease.

Drop a lettuce leaf into a pot of homemade soup to absorb excess grease from the top.

If time allows, the best method of removing fat is refrigeration until the fat hardens. If you put a piece of waxed paper over the top of the soup, etc. it can be peeled right off, along with the hardened fat.

Ice cubes will also eliminate the fat from soup and stew. Just drop a few into the pot and stir; the fat will cling to the cubes; discard the cubes before they melt. Or, wrap ice cubes in paper towel or cheesecloth and skim over the top.

If fresh vegetables are wilted or blemished, pick off the brown edges, sprinkle with cool water, wrap in paper towel and refrigerate for an hour or so.

Perk up soggy lettuce by adding lemon juice to a bowl of cold water and soak for an hour in the refrigerator.

Lettuce and celery keep longer if you store them in paper bags instead of cellophane.

To remove the core from a head of lettuce, hit the core end once against the counter sharply. The core will loosen and pull out easily.

Cream will whip faster and better if you'll first chill the cream, bowl, and beaters well.

Soupy whipped cream can be saved by adding an egg white, then chilling thoroughly. Re-beat for a fluffy surprise!

A few drops of lemon juice added to whipping cream helps it whip faster and better.

Cream whipped ahead of time will not separate if you add ¼ teaspoon unflavored gelatin per cup of cream.

A dampened and folded dish towel placed under the bowl in which you are whipping cream will keep the bowl from dancing all over the counter top.

Brown sugar won't harden if an apple slice is placed in the container.

But if your brown sugar is already brick-hard, put your cheese-grater to work and grate the amount you need.

KITCHEN HINTS

A slice of soft bread placed in the package of hardened brown sugar will soften it again in a couple of hours.

Potatoes will bake in a hurry if they are boiled in salted water for 10 minutes before popping into a very hot oven.

A leftover baked potato can be rebaked if you dip it in water and bake in a 350° oven for about 20 minutes.

A thin slice cut from each end of the potato will speed up baking time as well.

You'll shed less tears if you'll cut the root end off of the onion last.

No more tears when peeling onions if you place them in the deep freeze for four or five minutes first.

Scalding tomatoes, peaches, or pears in boiling water before peeling makes it easier on you and the fruit — skins slip right off.

Ripen green fruits by placing in a perforated plastic bag. The holes allow air movement, yet retain the odorless gas which fruits produce to promote ripening.

To hasten the ripening of garden tomatoes or avocados, put them in a brown paper bag, close the bag and leave at room temperature for a few days.

When pan frying always heat the pan before adding the butter or oil.

A little salt sprinkled into the frying pan will prevent spattering.

Meat loaf will not stick if you place a slice of bacon on the bottom of the pan.

Vinegar brought to a boil in a new frying pan will prevent foods from sticking.

Muffins will slide right out of tin pans if the hot pan is first placed on a wet towel.

No sticking to the pan when you're scalding milk if you'll first rinse the pan in cold water.

Add a cup of water to the bottom portion of the broiling pan before sliding into the oven, to absorb smoke and grease.

A few teaspoons of sugar and cinnamon slowly burned on top of the stove will hide unpleasant cooking odors and make your family think you've been baking all day!

A lump of butter or a few teaspoons of cooking oil added to water when boiling rice, noodles, or spaghetti will prevent boiling over.

Rubbing the inside of the cooking vessel with vegetable oil will also prevent noodles, spaghetti, and similar starches from boiling over.

A few drops of lemon juice added to simmering rice will keep the grains separate.

Grating a stick of butter softens it quickly.

Soften butter for spreading by inverting a small heated pan over the butter dish for a while.

A dip of the spoon or cup into hot water before measuring shortening or butter will cause the fat to slip out easily without sticking to the spoon.

Before measuring honey or other syrup, oil the cup with cooking oil and rinse in hot water.

Catsup will flow out of the bottle evenly if you will first insert a drinking straw, push it to the bottom of the bottle, and remove.

If you wet the dish on which the gelatin is to be unmolded, it can be moved around until centered.

KITCHEN HINTS

A dampened paper towel or terry cloth brushed downward on a cob of corn will remove every strand of corn silk.

An easy way to remove the kernels of sweet corn from the cob is to use a shoe horn. It's built just right for shearing off those kernels in a jiffy.

To determine whether an egg is fresh, immerse it in a pan of cool, salted water. If it sinks, it is fresh; if it rises to the surface, throw it away.

Fresh eggs' shells are rough and chalky; old eggs are smooth and shiny.

To determine whether an egg is hard-boiled, spin it. If it spins, it is hard-boiled; if it wobbles and will not spin it is raw.

Egg whites won't run while boiling or poaching if you'll add a little vinegar to the water.

Eggs will beat up fluffier if they are allowed to come to cool room temperature before beating.

For baking, it's best to use medium to large eggs; extra large eggs may cause cakes to fall when cooled.

Egg shells can be easily removed from hard-boiled eggs if they are quickly rinsed in cold water first.

For fluffier omelets, add a pinch of cornstarch before beating.

For a never fail, never weep meringue, add a teaspoon of cornstarch to the sugar before beating it into the egg whites.

Once your meringue is baked, cut it cleanly, using a knife coated with butter.

A meringue pie may be covered with waxed paper or plastic wrap with no fear of sticking, if you'll first grease the paper with oleo.

No "curly" bacon for breakfast when you dip it into cold water before frying.

Keep bacon slices from sticking together; roll the package into a tube shape and secure with rubber bands.

A quick way to separate frozen bacon: heat a spatula over a burner, slide it under each slice to separate it from the others.

Cheese won't harden if you'll butter the exposed edges before storing.

A cloth dampened with vinegar and wrapped around cheese will also prevent drying out.

Thaw fish in milk. The milk draws out the frozen taste and provides a fresh-caught flavor.

When browning any piece of meat, the job will be done more quickly and effectively if the meat is very dry and the fat is very hot.

You'll get more juice from a lemon if you'll first warm it slightly in the oven.

Popcorn will stay fresh and you will eliminate "old maids" if you store it in the freezer.

Running ice cold water over the kernels before popping will also eliminate "old maids".

After flouring chicken, chill for one hour. The coating adheres better during frying.

Empty salt cartons with spouts make dandy containers for bread crumbs. A funnel is used for getting the crumbs into the carton.

A sack of lumpy sugar won't be if you place it in the refrigerator for 24 hours.

CLEANUPS

Fill blender part way with hot water; add a drop of detergent; cover and turn it on for a few seconds. Rinse and drain dry.

Loosen grime from can openers by brushing with an old toothbrush. To clean blades, run a paper towel through the cutting process.

Don't panic if you accidentally scorch the inside of your favorite saucepan. Just fill the pan halfway with water and add ¼ cup baking soda. Boil awhile until the burned portions loosen and float to the top.

A jar lid or a couple of marbles in the bottom half of a double-boiler will rattle when the water gets low and warn you to add more before the pan scorches or burns.

To remove lime deposits from teakettles, fill with equal parts vinegar and water. Bring to a boil and allow to stand overnight.

Before washing fine china and crystal, place a towel in the bottom of the sink to act as a cushion.

To remove coffee or tea stains and cigarette burns from fine china, rub with a damp cloth dipped in baking soda.

To quickly remove food that is stuck to a casserole dish, fill with boiling water and 2 tablespoons of baking soda or salt.

To clear a sink or basin drain, pour ½ cup of baking soda followed by a cup of vinegar down the drain . . .let the mixture foam, then run hot water.

When a drain is clogged with grease, pour a cup of salt and a cup of baking soda followed by a kettle of boiling water.

Silver will gleam after a rubbing with damp baking soda on a soft cloth.

For a fast and simple clean-up of your hand grater, rub salad oil on the grater before using.

A toothbrush works great to clean lemon rind, cheese, onion, etc. out of the grater before washing it.

While baking fruit pies, does the juice runneth over? Shake salt into the spills. They'll burn to a crisp and can be easily scraped up with a spatula.

Grease splatters or other foods that have dried on the stove, burner rings, counter appliances, etc., may be removed by applying dry baking soda to the spots, then rubbing with a damp cloth. Rinse with clear water, dry and enjoy the like-new look.

CALORIE COUNTER

Almonds:
    roasted in oil, salted, 9-10 nuts 62
Apple butter, 1 tbsp. 33
Apple juice, canned or bottled, 1 cup 117
Apples:
    fresh, with skin, 1 average (2½" diameter) 61
    dried, cooked, sweetened, ½ cup 157
    dried, cooked, unsweetened, ½ cup 100
Applesauce, canned, sweetened, ½ cup 116
Applesauce, canned, unsweetened, ½ cup 50
Apricot nectar, canned or bottled, 1 cup 143
Apricots:
    fresh, 3 average (12 per lb.) 55
    canned, 4 halves with 2 tbsp. heavy syrup 105
    canned, water pack, ½ cup with liquid 38
Asparagus:
    canned, drained, cut spears, ½ cup 25
    frozen, 6 spears 23
Avocados, 3⅛" diameter 185

Bacon, fried, drained, 2 medium slices 86
Bacon, Canadian, fried, drained, 1 slice 58
Bagel, egg or water, 1 medium (3" diameter) 165
Bamboo shoots, raw, cuts, ½ cup 21
Bananas, 1 average 118
Bean sprouts, soy, raw, ½ cup 24
Beans, baked, canned:
    with pork and tomato sauce, ½ cup 156
Beans, green or snap:
    fresh, boiled, drained, cuts or French style, ½ cup .. 16
    canned, with liquid, ½ cup 22
Beans, lima, immature seeds:
    boiled, drained, ½ cup 95
    canned, with liquid, ½ cup 88
Beans, pea, navy, or white, dry, cooked, ½ cup 112
Beans, red kidney, canned, with liquid, ½ cup 115
Beef, choice grade cuts (without bone):
    brisket, lean only, braised, 4 oz. 253
    chuck, arm, lean only, pot-roasted, 4 oz. 219
    club steak, lean only, broiled, 4 oz. 277
    flank steak, lean only, pot-roasted, 4 oz. 222
    ground, lean (10% fat), broiled, 4 oz. 248
    porterhouse steak, lean only, broiled, 4 oz. 254
    rib, lean only, roasted, 4 oz. 273
    round steak, lean only, broiled, 4 oz. 214
    rump, lean only, roasted, 4 oz. 236
    short plate, lean only, simmered, 4 oz. 253
    sirloin steak, double-bone, lean only, broiled, 4 oz. .. 245
    sirloin steak, round-bone, lean only, broiled, 4 oz. . 235
    T-bone steak, lean only, broiled, 4 oz. 253
Beef, corned:
    boiled, medium-fat, 4 oz. 422
    canned, lean, 4 oz. 211
Beef and vegetable stew, canned, 4 oz. 90
Beets:
    boiled, drained, sliced, ½ cup 33
Blackberries:
    fresh, ½ cup 42
    canned, juice pack, ½ cup with liquid 68
Blueberries:
    fresh, ½ cup 45
    canned, water pack, ½ cup with liquid 47
Bologna, all meat, 4 oz. 315
Boysenberries:
    canned, water pack, ½ cup with liquid 45
    frozen, unsweetened, ½ cup 30
Braunschweiger (smoked liverwurst), 4 oz. 362
Brazil nuts (3 large nuts) 90
Bread, commercial:
    Boston brown, 1 slice 101
    cracked wheat, 1 slice, 20 per loaf 60
    French, 1 slice 44
    Italian, 1 slice 28

    pumpernickel, 1 slice 79
    raisin, 1 slice, 20 per loaf 60
    rye, light, 1 slice, 20 per loaf 56
    white, firm-crumb type, 1 slice, 20 per loaf 63
    whole wheat, firm-crumb type, 1 slice, 20 per loaf .. 56
Bread stuffing, mix, mixed with butter, water, ½ cup . 250
Broccoli:
    raw, 1 large spear 32
    boiled, drained, cut spears, ½ cup 20
Brussels sprouts boiled, drained ½ cup 28
Butter, 1 Tbsp. 100
Butter, whipped, 1 tbsp. 67

Cabbage:
    red, raw, chopped or shredded, ½ cup 14
    white, raw, chopped or shredded, ½ cup 11
Cake, mix, prepared as directed on package:
    angelfood, without icing, 3½-oz. serving 269
    coffee cake, 3½-oz. serving 322
    devil's food, with chocolate icing, 3½-oz. serving . 369
    white, with chocolate icing, 3½-oz. serving 351
    yellow, with chocolate icing, 3½-oz. serving 365
Candies, 1-oz. serving:
    almonds, chocolate-covered 161
    butter mints, after dinner (Kraft) 106
    butterscotch 112
    cherries, dark chocolate-covered (Welch's) 115
    chocolate, milk 147
    chocolate, semi-sweet 144
    coconut, chocolate-covered 124
    fudge, chocolate, with nuts 121
    gum drops 98
    jelly beans 104
    licorice (Switzer) 101
    Life Savers, all flavors except mint 111
    Life Savers, mint 108
    mints, chocolate-covered 116
    marshmallows (Campfire) 100
    peanut brittle 119
    peanut cluster, chocolate-covered (Kraft) 151
    raisins, chocolate-covered 120
    toffee, chocolate (Kraft) 111
Cantaloupe, fresh, ½ melon, 5" diameter 58
Carrots:
    raw, 1 average 21
    boiled, drained, diced, ½ cup 23
Catsup, tomato, bottled, 1 tbsp. 16
Cauliflower:
    raw, flowerbuds, sliced, ½ cup 12
    boiled, drained, flowerbuds, ½ cup 14
Celery, raw, 1 outer stalk (8" long) 7
Cereals:
    All-bran, 1 cup 192
    bran, 100% (Nabisco), 1 cup 150
    bran flakes, 40%, 1 cup 106
    bran flakes with raisins, 1 cup 144
    corn flakes, 1 cup 97
    corn flakes, sugar coated, 1 cup 154
    Cream of Wheat, cooked, 1 cup 133
    farina, quick-cooking, cooked, 1 cup 105
    oat flakes, (Post), 1 cup 165
    oatmeal or rolled oats, cooked, 1 cup 132
    rice, puffed, 1 cup 60
    wheat flakes, 1 cup 106
    wheat, puffed, 1 cup 54
    wheat, puffed, presweetened, 1 cup 132
    wheat, shredded, 1 biscuit (2½" x 2" x 1¼") 89
Cheese:
    American, processed, 1 oz. 105
    blue or Roquefort type, 1 oz. 104
    brick, 1 oz. 105
    cheddar, domestic, 1 oz. 113
    cottage, creamed, small curd, ½ cup 112

CALORIE COUNTER

cream, 1 tbsp. 52
cream, whipped, 1 tbsp. 37
Gouda, 1 oz. 108
Monterey Jack, 1 oz. 103
Mozzarella, part-skim, 1 oz. 85
Muenster, 1 oz. 100
Neufchatel (Borden's), 1 oz. 73
Old English, processed, 1 oz. 105
Parmesan, grated, 1 Tbsp. 23
pimiento, American, processed, 1 oz. 105
Provolone, 1 oz. 99
ricotta, moist, 1 oz. 45
Romano, 1 oz. 110
Roquefort, 1 oz. 105
Swiss, domestic, 1 oz. 104
Cheese food, American, processed, 1 oz. 92
Cherries:
    sweet, fresh, whole, ½ cup 41
Cherries, maraschino, bottled, 1 oz. with liquid 33
Chestnuts, fresh, 10 average 141
Chicken:
    broiled, meat only, 4 oz. 154
    roasted, dark meat, 4 oz., no skin 204
    roasted, light meat, 4 oz., no skin 207
Chili, with beans, canned ½ cup 170
Chili, without beans, canned, ½ cup 255
Coconut:
    dried, sweetened, shredded, ½ cup 258
Cod (meat only):
    broiled, with butter, fillets, 4 oz. 192
    frozen, fish sticks, breaded, 5 sticks, 4 oz. 276
Coffee, prepared, plain, 1 cup 2
Coleslaw, commercial, with mayonnaise, ½ cup 87
Cookies, commercial:
    brownies, from mix, with nuts and water, 1 oz. 114
    butter thins, 1 piece (2" diameter) 23
    chocolate chip, 1 piece (2¼" diameter) 50
    coconut bar, 1 oz. 140
    fig bar, 1 average piece 50
    gingersnaps, 1 piece (2" diameter) 29
    graham cracker, plain, 1 piece (5" x 2½") 55
    ladyfinger, 1 piece 40
    macaroon, 1 piece (2¾" diameter) 91
    oatmeal with raisins, 1 piece (2⅝" diameter) 59
    peanut sandwich, 1 piece (1¾" diameter) 58
    shortbread, 1 average piece 37
    vanilla wafer, 1 piece (1¾" diameter) 19
Corn:
    boiled, drained on cob, 1 ear (5" x 1¾") 70
    boiled, drained, kernels, ½ cup 69
    canned, cream style, ½ cup 105
Corn chips (Fritos), 1 oz. 166
Crackers:
    bacon-flavor, 1 oz. 127
    butter, round, 1 piece (1⅞" diameter) 15
    cheese, round, 1 piece (1⅝" diameter) 17
    Melba toast, white, regular, 1 piece 15
    Rye-Krisp, 1 piece (1⅞" x 3½") 21
    saltines, 1 piece 12
    whole wheat, 1 oz. 114
Cranberry juice cocktail, canned or bottled, 1 cup 164
Cranberry sauce, canned, strained, ½ cup 202
Cream:
    half and half, ½ cup 162
    sour, 1 tbsp. 26
    whipping, light, ½ cup unwhipped 358
    whipping, heavy, ½ cup, unwhipped 419
Cream substitute, non-dairy, dry, 1 tbsp. 33
Cucumber, with skin, 1 large (8¼" long) 45

Dates, domestic, 10 average 219
Duck, domestic, roasted, meat only, 4 oz. 352

Eclair, custard filled, with chocolate icing, 1 average . 239
Eggnog, 8% fat (Borden's), ½ cup 171
Eggplant, boiled, drained, diced, ½ cup 19
Eggs, chicken:
    boiled or poached, 1 large egg 82
    fried, with 1 tsp. butter, 1 large egg 99
    scrambled, with 1 tsp. butter, 1 large egg 111
Endive, raw, 10 small leaves 5
Escarole, raw, 1 large leaf 4

Fat, vegetable shortening, 1 tbsp. 111
Figs:
    dried, 1 large fig (2" x 1") 57
Fish cakes, fried, frozen, reheated, 4 oz. 306
Flour:
    all-purpose, sifted, 1 cup 419
    buckwheat, dark, sifted, 1 cup 326
    cake or pastry, sifted, 1 cup 349
    rye, dark, unsifted, 1 cup 419
    wheat, self-rising, sifted, 1 cup 405
Frankfurters, all-meat, 1 average (10 per lb.) 133
Fruit cocktail, canned, water pack, ½ cup with liquid . . 46
Fruit, mixed, frozen, sweetened, 4 oz. 125

Gelatin dessert, flavored, prepared with water, ½ cup . 71
Gooseberries, fresh, ½ cup 30
Grape drink, canned, 1 cup 135
Grape juice, canned or bottled, 1 cup 167
Grapes:
    fresh (Concord, Delaware, etc.), 10 18
    fresh (Thompson seedless, etc.), 10 34
Grapefruit juice:
    canned, sweetened, 1 cup 133
    canned, unsweetened, 1 cup 101

Haddock, fried, breaded fillets, 4 oz. 187
Halibut, fillets, broiled with butter, 4 oz. 194
Halibut, frozen, steak, 4 oz. 254
Halibut, smoked, 4 oz. 254
Ham:
    boiled, packaged, 4 oz. (about 4 slices) 266
    fresh, medium-fat, roasted, 4 oz. 426
    picnic, cured, medium-fat, roasted, 4 oz. 368
    canned, cured, lean only, roasted, 4 oz. 241
    canned, deviled, 4 oz. 398
Herring:
    canned, plain, 4 oz. with liquid 236
    pickled, Bismark-type, 4 oz. 253
    smoked, hard, 4 oz. 340
Hickory nuts, shelled, 4 oz. 763
Honey, strained or extracted, 1 tbsp. 64
Honeydew melon:
    fresh, 1 wedge (2" x 7") 49

Ice cream:
    hardened, rich, 16% fat, ½ cup 165
    soft-serve (frozen custard), ½ cup 167
Ice cream bar, chocolate coated, 3-oz. bar 162
Ice cream cone, sugar 1 cone 37
Ice cream cone, waffle, 1 cone 19
Ice milk, hardened, 5.1% fat, ½ cup 100
Ice milk, soft-serve, 5.1% fat, ½ cup 133
Ice milk bar, chocolate coated, 3-oz. bar 144

Jams and preserves, all flavors, 1 tbsp. 54
Jellies, all flavors, 1 tbsp. 49

Kale:
    fresh, leaves only, 4 oz. 80
    fresh, with stems, boiled, drained, ½ cup 16
Knockwurst, 1 link (4" x 1⅛" diameter) 189
Kumquats, fresh, 1 average 12

CALORIE COUNTER

Lamb, retail cuts:
    chop, loin, lean only, broiled, 2.3 oz. with bone 122
    leg, lean and fat, roasted, boneless, 4 oz. 317
    shoulder, lean only, roasted, boneless, 4 oz. 233
Leeks, raw, 3 average 52
Lemon juice:
    fresh, 1 tbsp. 4
Lemonade, frozen, diluted, 1 cup 107
Lemons, fresh, 1 average (2⅛" diameter) 20
Lentils, whole, cooked, 1 cup 212
Lettuce:
    iceberg, 1 leaf (5" x 4½") 3
    romaine, 3 leaves (8" long) 5
Limes, fresh, 1 average (2" diameter) 19
Liverwurst, fresh, 4 oz. 348
Lobster, cooked in shell, whole, 1 lb. 112
Lobster, cooked or canned, meat only, cubed, ½ cup . 69

Macadamia nuts, 6 average nuts 104
Macaroni, boiled, drained, ½ cup 96
Macaroni and cheese, canned, ½ cup 114
Mackerel, fresh or frozen, broiled with butter, 4 oz. . . 268
Mangos, whole, 1 average (1½ per lb.) 152
Margarine, salted or unsalted, 1 tbsp. 102
Marmalade, citrus flavors, 1 tbsp. 51
Milk, chocolate, canned, with skim milk, 1 cup 190
Milk, chocolate, canned, with whole milk, 1 cup 213
Milk, cow's:
    whole, 3.5% fat, 1 cup 159
    buttermilk, cultured, 1 cup 88
    skim, 1 cup 88
    skim, partially, 1 cup 145
    canned, condensed, sweetened, 1 cup 982
    canned, evaporated, unsweetened, 1 cup 345
    dry, whole, 1 tbsp. dry form 35
    dry, nonfat, instant, 1 envelope (3.2 oz.) 327
Milk, malted, beverage, 1 cup 244
Muffin, corn, mix, made with egg, milk, 1.4 oz. muffin 130
Mushrooms, raw, sliced, chopped or diced, ½ cup . . . 10
Mushrooms, canned, with liquid, ½ cup 21
Mustard greens, boiled, drained, ½ cup 16

Nectarines, fresh, 1 average (2½" diameter) 88
Noodles, chow-mein, canned, ½ cup 110
Noodles, egg, cooked, ½ cup 100

Oil, cooking or salad:
    corn, safflower, sesame or soy, 1 tbsp. 120
    olive or peanut, 1 tbsp. 119
Olives, pickled, canned or bottled:
    green, 10 large (¾" diameter) 45
    ripe, salt-cured, Greek style, 10 extra large 89
Onions, mature:
    raw, 1 average (2½" diameter) 40
    raw, chopped, 1 tbsp. 4
Orange juice:
    fresh, California, Valencia, 1 cup 117
    fresh, Florida, Valencia, 1 cup 112
    canned, sweetened, 1 cup 130
    canned, unsweetened, 1 cup 120
    frozen, concentrate, unsweetened, diluted, 1 cup . 112
Oranges, fresh, 1 average 71

Pancakes, prepared from mix as directed on package:
    plain and buttermilk, 4" diameter cake 61
    buckwheat and other flours, 4" diameter cake 54
Papaya juice, canned, 1 cup 120
Papayas, fresh, whole, 1 papaya (3½" x 5⅛") 119
Peach nectar, canned, 1 cup 120
Peaches:
    fresh, 1 average 38
    canned, in juice, 2 peach halves with 2 tbsp. juice . . 45
    dried, ½ cup 210

Peanut butter, commercial, 1 tbsp. 94
Peanuts:
    roasted, in shell, 10 nuts 105
    roasted, chopped, 1 tbsp. 52
Pear nectar, canned, 1 cup 130
Pears:
    fresh, Bartlett, 1 pear (2½" diameter) 100
    canned, in heavy syrup, 1 pear half and 2 tbsp. syrup 71
    dried, ½ cup 241
Peas, green:
    boiled, drained, ½ cup 57
Peas, split, cooked, ½ cup 115
Pecans:
    shelled, 10 large nuts 62
    chopped, 1 tbsp. 52
Peppers, hot, chili:
    green, raw, seeded, 4 oz. 42
    green, chili sauce, canned, ½ cup 25
    red, chili sauce, canned, ½ cup 26
Peppers, sweet, green:
    raw, fancy grade, 1 pepper (3" diameter) 36
Peppers, sweet, red:
    raw, fancy grade, 1 pepper (3" diameter) 51
Perch, ocean, Atlantic, frozen, breaded, 4 oz. 382
Perch, white, raw, meat only, 4 oz. 134
Pickle relish:
    hamburger (Heinz), 1 tbsp. 17
    sweet, 1 tbsp. 21
Pickles, cucumber:
    dill, 1 large (4" long) 15
    sweet gherkins, 1 small (2½" long) 22
Pies, frozen:
    apple, baked, 3⅛" arc (⅛ of 8" pie) 173
    cherry, baked, 3⅛" arc (⅛ of 8" pie) 211
    coconut custard, baked, 3⅛" arc (⅛ of 8" pie) 187
Pimientos, canned, drained, 1 average 10
Pineapple:
    fresh, sliced, 1 slice (3½" diameter x ¾") 44
    canned, heavy syrup, chunks or crushed, ½ cup . . 95
    canned, water pack, tidbits, ½ cup with liquid 48
Pineapple juice, canned, unsweetened, 1 cup 138
Pistachio nuts, chopped, 1 tbsp. 53
Plums:
    damson, fresh, whole, 10 plums (1" diameter) 66
    canned, purple, 3 plums and 2¾ tbsp. liquid 110
Popcorn:
    popped, plain, 1 cup 23
    popped, with oil and salt added, 1 cup 41
Pork:
    Boston butt, lean only, roasted, 4 oz. 279
    chop, lean only, broiled, 4 oz. with bone 308
    loin, lean only, roasted, 4 oz. 288
Potato chips, 10 chips (2" diameter) 114
Potato sticks, ½ cup 95
Potatoes, white:
    baked, in skin, 1 long 145
    boiled, in skin, 1 round 104
    fried, ½ cup 228
    frozen, hash brown, cooked, ½ cup 174
    mashed, with milk and butter, ½ cup 99
Potatoes, sweet:
    baked, in skin, 1 average 161
    boiled, in skin, 1 average 172
    boiled, in skin, mashed, ½ cup 146
    candied, 1 piece (2½" long x 2") 176
Pretzels, commercial varieties:
    rods, 1 pretzel (7½" long) 55
    twisted, 3-ring, 10 pretzels 117
Prune juice, canned or bottled, 1 cup 197
Prunes, dried, medium-size, 1 average 16
Pumpkin, canned, ½ cup 41
Radishes, raw, whole, 10 medium 8
Raisins, seedless (½ cup) 210

CALORIE COUNTER

Raspberries:
  black, fresh, ½ cup 49
  red, fresh, ½ cup 35
  canned, black, water pack, 4 oz. with liquid 58
  canned, red, water pack, ½ cup with liquid 43
  frozen, red, sweetened, ½ cup 123
Rhubarb, cooked, sweetened, ½ cup 191
Rice, cooked (hot):
  brown, long grain, ½ cup 116
  white, long grain, ½ cup 112
  white, parboiled, long grain, ½ cup 93
Rolls and buns, commercial (ready to serve):
  frankfurther or hamburger, 1.4 oz. roll 119
  hard, rectangular, ⅞-oz. roll 78
  raisin, 1-oz. roll 78
  sweet, 1-oz. roll 89
  whole wheat, 1-oz. roll 73

Salad dressings, commercial:
  blue cheese, 1 tbsp. 76
  French, 1 tbsp. 66
  Italian, 1 tbsp. 83
  mayonnaise, 1 tbsp. 101
  Roquefort cheese, 1 tbsp. 76
  Russian, 1 tbsp. 74
  Thousand Island, 1 tbsp. 80
Salami:
  cooked, 1 slice (4" diameter) 68
  dry, 1 slice (3⅛" diameter) 45
Salmon, smoked, 4 oz. 200
Sauces:
  barbecue, 1 tbsp. 17
  soy, 1 tbsp. 12
  tartar, 1 tbsp. 74
  tomato, canned (Hunt's), ½ cup 35
Sauerkraut, canned, ½ cup with liquid 21
Sausages:
  polish, 2.7 oz. sausage (5⅜" long x 1" diameter) .. 231
  pork, cooked, 1 link (4" long x ⅞" diameter) 62
  pork, cooked, 1 patty (3⅞" diameter x ¼") 129
  pork and beef, chopped, 4 oz. 383
  Vienna, canned, 1 sausage (2" long) 38
Sherbet, orange, ½ cup 130
Shrimp:
  fresh, breaded, fried, 4 oz. 255
  canned, drained, 10 medium shrimp 37
Soft drinks:
  cola, 1 cup 96
  cream soda, 1 cup 105
  fruit flavored (citrus, cherry, grape, etc.), 1 cup 113
  root beer, 1 cup 100
  Seven-Up, 1 cup 97
Soup, canned, condensed, diluted with equal part water:
  asparagus, cream of, 1 cup 65
  beans with pork, 1 cup 168
  beef broth, bouillon or consomme, 1 cup 31
  beef noodle, 1 cup 67
  celery, cream of, 1 cup 86
  chicken consomme, 1 cup 22
  chicken, cream of, 1 cup 94
  chicken gumbo, 1 cup 55
  chicken noodle, 1 cup 62
  chicken vegetable, 1 cup 76
  chicken with rice, 1 cup 48
  clam chowder, Manhattan type, 1 cup 81
  minestrone, 1 cup 105
  mushroom, cream of, 1 cup 134
  onion, 1 cup 65
  pea, split, 1 cup 145
  tomato, 1 cup 88
  vegetable beef, 1 cup 78
  vegetarian vegetable, 1 cup 78

Spaghetti:
  plain, boiled 8-10 minutes, drained, ½ cup 96
  canned, in tomato sauce with cheese, ½ cup 95
  canned, with meatballs in tomato sauce, ½ cup ... 129
Spinach:
  boiled, drained, leaves, ½ cup 21
Squash, summer:
  scallop variety, boiled, drained, sliced, ½ cup 15
  yellow, boiled, drained, sliced, ½ cup 14
  zucchini, boiled, drained, sliced, ½ 11
Squash, winter:
  acorn, baked, ½ squash (4" diameter) 86
  acorn, boiled, mashed, ½ cup 42
  butternut, baked, mashed, ½ cup 70
  butternut, boiled, mashed, ½ cup 50
Strawberries:
  fresh, whole, ½ cup 28
  canned, water pack, ½ cup with liquid 27
Sugar, beet or cane:
  brown, ½ cup firm packed 411
  brown, 1 tbsp. firm packed 52
  granulated, ½ cup 385
  granulated, 1 tsp. 15
  powdered, unsifted, ½ cup 231
  powdered, stirred, 1 tbsp. 31
Sunflower seed kernels, in hull, ½ cup 129
Sunflower seed kernels, hulled, ½ cup 406
Syrups:
  chocolate, thin-type, 1 tbsp. 46
  corn, light or dark, 1 tbsp. 58
  maple, 1 tbsp. 50
  molasses, blackstrap, 1 tbsp. 43
  molasses, light, 1 tbsp. 50
  molasses, medium, 1 tbsp. 46
  sorghum, 1 tbsp. 53

Tangerines, fresh, 1 average (2⅜" diameter) 39
Tomato juice, canned or bottle, 1 cup 46
Tomato juice cocktail, canned or bottled, 1 cup 51
Tomato paste, canned, ½ cup 108
Tomato puree, canned ½ cup 49
Tomatoes, ripe:
  raw, whole, 1 average (about 2⅖" diameter) 20
  canned, ½ cup with liquid 26
Toppings: dessert:
  butterscotch, 1 tbsp. 52
  caramel, 1 tbsp. 72
  chocolate fudge, 1 tbsp. 62
  pineapple, 1 tbsp. 56
Tuna, canned:
  in oil, solid pack or chunk style, drained, ½ cup ... 158
  in water, all styles, with liquid, 4 oz. 144
Turkey:
  dark meat, roasted, 4 oz. 230
  light meat, roasted, 4 oz. 200
  canned, boned, ½ cup 207
Turnip greens:
  fresh, boiled in small amount water, drained, ½ cup . 15
Turnips, boiled, drained, cubed, ½ cup 18

Vegetable juice cocktail, canned, 1 cup 41
Vegetables, mixed, frozen, boiled, drained, ½ cup ... 58

Waffles, baked from mix:
  made with egg and milk, 1 round (7" diameter) 206
Walnuts, 10 large nuts 322
Watermelon, with rind, 1 wedge (4" x 8") 111
Wheat bran, commercially milled, 4 oz. 242
Wheat germ, toasted, 1 tbsp. 23

Yogurt, plain:
  partially skim milk, 8-oz. container 113
  whole milk, 8-oz. container 140

*This Cookbook is a perfect gift for Holidays,
Weddings, Anniversaries & Birthdays.*

*To order extra copies as gifts for your friends,
please use Order Forms on reverse side
of this page.*

* * * * * * * * * *

TO ORDER COOKBOOKS

Name _____

Address _____

City, State, Zip _____ Telephone: _____

Please send:

Recipes From Our House	Quantity	Price	Tax (Colo. residents)	Total
	_____	$12.00	$.88 each	$_____
	plus $2.00 each, shipping & handling			$_____
	TOTAL ENCLOSED			$_____

Please make checks payable to:

Assistance League of Denver. (Please do not send cash. Sorry no C.O.D.'s)

Send to:
Recipes From Our House
Assistance League of Denver
1400 Josephine St.
Denver, CO 80206

- -

TO ORDER COOKBOOKS

Name _____

Address _____

City, State, Zip _____ Telephone: _____

Please send:

Recipes From Our House	Quantity	Price	Tax (Colo. residents)	Total
	_____	$12.00	$.88 each	$_____
	plus $2.00 each, shipping & handling			$_____
	TOTAL ENCLOSED			$_____

Please make checks payable to:

Assistance League of Denver. (Please do not send cash. Sorry no C.O.D.'s)

Send to:
Recipes From Our House
Assistance League of Denver
1400 Josephine St.
Denver, CO 80206

1413-96

We Can Create a Cookbook For You Too!

Our Fundraising Personalized Cookbook Program is Fun, Easy, AND Profitable!

You furnish the recipes—and we do the rest! We even supply you with FREE recipe forms!! Your organization's name can be on the front cover of your very own cookbook. AND the names of the recipe contributors appear with their submitted recipes.

YOUR BOOKS ARE SELF-FINANCING

You figure the cost of your books from our Price Chart. Costs are based on the number of recipes you want printed and the number of books you want to order.

NO DOWN PAYMENT
NO INTEREST OR HANDLING CHARGES

One-half of balance 37 days after books are shipped—remaining balance, 67 days after books are shipped. Thirty-day extension on written request if needed (making a total of 97 days).

For your FREE Step-by-Step Personalized Cookbook Instruction Kit return the postage-paid card today or call toll-free
1-800-227-7282

 Interested in additional fundraising ideas? Just ask us about our other fundraising programs when you call, or simply check the appropriate box on the opposite side of the business reply card shown below, then drop the card in the mail today.

(Tear along perforation, fill in reverse side and mail)

BUSINESS REPLY MAIL

FIRST-CLASS MAIL PERMIT NO. 4483 SHAWNEE MISSION KS

POSTAGE WILL BE PAID BY ADDRESSEE

COOKBOOK PUBLISHERS INC
10800 LAKEVIEW AVE
PO BOX 15920
LENEXA KS 66285-9802

NO POSTAGE
NECESSARY
IF MAILED
IN THE
UNITED STATES